KT-504-888

Tourism and the Media

Tourist decision-making, information, and communication

Christian Nielsen

HOSPITALITY
P R E S S
MELBOURNE

Hospitality Press Pty Ltd
38 Riddell Parade
PO Box 426
Elsternwick VIC 3185
Australia
Telephone (+61 3) 9528 5021 Fax (+61 3) 9528 2645
email hosppress@access.net.au

Australian Studies in Tourism Series No 2
Tourism and the Media
First published 2001

This book is copyright.
© Hospitality Press Pty Ltd 2001

Copying for educational purposes
The Australian *Copyright Act* 1968 (the Act) allows a maximum of one chapter or 10% of this book, whichever is greater, to be copied by any educational institution for its educational purposes provided that that educational institution (or the body that administers it) has given a remuneration notice to Copyright Agency Limited (CAL) under the Act.

For details of the CAL licence for educational institutions contact:

Copyright Agency Limited
Level 19, 157 Liverpool Street
Sydney NSW 2000
Telephone (02) 9394 7600 Fax (02) 9394 7601
email info@copyright.com.au

Copying for other purposes
Except as permitted under the Act (for example a fair dealing for the purposes of study, research, criticism or review) no part of this book may be reproduced, stored in a retrieval system, or transmitted in any form or by any means without prior written permission. All inquiries should be made to the publisher at the address above.

National Library of Australia
Cataloguing-in-publication data:

Nielsen, Christian, 1968–
Tourism and the Media: tourist decision-making,
information, and communication.

   Bibliography.
   Includes index.
   ISBN 1 86250 487 3.

1. Tourism. 2. Mass media and business. 3. Advertising —
Tourism. I. Title.

338.4791

Edited by Ross Gilham (Ginross Editorial Services), Torquay, Vic
Designed and typeset by Egan-Reid Ltd, Auckland, New Zealand
Printed in New Zealand by Publishing Press, Auckland
Published by Hospitality Press Pty Ltd (ABN 69 935 151 798)

338.4791
(Niz)

SM 02000842
12/02
£24-95

BZW
(Niz)

0219153

Tourism and the Media

Long Loan

This book is due for return on or before the last date shown below.

1 0 SEP 2003
CANCELLED

3 0 SEP 2004
- 7 APR 2008

AMBLESIDE LIBRARY

ST MARTINS SERVICES LTD

Contents

About the Author

Australian-born Christian Nielsen obtained a bachelor's degree in business (specialising in tourism management) at Victoria University before moving to Brussels to complete a master's degree in industrial locations and development at Free University.

Following a stint as report writer on a media research project for the 1996 Olympics, Christian worked as a business communications consultant and joined the Tourism Research Group—a regional tourism research unit of Limburg University Centre, Belgium. While studying for a diploma in journalism, he worked as a copy editor for the *Wall Street Journal* Europe, and has written for Belgian and Australian publications.

Embracing the new economy, Christian has recently taken up a position as a marketing and communications consultant for Europe Unlimited, a Brussels-based research company and organiser of investment events, promoting European high-tech growth companies.

Introduction

The key to an organisation's success is an understanding of its potential clients. The organisation needs to know how its clients make decisions—such as how to spend their scarce resources of time, money, and effort—and how clients assess the benefits that they expect to derive from those decisions. The tourism industry is no exception to this. An understanding of the determinants of demand for tourism inherently improves decision-making and communication among interested parties.

The aim of this book is to examine the relationship between tourism and the media. The influence of the media is a key element in the study of tourism today, and this book aims to provide both the theoretical foundation of this relationship, and an empirical understanding of it. Previously, there has been some interest in the relationship between the media and consumer decision-making—but with little in the way of definitive research related specifically to tourism. Taking an analytical and discursive approach, this book attempts to explain the communication of media events—and the ensuing relationship between tourism and the media. However, it must be acknowledged that ' . . . no unified theory of effects exists today' (Merrill, Lee & Fiendlander 1990).

The following quotations from the reputable Australian daily newspaper, the *Age*, offer a poignant introduction to the triangle of relationships that exist among an event, the media, and tourism. First, an image of tourism in the former Yugoslavia:

> Before the war, charter flights and buses brought visitors by the thousands to enjoy . . . sunny beaches . . . charming villages . . . Dubrovnik, the medieval walled city.
>
> Morison 1995

Then follows an image of post-war Croatia:

> To those of us scanning television and the newspapers, it looked like hell. Dead: 250 000. Displaced: perhaps 2.5 million. It was hell.
>
> Morison 1995

Initially, we have a clear example of informal media coverage of a previously beautiful tourist attraction. Following this is a description of an event—an horrific civil war. Reference to our previous understanding of the event via television and newspapers is also made. The direct and irrefutable effect of political turmoil and war on tourism becomes clear:

> In the best pre-war year, Dubrovnik attracted six million 'overnights' (individual nights spent by visitors). This year [1995], the total will be around 300 000, down by 95%. That's tourism as war.
>
> Morison 1995

These figures speak for themselves. However, it is important for those involved in tourism—participants, information providers, educators, and students—to understand the interrelationships among tourism, an event, and the media in order to make informed decisions. The following chapters go some way towards melding available data on this expansive subject into a document of value to those interested in knowing the links between communication and tourism.

PART I

Introduction to Tourism, the Media, and Decision-Making

1

Tourism Theory

SYNOPSIS OF CHAPTER

- Why tourism is difficult to define

- Tourism can be defined from at least six points of view

- A simple tourism flow-model

- *Focus* on International Tourism; world tourist arrivals, receipts and the World Tourism Organization (WTO)

- *Fast Facts* on Australian tourism definitions, trends, and forecasts

What is Tourism?

When a person visits friends in another city, is that person a tourist? If a person travels to another country on a brief work assignment, is that person a tourist? If a family goes to Indonesia for a week of rest and sun, are they tourists? The probable answer to all of these questions is *yes*. Were the Crusaders tourists? Perhaps!

So what, then, is tourism?

Modern tourism boasts an interesting historical and social heritage—dating back to before the Industrial Revolution, when a jaunt across Europe was considered an integral part of the education of the ruling classes. After the Industrial Revolution, changes in the patterns of work and leisure set the wheels of tourism in motion. Work cycles became adjusted to suit machine-paced labour—rather than on the traditional measurements of time based on the individual's subsistence or semi-subsistence lifestyle. Later developments—in economics, labour laws (such as paid holidays), transportation, communications, and awareness of other cultures—opened up tourism, and made it more accessible to the masses (Laws 1991).

Tourism in this post-Industrial era can trace its origins back to Thomas

Cook's earliest foray into organised tours—which marked the birth of mass tourism. It has been recorded that Cook used the printing machines in his own print shop to compose an early form of brochure, promoting a day-trip train journey. The success of this venture gave early evidence of the power of advertising and channels of distribution. It also establishes an early link between the growth in mass tourism and, in turn, mass media (see Part II).

Tourism, as we see it today, has developed into a phenomenon of incredible proportions. Ritchie states that:

> . . . with economic activity measured at [US$]2.75 trillion . . . [tourism] can claim to be the 'world's largest industry'.
>
> Ritchie 1990

Tourism encompasses a vast array of activities and travel situations carried out for family, business, and leisure purposes. As such, defining it presents a problem.

Tourism Defined

In defining tourism, many approaches have been taken by researchers over the years. At least six different viewpoints can be used:

- economic;
- technical;
- experiential;
- psychological;
- holistic; and
- communicative.

Economic Definition

Viewing tourism as an economic activity recognises it primarily as an industry like any other industry. Ryan offers the following definition:

> . . . a study of the demand for, and supply of, accommodation and supportive services for those staying away from home, and the resultant patterns of expenditure, income creation and employment.
>
> Ryan 1991a

This is a rather bland definition. It is to be noted that it excludes any reference to enjoyment and leisure. It does, however, cover other key ingredients—such as demand and supply, and stays away from home. Omission of the words *travel, trip, journey* (or any other form of movement) is an important shortcoming of this definition—particularly in light of one of the basic models of tourism proposed by Laws (1991) in Figure 1.1. This model distinguishes between home and some other destination, and indicates the physical effort involved in moving to and from home.

Figure 1.1   The basic tourism model

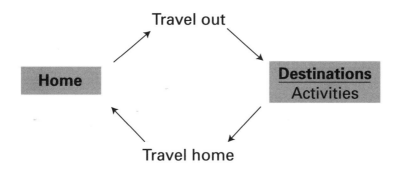

Source: Laws 1991

Technical Definition

Tourism planners have different interpretations of tourism in accordance with their individual needs and orientation. As such, their approach to defining tourism will reflect more specific technical attributes.

Tourism can be defined in terms of one's reason for travelling—whether it be for leisure, family reasons, or business. For example, American Express claims that:

> Travel and tourism is a vast complex network of business engaged in the lodging, transportation, feeding and entertainment of travellers.
>
> American Express, quoted by Ryan 1991a

Although brief, this definition succinctly states the general areas of operation of American Express, and also represents a good overall business definition of tourism. However, the definition is a little too broadly stated to satisfy the specific needs of certain tourism participants. Economists might require a more exacting understanding of tourism. And tourists might not appreciate the thought of being part of a 'network of business' as they take their dream holiday—for them, the business side needs to be under-emphasised, not put forward as a technicality that they are 'engaged in'.

Economists might find the next definition more exacting for their needs. It is another example of a technical definition, stated in statistical terms by the British Tourist Authority. According to this definition:

> . . . a tourist trip is a stay of one or more nights away from home for holidays, visits to friends or relatives, business conferences or any other purpose, except . . . boarding education or semi-permanent employment.
>
> British Tourist Authority, quoted in Ryan 1991a

This definition illustrates the attention given to tourism by business and government. It affects groups from a range of enterprises—those mentioned in the definition, as well as entertainment, accommodation, transport, catering, and sport.

These definitions do not, however, thoroughly explain all that is involved in tourism. There is a user-specific nature in such definitions that, although functional for specific organisations applying them, omit more personalised explanations for travel and tourism.

Experiential Definition

Recognising that every individual is different, tourism can be defined to accommodate the impact of each person's experience. The desire for sensual gratification is a major component in the 'holiday' travel industry, in which the primary motivation is rest, pleasure, adventure, and discovery. As such, another definition of tourism could be:

> . . . benefits that arise from experiencing new places, and new situations that are of a temporary duration, whilst free from the constraints of work, or normal patterns of daily life at home.
>
> Ryan 1991a

This definition aptly encapsulates an underlying element of escapism—the concept of escaping the rigmarole of daily routine in order to act out some kind of fantasy. Emotional wellbeing and development is inherent in this definition, and deserves further examination.

Psychological Definition

The psychological benefits of tourism, as linked to holiday travel, can also be tied into the determinants of motivation, and economic demand for travel, as explained below:

> An analysis of the motivational stage [which generates the whole process] can reveal the way in which people set goals for their destination-choice and how these goals are then reflected in both their travel choice and travel behaviour.
>
> Mansfeld 1992

Clearly, this has implications for how tourism planners understand their trade, and how they relate planning activities to tourist goals, needs and real expectations (Goodall & Ashworth 1988). Travel motivation and tourist decision-making can be attributed to what van Raaij and Francken (1984) called the 'vacation sequence' which, in turn, is related to various 'push' and 'pull' factors (see pages 126, 127)

A simple example of a psychological definition was one given to the author during an interview with the ex-airport manager for Air New Zealand:

> ... [people go to] places they have always wanted to go. A great many Australians go to Europe—Italians, Greeks, Yugoslavs—not so much now ...
>
> Interviews, Holt 1995

This is a combination of experiential and psychological reasoning, perhaps underscored by an element of childhood dreaming—the desire, since early childhood (when fantasies ran wildest), to see something. Although eloquent in its simplicity, the above definition also fails to capture the true essence of tourism. It fails to explain *why* they have always wanted to go to a particular place. Is it because their parents came from the place (which is highly likely in the Australian case)? Or because they have seen it on television or in a magazine? Or overheard their neighbours discussing the place? Or simply the thought of getting away? There is a plethora of possibilities. Motivation for travelling is much more complex than presented in the above quotation and requires more analysis (see Chapter 3, Tourist Decision-Making).

Holistic Definition

A holistic approach, broad-reaching in its terminology, and assimilating various interpretations into a general definition, was first taken by the Tourism Steering Group to Stratford-upon-Avon District Council in England. In its 1978 report, the group agreed to the following definition:

> ... day trippers from the cities of the Midlands, evening theatregoers from London, coach-tour passengers from all over the world hurtling through the country, conference delegates and longer-stay customers of the whole price range of serviced and unserviced accommodation ... a visitor to the District for whatever reason he or she comes, for however long he or she may stay, and by whatever means he or she may come ...
>
> Tourism Steering Group, 1978, quoted by Ryan 1991a

This very general definition covers tourism and travel at various levels—including the aim and the means of travel, duration intended, price range, accommodation style, and tourism type (cultural tourism, adventure tourism, day-tripping, and so on). It provides sufficient detail and scope. It does not refer specifically to the business side of tourism but, for the purpose of introducing a newcomer to the study of tourism, it is a useful description. The definition could, perhaps, be criticised as being too long, but this is justified in order to cover the many facets of tourism.

Marketing/Communications Definition

One final interpretation that is appropriate in the context of this book is to explain tourism as a function of marketing or, more broadly, as a communication experience. In an attempt to convey the concept of tourism to multiple users (students, professionals, academics, businesses, governments, and the media), a market or communications definition might be the best way to understand tourism as an act or intention. For example, tourism might well be a form of self-expression (like art, writing, or speech); a desire to exercise the many freedoms we enjoy in modern society (a freedom to spend; freedom of movement; freedom to experience the sense of the new, the old, or the other); and to communicate these present or future desires in commercial, aesthetic, physical, virtual, real, and emotional travel and tourism decisions and actions.

This definition borders on the experiential and psychological definitions, and certainly touches on the business/commercial side of tourism. It is not above criticism, but it introduces some new elements to a tourism definition via the fundamental freedoms, and through the dualisms of 'physical/aesthetic', and 'self/other'—which, it could be argued, are at the heart of tourists' communicating their will through experience and the motivations that lead to tourism decisions and actions. Tourism communications specialists would like to understand the critical connection between tourist/consumer behaviour and these expressions of free will. The definition introduces the concepts of time (represented as present or future tourism potentialities), and real versus virtual tourism (virtual tourism being computer simulations that allow holiday sensations to be experienced as though they were real).

Focus on International Tourism

World Tourism Arrivals (WTA) and the World Tourism Organization (WTO)

Definition of International Tourism

International tourism involves the temporary movement of persons to a destination located beyond the national borders of the persons' normal country of residence or citizenship for the purpose of activities except work or schooling. International tourism includes travel for leisure and business purposes.

The basic tourism system of travel to and from a destination can be expanded to include other important tourism components, as shown in Figure 1.2.

Figure 1.2   Simple tourism model including international tourism

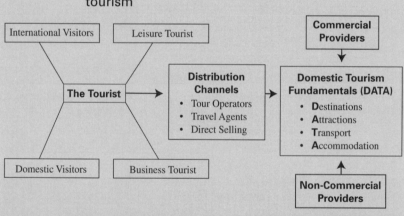

Source: Author's presentation

International Tourism Arrivals

The measurement of worldwide tourism movements is called the International Tourism Arrivals (ITA) and is calculated by the World Tourism Organization (WTO) as a barometer of tourism activity. The evolution of ITAs from 1950 is shown in Table 1.1.

Table 1.1 International tourist arrivals (ITAs) worldwide 1950–98

Year	Arrivals (millions)	Yearly Growth (%)	Receipts (millions US$)	Yearly Growth (%)
1950	25.3	–	2.1	–
1960	69.3	10.6	6.9	12.58
1961	75.3	8.7	7.3	6.1
1962	81.4	8.1	8.0	10.2
1963	90.1	10.7	8.9	10.7
1964	104.6	16.1	10.1	13.4
1965	112.9	7.9	11.6	15.2
1966	120.0	6.3	13.3	15.0
1967	129.8	8.2	14.5	8.4
1968	131.2	1.1	15.0	3.7
1969	143.5	9.4	16.8	12.1
1970	165.8	15.5	17.9	6.6
1971	178.9	7.9	20.9	16.5
1972	189.1	5.7	24.6	18.1
1973	198.9	5.2	31.1	26.1
1974	205.7	3.4	33.8	8.9
1975	222.3	8.1	40.7	20.3
1976	228.9	3.0	44.4	9.2
1977	249.3	8.9	55.6	25.2
1978	267.1	7.1	68.8	23.7
1979	283.1	6.0	83.3	21.1
1980*	285.3	0.8	105.3	26.4
1981*	286.4	0.4	107.5	2.0
1982*	285.3	–0.4	100.9	–6.1
1983*	289.0	1.3	102.5	1.6
1984*	315.9	9.3	112.7	10.0
1985*	326.7	3.4	117.9	4.6
1986*	338.4	3.4	143.2	21.5
1987*	363.3	7.4	176.3	23.1
1988*	394.3	8.5	203.8	15.6
1989*	426.0	8.0	220.8	8.3
1990*	457.6	7.4	268.3	21.5
1991*	463.3	1.2	276.8	3.2
1992*	502.3	8.4	313.5	13.3
1993*	518.1	3.1	321.1	2.4
1994*	549.6	6.1	352.6	9.8
1995*	563.6	2.6	401.5	13.9
1996*	594.8	5.5	433.9	8.1
1997	610.8	2.6	436.0	4.8
1998	625.2	2.4	444.7	2.0

Note: *revised figures

Source: WTO, Tourism Compendium 1999

Column two of this table presents the total number of arrivals from foreign countries (same-day visitors excluded) per year for the world—and serves as a good indicator of tourist activity around the world.

Column three indicates the yearly change. This column indicates that world tourism has consistently grown from 1960 to 1997 with the exception of 1981–82 (perhaps due to economic factors including the oil crisis), and that the highest growth from one year to the next was 1969–70 (probably coinciding with the introduction of Boeing 747s which revolutionised long-haul travel).

Column four presents the total receipts from international tourism (international transport excluded), which has also shown a constant growth trend (again except for 1981–82).

The international arrivals can also be broken down by region—Africa, Americas, Europe, East Asia/Pacific, Middle East, and South Asia (WTO classifications). This is show in Figure 1.3

Figure 1.3   International Tourist Arrivals by WTO's classified region

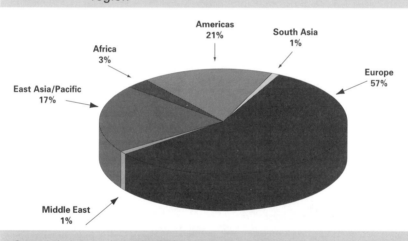

Source: Author's presentation based on WTO statistics, 1997

In terms of tourism spending on a worldwide basis, Australia competes relatively well. In 1996, Australia ranked 19th in the world—down from 16th in 1980 when Australia's economy was booming. Germany is at the top of the list.

In 1996, Australia was ranked 12th in terms of tourism earnings, up from 24th in 1980. The USA held the number one place.

As far as being one of the world's top tourism destinations, Australia still has some catching up to do. In 1996, Australia was in 30th position, up from 53rd in 1980. France consistently holds the number one position (WTO Yearbook, 1998)—solidified in place by the 1998 soccer World Cup in Paris.

The World Tourism Organization (WTO)

The WTO, based in Madrid, is the largest governmental organisation dealing exclusively with tourism. It has a membership of 133 countries and territories. This does not include Australia—which left in 1990 because it believed that the WTO, based in Madrid, was not serving Australian tourism adequately. As an executive agency of the United Nations Development Program (UNDP), the WTO is composed of three core groups: General Assembly, Executive Council, and Regional Commission.

The Regional Commission is composed of the six regions noted above. The WTO's chief mission is to:

> ... promote and develop tourism as a significant means of fostering international peace and understanding, economic development and international trade.
>
> WTO 1997

The Regional Commission executes this mission through the following broad activities:

- establishing inventories of existing and potential tourism resources;
- providing a framework for national tourism administration, legislation (regulation) and corporations;
- evaluating the impact of tourism on economies and the environment;
- supporting training and feasibility research for schools and management;
- social planning and management at local, regional, and national level;
- developing new tourist sites and products;
- standardising and planning tourist accommodation and classification systems;
- investigating and sourcing finance and investments in tourism; and
- ensuring safety of tourists and tourist facilities.

The WTO's tourism figures *do* include the following:

- excursionists: cruise passengers, day visitors, crews;
- tourists: non-residents, nationals resident abroad, crew members (non-resident);
- purpose: holidaymakers, business travellers, health tourists, students, delegates to meetings and congresses, visiting friends and relatives (VFR), religious travellers, sports travellers, others.

The WTO's tourism figures *do not* include the following:

- border workers, transit passengers, nomads, refugees, members of armed forces, consular employees, diplomats, temporary immigrants, permanent immigrants.

Figure 1.4 illustrates the WTO classification of tourists.

Figure 1.4 WTO classification of tourism

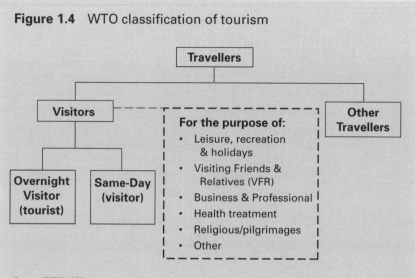

Source: WTO 1997

Fast Facts on Australian Tourism: Definition, Trends and Forecasts

Definition

The Australian Tourism Commission (ATC) defines tourism as:

> ... encompassing all travel more than 40 kilometres away from the normal place of residence, except that undertaken to commute to and from the usual place of work. It includes both domestic and international travel, whether for business or pleasure.
>
> ATC, cited in Commonwealth Department of Tourism 1992

It should be noted that tourism:
- is a significant employer and producer in the global economy—in 1997, of the 262 million jobs worldwide, tourism provided approximately 10.3 per cent;
- is often service-orientated and, therefore, labour-intensive;
- can function on minimum direct financial assistance from government;
- consists mainly of small-to-medium businesses—although there are moves towards big business through integration;
- is a 24-hour-a-day, seven-day-a-week industry;
- is a seasonal industry;

- has relatively few barriers to entry;
- is decentralised (and, hence, very flexible in regional economies); and
- can be an important means of education and cultural exchange.

Tourism in Australia does not, as many would expect it, involve only hotels, restaurants, catering, and airlines. It touches many businesses and many people directly and indirectly. As the tourist spends money, the effect filters into the economy—which has a 'multiplier effect' on the initial expenditure. The end result is that tourism affects a much wider cross-section of the economy than might be imagined. This is illustrated in Figure 1.5.

Figure 1.5   The core Australian tourism businesses (primary, secondary & tertiary)

Primary (Core)	Secondary	Tertiary
Accommodation	Hotel & Restaurant	Construction/real estate
– Hotels/resorts	suppliers	Distillers/brewers/bottlers
– Motels	Taxi services	Vehicle manufacturers
– Hostels	Cameras & film	Fuel producers
– Caravans	Maps, travel books	Clothing manufacturers
– Camping	Shopping malls	Communication networks
Transport	Service stations	Education & training
– Airlines	Sporting events	Recreation/sports goods
– Cruise ships	Banking services	Food producers
– Rail	Reservation systems	Advertising/media
– Car rentals	Auto clubs/insurers	Cartographers/printers
– Bus/coaches	Entertainment & arts	
Attractions	venues	
– Man-made	Museums/historical sites	
– Natural	National parks	
Food & Beverage		
– Restaurants		
– Fast foods		
– Wine merchants/bars/		
clubs		
Travel agencies		
Tour operators		
Souvenirs		
Luggage		

Source: Influenced by Commonwealth Department of Tourism 1992

Conclusions

From the vast array of information available on this growing industry, tourism can be defined from various standpoints—technical, holistic, psychological, experiential, economic, and communicative. Although technical and financial details are important to business and economists, tourists might find a more general explanation more suitable to their needs. Any definition of tourism ultimately depends on the perspective and purpose requiring explanation. The holistic definition is a compromise between multiple purposes and users, and the communicative definition introduces some important philosophical tenets into tourism theory.

The best definition is the one that suits the individual or organisation seeking to define tourism. For example, tourism could be the experience being contemplated by a person who wants to get away from home, relax, have some fun, see some sights, and spend some hard-earned money. It does not need to be a formalised definition to communicate the desired intention. Anything is possible. In the future, tourism could be defined as the latest pill that can be taken, or as the virtual-reality centre that simulates the tourism and travel once taken in the twentieth century. The final word on tourism definitions, therefore, is that it depends on different circumstances, and changes with time.

Discussion Time

- Why is it important to define tourism at all? Who stands to benefit by delineating tourism? Discuss these questions in small groups.
- Again in small groups, simulate a brainstorming exercise to redefine tourism for the following entities:
    - special-interest groups (for example, disability tourism, ethnic tourism, or make up your own);
    - a tour operator;
    - a charter airline;
    - a terrorist group;
    - a television producer.

2

Media Theory

What are the Media?

A person's basic understanding of the media often emanates, ironically, from the media themselves. The term 'the media' is a title attached to the type and format of communication going on all around us. Sometimes consciously and sometimes subconsciously, in formal and informal communication, we are made aware of our surroundings. As part of this awareness, we formulate ideas and attitudes that lead to an interpretation of our surroundings. In making this interpretation, we assign a meaning to the words 'media' or 'the media', we have (perhaps unconsciously) responded to the media as a function, which is to inform.

The term 'medium' refers to a channel of communication, or the means of information exchange between parties. The term 'the media' (or the 'mass media'), as an entity, describes the various modes of communication as an industry in the public domain. This is taken to mean print media (primarily newspapers, magazines, brochures, journals, direct mail, newsletters, and so on), broadcast media (radio, television), and the Internet. These are examples of the formal modes of mass communication.

Describing the media in terms of their communication value, we should add:

- public relations, which is the monitoring and promotion of informal (uncommissioned) information in the public media with the intention that an interested party be presented favourably; and
- advertising, which is commissioned formal communication.

To further our understanding of how the mass media actually work, we should look at what communication means, and some definitions.

Media Defined

The mass media are multifaceted but, central to all interpretations, is the communication process. Communication is, therefore, an appropriate place to begin the theoretical introduction.

Communication

Communication can be defined in complex terms (such as 'encoding', 'decoding', 'discounting cues', and 'dissociation') but, for clarity, the simplest explanation is often the best. Reilly (1990) describes communication as 'the transmitting of ideas and information'. However, Reilly adds a cautionary note to his definition when he notes that the act of communication itself is a complicated process to perform effectively when the audience is often distant and diverse. Communication thus exists at a mass level (the public media or non-personal media), between individuals (interpersonal or personal media), and between limited numbers of people (small group).

There are many communication 'roadblocks' (or barriers). Some of these are interpersonal, some technical (especially in the case of mass audience diversity), and some could be a matter of group or interpersonal dynamics.

An example of a *personal* barrier to communication is someone trying to express himself or herself to an authority figure who behaves unsympathetically (for example, motorist and policeman, or student and teacher). The individual, in this case, probably experiences a feeling of anxiety and possibly even some physical symptoms (such as difficulties in vocalisation, dry mouth, stammered words, and so on). The barriers here could stem from a number of sources—physical or psychological.

A *technical* barrier might simply be a breakdown in the transmission—interference from outside noises, radio waves, or mixed and/or confused messages. The use of communication models has enhanced our understanding of the communication process, as well as its tendency towards dysfunction. For now, we will look at the model of Basic Communication and, in Part II, we will examine some of the 'roadblocks' in greater detail.

Figure 2.1   Basic communication

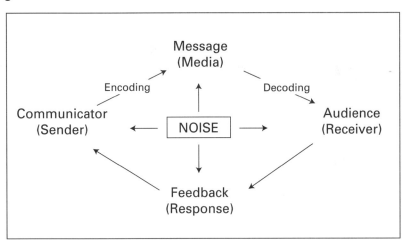

Legend: Communicator (Sender): party sending the message to another party; Encoding: converting thoughts and ideas into symbolic form; Message: information relayed symbolically from the sender; Media: channels of communication transporting a message from sender to receiver; Decoding: assigning meaning to the symbolic message encoded by the receiver; Audience (Receiver): party receiving the message sent by another party; Response: receiver's reaction to the message; Feedback: receiver's response relayed back to sender; Noise: interruption of the message resulting in distortion of the communication exchange and possible misinterpretation of the message and response

Source: Based on Reilly 1990 and Kotler, Bowen & Makens 1999

In Figure 2.1, we have an example of two-way communication which, through feedback (such as questions by the receiver), is a continuous process. Instantaneous feedback is generally preferable—such as a teacher gauging the class's attention by the level of restless movement, or a speaker counting yawns in the audience. Although simple in interpersonal communication, feedback is more difficult with the mass media—where the kind of feedback an editor can expect from sales charts is often delayed and patchy.

The sender's message is vitally important. The sender must be capable of effectively saying what is intended, or employ an expert to do so. The receiver must, first, be able to understand the message and, assuming the receiver finds the sender credible, to perceive a benefit in complying, before acting upon the message received (Reilly 1990).

The relationship between sender and receiver is also very important. How they view each other can significantly influence the communication experience. The likelihood of compliance to a request from a person who is not liked or respected is much less than a similar request from someone with whom there is empathy. For effective communication, it is extremely important to develop an understanding of *active participation* in the communication exchange—which implies active listening by both sender and receiver. This is important to tourist information providers in assessing the information needs of potential tourists. However, it is not as simple as it might seem at an interpersonal level. Communications experts claim that one of the greatest hurdles in communication is *selective understanding* linked to poor listening skills.

Some of the typical barriers to communication can also be applied in a learning context. Some people believe their status entitles them to speak without listening—that they know what is best.

Active (rather than *passive*) listening, and *direct* (rather than *indirect*) listening, are also understandably difficult in the case of the mass media— where the audience is often remote. However, an editor or network director who perfects a way to actively listen to the audience, rather than merely monitoring it, may derive a great advantage over the competition.

> The communication process involved in the mass media has some of the characteristics of both a formalised and an informal network. On the one hand, they are directional [from a newspaper to its readers, for example]. On the other, they are mainly concerned with relatively non-essential ideas, which to most people may be interesting or entertaining, but do not usually require direct or immediate action by the majority of the readers or audience. There is also the element of choice, so that one can opt in or out of the audience at any time, at the turn of a switch, or the failure to pay a newspaper bill.
>
> Carter 1971

Perhaps, to better understand what is being said here, we should look at what the mass media means in a communication event.

Mass Media

According to the American sociologist, Dr Wilbur Schramm:

> A mass medium is essentially a working group organised round some device for circulating the same message at about the same time, to large numbers of people.
>
> Schramm 1960

Although a good definition, it fails to address some of the more 'natural' means of mass communication—such as that in education, the church, and through word-of-mouth or rumour, to name three. The effect of word-of-mouth in tourism communications will be developed in Chapters 4, 5, and 7.

Criticism has been directed at definitions of communications that contain the word 'mass'—on the grounds that the word depreciates the value of individuality within society. Such criticism claims that people do not buy newspapers and watch television as members of a large group, that their personalities are not imperceptibly coated in the same colour—but are more like an abstract matrix. As it is, the mass media represent a peep show, a look into the keyhole, at what is happening outside one's own personal communication networks. But it is important to know where to look, if one is to understand what is really being looked at.

The mass media are divided into print and electronic media as follows:

Figure 2.2   Mass media formats

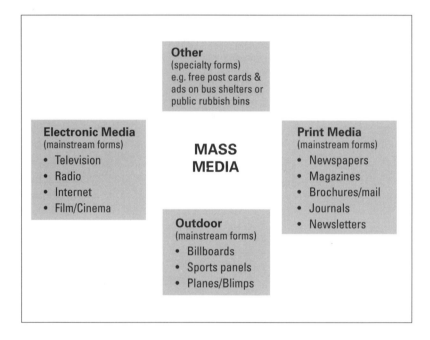

Source: Author's presentation

Mass Media Efficacy

Despite the term, the 'mass media' by no means make up a generic entity. Different formats and applications of various media render different results—which makes media choice and application a vital part of the marketing and communications process. Table 2.1 presents a useful guide to the comparative efficacy of the mass media, illustrating the advantages, limitations, and the volume of business generated by each medium.

Table 2.1. Summary of most important mass media types, costs, and advantages

Medium	Volume (US$ bill)	%	Examples of cost	Advantages	Limitations
			⌐or 1 page in *Chicago*	Flexibility; timeliness; good local market coverage; broad acceptance; high believability	Short lift; poor reproduction quality; small pass-along audience (from one to other)
			⌐ 30 of prime ⌐hicago	Combines sight, sound & motion; appealing to the senses; high attention; high reach	High absolute cost; high clutter; fleeting exposure; less audience selectivity
			⌐ the names ⌐es of ⌐terinarians ⌐le	Audience selectivity; flexibility; no ad competition within same medium; personalisation	Relatively high cost; junk-mail image; clutter if bulk delivered by distributor
Radio	8.7	6.6	$700 for 1 minute of drive time (during peak hour commute a.m. & p.m.) in Chicago	Mass use; high geographic and demographic selectivity; low cost	Audio presentation only; lower attention than TV; non-standardised rate structures; fleeting exposure
Magazines	7.0	5.3	$84 390 for one page, four colours, in *Newsweek*	High geographic and demographic selectivity; credibility and prestige; high-quality reproduction; long life; good pass-along readership	Long advertisement purchase lead time; some waste circulation; no guarantee of position
Outdoor	1.0	0.8	$25 500 per month for 71 billboards in metropolitan Chicago	Flexibility; high repeat exposure; low cost; low competition	No audience selectivity; creative limitations
Other	29.1	22.2			
Total	131.3	100.0%			

Source: Columns 2 & 3 from Cohen 1993; rest of table adapted from Kotler, Bowen & Makens 1999

Print Media

In general, the term 'print media' is taken to mean newspapers, magazines, brochures, journals, newsletters and, to a lesser degree, direct mail. The print media originated in Britain with the invention of letterpress techniques in 1476. It was followed by the first, crude, newspapers in the early 1620s.

Newspapers

In 1665, the *London Gazette* was the first newspaper to be printed on larger sheets aimed at the more general reader. Circulation of newspapers remained small, but sufficient to warrant daily publication by 1702— marking the first regular daily paper, the *Daily Courant*.

Newspapers became more viable with time, with the advent of improved postal services, more efficient news-gathering methods, better means of distribution, and paid advertising. By the beginning of the nineteenth century, newspapers had become a firmly established middle-class institution with considerable political influence (Carter 1971).

Historically, the growth of the press did not rely entirely on technological developments leading to improvements in printing and paper-making machinery. It depended (as heavily then as it does now) on its ability to communicate to the masses, or the mass of individuals. This means the ability of journalists, photojournalists, editors, and advertisers to inform, entertain, and persuade—and, in turn, the newspaper's capacity to interest readers in purchasing the product.

Readership of newspapers is high, especially in Europe. For example, in Sweden, readership is as high as 487 copies circulated per 1000 inhabitants. That is, almost one in two Swedish people buy newspapers— which could mean an even higher readership because newspapers are often passed on and used in public areas (Swedish Consulate 1996).

In the travel industry, virtually every member uses newspapers (Reilly 1990). It represents the dominant medium for travel principals— particularly for advertising. Potential travellers have an understanding of this close relationship, and are conditioned to look to newspapers for travel information.

There are several limitations to newspapers—including poor reproduction, criticism about sensationalism, and reduced visual impact due to advertising clutter. From a commercial point of view, newspapers are also not the best means of showing a product in colour and, when used in nationwide advertising campaigns, can present production problems with different measurement requirements being required. In addition to the above problems, a further disadvantage of newspaper advertising is that its wide readership might also be *wasted* readership, with no guarantees of target audience.

Magazines

Magazines overcome some of the problems in newspapers. Because of this, and as a result of increasing designer needs of audiences, magazines. specific newsletters, and journals have experienced growth in the years since the earliest *Harper's Bazaar* rolled off the press in 1867.

Colour is clearer and more attractive in magazine glossy form. They are more audience-specific, and generally have a longer shelf-life. Readers of magazines are usually more affluent, which offers many opportunities for advertising.

However, magazines also encounter certain problems as a communication channel. They are more costly to produce, and this makes placement costs higher. There is also a problem with overlapping audiences for certain advertising placements which, as Reilly (1990) states, might not be such a bad thing from the perspective of persuasiveness.

Radio

Radio, as a medium, is experiencing a return to favour. It has fought its way back from relative obscurity in the wake of the television boom. Marconi arrived in the United Kingdom in the early 1900s to demonstrate his incredible invention—the sending of electromagnetic waves from Cornwall to Newfoundland. Radio was soon used in wider mass communication in the 1920s and, within years, broadcasting stations had sprung up throughout the world, most of them in the United States of America which experienced an explosion in commercial radio. The British avoided the cluttered airwaves problem by setting up the British Broadcasting Corporation (BBC) in 1922, which still broadcasts around the world today.

Radio was (and still is) an accessible medium. Some have described it as an intimate and selective medium. Other advantages are that it is flexible, that transmission can be altered on very short notice and, with portable radios so prevalent nowadays, that audiences are more portable.

Radio is relatively inexpensive to produce. Receivers are also inexpensive—with AM/FM band radios being sold in Western markets for as little as $10.00. Electronics companies in low-cost producing countries in South-East Asia can manufacture what have become virtually disposable electronic goods.

With both public and commercial radio networks worldwide, there is a wide variety of choice for audiences. For example, the BBC can be heard virtually all over the world, 24 hours a day.

However, as a medium, radio also has some disadvantages. Reilly describes them in this way:

There are, however, time restrictions as to length of message, no visual appeal, and no means of referring back to the message.

Reilly 1990

Reilly's observation touches on what we have previously referred to as the problem of *feedback* in the mass media.

Reilly also deals specifically with the travel industry's under-use of radio:

For travel advertising radio, with its unique property of conjuring up images with sound, could be used more than it is.

Reilly 1990

Television

It is recognised by most (if not all) commentators on the use of mass media, that television is the most significant medium in its power to lure an audience. Television is continuing to grow in audience size—despite pressure from multimedia higher technology (such as the Internet and email network) spreading at a rapid rate throughout the world. Television's long 'growth' phase in the product life-cycle can be accredited to;

- the ability of networks (and later cable and satellite operators) to supply a communications product in line with audience taste; and
- the power of persuasion.

As far back as 1925, a little-known development was taking place within the walls of Television Limited, a start-up company run by a Scottish engineer, John Baird. Across the Atlantic, in the USA, the Radio Corporation of America (RCA), Electronical Musical Industries (EMI, est. 1931), and the Marconi Company, were also very interested in this new technology called television. Competing standards led to a committee decision to use the 405-line picture (with 50 frames), as used by EMI–Marconi, rather than Baird's 30-line system.

As an influence on societal thinking, television grew slower than did the technology. The units were initially expensive, and World War II led to the immediate closure of the BBC. Television's rise to fame came after the war ended, spearheaded first by the American commercial networks, and later spurred on by cable television and, eventually, by international satellite television that was capable of being beamed around the world.

The Gulf War was not a big-enough conflict to close television stations, but it was an early sign of things to come—with scenes of the battles being televised directly via Cable News Network (CNN) satellite around the world. This was instantaneous and graphic information—a sign of things to come.

As a commercial tool, television communicates like no other. Television commercials combine sound and picture; television is popular among all ages, economic levels, and cultural groups; and television uses colour and images very well. It can demonstrate a product or a scene in motion or in use, has huge audiences worldwide, and is a strong means of identification. Some research indicates that television also possesses impact, but this is a point of contention.

Others argue that, as with other forms of mass media, the measurement of television's impact on its audience is a very difficult task indeed. The following quotation illustrates the point:

> Definition of the media-effects perspective is a task made difficult by the great diversity in theoretical styles, research questions and methods of gathering evidence and making inferences.
>
> McLeod, Kosicki & Zhangdang 1991

A discussion on understanding and misunderstanding media effects will be developed more fully in Chapter 5.

Focus on Television Ratings

The Nielsen Ratings in the USA

> You just heard that a TV Show was ranked #1 in the Nielsen TV ratings. What does that mean?
>
> Nielsen Media 1998

There is a unique and strong partnership between audience ratings research and the television business for a very good reason. Television principals, who have a very heavy financial stake in the success of their programming, want to leave as little as possible to chance when it comes to knowing what their target public wants to watch.

Nielsen Media Research, founded in 1936 by Arthur C. Nielsen, was one of the first to measure radio audiences. In 1950, it jumped on the burgeoning television broadcasting business and remains the official national measurement standard.

How are Viewers Measured?

Unlike printed media, where copies can be counted to establish a circulation figure, television is distant and diffused across many sub-media (cable, satellite, or terrestrial). This makes it difficult to count how many people viewed a particular program at a particular moment. A 'TV Rating' is then given to a specific program based on a count that is made of a sample of pre-selected 'voters' (known as the 'Nielsen TV families') and converted into an average rating. In other words, a rating is:

... how many people watched ... a particular program during the average minute.

Nielsen Media website 1998

This means a 'top-ranked' show has received more viewers than any other on any other channel at that given time slot.

What is the Sampling Method?

Obviously Nielsen Media Research cannot count every one of the 98 million American households watching television, so it has to take a sample of viewers. US national ratings are calculated from a sample of more than 5000 households, containing over 13 000 people. This relatively low sample figure is considered representative because everyone in the USA has an equal chance of being in the sample, and because Nielsen has matched its samples with US Census Bureau data.

Nielsen studies more than 17 000 US television stations and 11 000 cable systems to collect its programming information.

Other research methods used by Nielsen are:

- the use of metering devices on television sets to ascertain when they are on, and to which channel the set is tuned;
- passive commercial identification using 'fingerprints' or chronometered video cassettes; and
- diaries (viewers who record their viewing habits and submit the diary).

How are the Data Used?

Both television programmers and television advertisers are interested in ratings data. The relationship is simple. An advertiser wants to put an advertisement in a popular program time to secure high visibility for the product. The television channels are able to charge a higher premium for higher-rated timeslots or for programs occupying that timeslot—such as in 'prime time' (that is approximately 6 p.m. to 10 p.m.).

Based on Nielsen rating information, certain programs are valued more highly by the viewing public and by the producers of the program. Producers continue to produce successful shows, but drop the budget on the 'losers'.

It is thus apparent that much value is attached to the idea of 'media effects' in the television, advertising, and marketing businesses. However, not everyone agrees that this relationship is irrefutable. Critiques of 'media effects' are discussed in more detail in Chapter 5 of this book.

Nielsen Media 1998

The Internet

The Internet (or 'Net') is, without a doubt, one of the most exciting developments in the world of mass communications. However, it is not necessarily a very recent phenomenon. Since the late 1980s, and before this in the United States military and some multinational enterprises (MNEs), one could gain access to the vast world of the Internet with a telephone modem link, computer software, and a server. But what exactly is the Internet?

According to Williams et al.:

> The Internet can be defined as a computer network consisting of millions of hosts from organisations and countries around the world transporting data across computers . . . [supporting] the Worldwide Web (WWW), Electronic Mail (email), Usenet, Gopher, Telnet, and File Transfer Protocol (FTP) . . . similar to a global library with millions of books, records, movies [and so on] open all day, every day of the year.
>
> Williams et al. 1996

According to Berthon, Pitt & Watson (1996), the fundamental differences between the Internet and other media faculties are that:

- access opportunities are, theoretically speaking, egalitarian; and
- the audience or users have a uniform voice.

Some additional differences can be seen in the *interactivity* achievable with the Internet. Whether an Internet user is buying something or simply researching, there is an ongoing opportunity for feedback. Internet site managers normally solicit feedback from people who visit (or 'hit') their sites. This feedback can be virtually instantaneous and direct—depending on whether the site manager is monitoring the site at the time a reply is submitted. Records are also kept of the number of 'hits' that a particular site receives from browsers. This is similar to an instantaneous circulation update (if viewed from a print media perspective), or like gaining a new set of ratings each day or even every minute (from a television or radio perspective).

Other possible advantages are that the Internet can be as colourful as a magazine, can be moving like television or film, and can transmit sound with the quality of hifi stereo or radio. And, with the exception of the costs of getting online (buying the computer and the communication equipment, and paying a distributor to access the Net), it is probably one of the cheaper forms of mass media. Advertising on certain popular sites—such as the search engines (AltaVista, Lycos, Yahoo, and so on) or travel links—can sometimes incur high fees, but the Net does not prohibit self-advertising, nor promotion of individuals or small companies. Choice abounds.

One of the chief criticisms of the Net is that it is essentially unregulated. This has been debated at length by opponents of the Net on the grounds of public decency and protection of minors from pornographic and violent websites, or even on the grounds of certain people using the Net to prey on their victims. As with film and television, it is inevitable that some form of restriction will be put on the Net to protect the innocents, but just how this will be achieved is another question. In the US, close watch is maintained over sites worldwide (in search of, for example, child pornography), so it is possible that the Internet will not continue to be as liberal a form of mass media as assumed.

Another problem often cited is that of 'spamming'. This refers to those who take advantage of the free nature of many websites, and the seemingly ever-expanding commercial potential. For example, Microsoft's free 'Hotmail' service offers email access via the net to anyone anywhere in the world. There are many conditions of use, mostly related to security and civil law protection for the host but, in principle, a major concern is 'spamming' from the expanding Microsoft database of subscribers. The Hotmail site is, of course, a forum for advertising and information-gathering, but users subscribe knowing this in advance.

Another criticism is that, in using the Net as a marketing tool, reaching the correct target audience is very difficult. However, this is changing as site managers become more experienced with basic biodata and demographic information collection before allowing people to enter certain sites, or segments within the site. Like conventional media forms, competitions and research surveys are also being used on the Net to furnish marketers with invaluable demographic background information.

One final criticism, made by Kotler, Bowen & Makens (1999), is that the Internet can be a damaging source of negative propaganda against companies or individuals. For example, Microsoft receives a lot of bad

Figure 2.3   How does the Internet work?

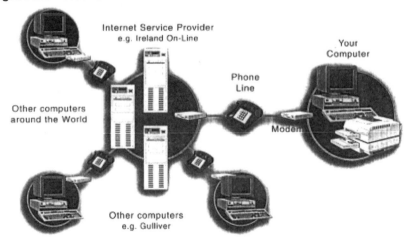

Source: Internet Link 1997, published with permission of Irish Tourist Board

publicity via the Internet. The above-mentioned 'Hotmail' email system has spawned a replica webpage that looks virtually the same as the 'Hotmail' homepage—except that it is called 'Crapmail'. Individuals will go to great lengths to harm an organisation's image.

Advertising

A discussion on the mass media would not be complete without mention of advertising. Advertising includes formal paid advertising, as well as informal and non-commercial information exchange. Advertising and the media are natural partners. Both seek to spread their message to a broad audience. Advertising makes the commercial mass media possible by providing valuable returns from selling advertising space. Revenues from subscriptions and counter sales are usually insufficient to guarantee continued business success in the media industry.

Advertising Agencies

The largest advertising agency in the USA is Young & Rubicam, which has an annual worldwide billing (the value of advertising placements for clients) of US$6 billion. The largest in the world, Dentsu, places US$10 billion annually (Konrad, quoted by Kotler, Bowen & Makens 1999). Advertising agencies were started in the mid-to-late nineteenth century by sales people who, as time went by, gained some insight into how layout and design of advertising could translate into greater returns. Although advertising is often handled in-house through marketing departments, many companies (especially tourism-related) employ specialists for expensive and important campaigns.

Advertising agencies are often divided into four sections:

- creative (advertisement development);
- media (advertisement placement);
- research (audience and market characteristics); and
- business (administration and business).

A commission fee structure has been traditional between the advertising agency and the client but, due to increasing costs and dissatisfaction with this system, more deals are being settled via a straight fee, or a combination of fee and commission.

Message Delivery

Creative staff in advertising agencies focus on several important characteristics in delivering their message to the audience. Setting the right tone and style, using the right images, voices and words, and finding the right timing and medium are just a few of the concerns. Kotler, Bowen &

Makens (1999) have provided some interesting message-diffusion tactics that work particularly well in the tourism business.

- *Slice-of-life:* 'normal' people visiting the resort being advertised (for example, a happy family sunbathing on the beach);
- *Lifestyle:* tries to match the tourist product with a lifestyle depiction conforming with that of their target audiences (for example, Diner's Club showing members of its special club as all business people from around the world);
- *Fantasy:* a dream world connected to the tourist product (for example, Sheraton Mirage Port Douglas in 1990 had a handsome man deliver a cocktail to a beautiful woman lounging by the lagoon swimming pool, with the slogan: 'Too good to be true');
- *Mood or image:* attaches an emotion or feeling to the image being delivered (for example, the calm of the Mediterranean or the romance of a Caribbean cruise);
- *Musical:* using music and complementary scenes to deliver the message (such as fast and 'rocky' for popular, youth-directed products, and slow and mellow for mature audiences);
- *Personality symbol:* build a character or mascot to represent the product (for example, Richard Branson as his own frontline character for his company Virgin);
- *Technical expertise:* espousing the expertise of the hotel, travel agent, or tour operator in handling certain holiday types for example (for example, Swissair has traditionally made use of its technical reputation for quality, and that 'Swiss-made' has traditionally meant quality);
- *Scientific evidence:* uses research to prove a point valued by the company (for example, that people who holiday more often have a lesser chance of dying from heart disease);
- *Testimonial evidence:* uses a well-known and believable person to endorse a product (for example, the McDonnell Douglas advertisement uses a famous astronaut to reassure audiences of the safety of their planes after negative press; see Chapter 4).

Based on Kotler, Bowen & Makens 1999

In choosing an appropriate medium to deliver their message, advertisers evaluate the reach, frequency, and impact of a potential advertisement. The *reach* is a measurement of the percentage of people contacted by an advertisement over a specified period of time (see Nielsen ratings, page 33). The *frequency* refers to how often an advertisement should be repeated (this being examined carefully to avoid saturation). The desired *impact* is a critical issue in the advertising process, but is very difficult to ascertain. Feedback can often be measured in terms of changed sales before and after the advertisement.

Conclusion

The various forms of media offer advantages and disadvantages to media operators. According to tourism practitioners, television is generally held to be the most effective advertising medium—entering more houses and thus gaining access to greater audiences. However, the phenomenal growth and impact of the Internet cannot be ignored by media practitioners as being the way forward in communications in general, and tourism communications in particular.

It must be understood, however, that a great divide still exists between merely exposing a public or audience to a message, and the desired influence of this message. This is examined further in Chapter 5.

Based on this understanding of communications and the mass media, the following chapter introduces decision theory, the many different approaches to defining and understanding tourist decision-making, and the associated difficulties.

Discussion Time

- Divide the group into three. Each group prepares a sales presentation (preferably in separate rooms) on an invented travel product. The groups then take it in turns to do a sales presentation of their product—its qualities, price, distribution, target market, and so on. While a group presents, one of the remaining two groups acts as the audience of potential buyers of the product (asking questions, evaluating the product, assessing its value for money). The third group takes the role of a panel of judges whose task is to assess the communication skills (believability, audience interest, appropriateness of the product for their audience, sales skills, and so on) of the presenting group. The activity rotates so that each group has a turn at playing each of the three roles. (A tip for the presenting group is to allocate the audience a specific market role so the audience knows from which perspective to evaluate the product; for example, 'This product is designed for the under-30s single market or the over-50s retired market'.)
- You are the editors of a publishing house. You are not completely satisfied with the definition of the media presented in this book. Together as a group, discuss the problems in the definition and come up with one of your own to rectify it. Discuss the difficulties experienced in formulating your own definition.

3

Tourist Decision-Making

SYNOPSIS OF CHAPTER

- The difficulties in isolating tourist decision-making

- The development of tourist-classification techniques

- The connection between information and tourist image perceptions

- Influence and the tourist decision process—aims + means = desire

- *Focus* on research on travel motives, Australian example

- *Fast Facts* on travel health and safety abroad

What is Decision-Making?

Some of the most difficult moments in life are those marked by indecision. Individuals make decisions every day on how to live their lives; what to eat and wear; what to watch on television; and who they spend time with, where, and for how long. Individuals are identified by their ability to make decisions, and their ability to select from the masses of options presented to them daily.

In tourism, as in other business enterprises, interested parties need to understand how the tourist population reaches these decisions—their motives, behaviour, and expectations—and also need to be aware of the broader trends affecting the industry. Tourism operators face difficulties in these tasks because this characteristic human ability, the ability to think, also makes each individual different from another. Individuality might be a useful tool in differentiation theory, but it is a thorn in the side of managers wanting to make decisions on products and services—what to offer, to whom, when and where to supply the products, and in what quantities.

Marketing and researchers have helped in this process by segmenting potential tourists (customers) into discernible classes based on such criteria as demographics, psychographics, behavioural/operational typologies, escape–reward models and institutional preferences—to name a few. Researchers have also contributed a great deal of time and effort into establishing a theoretical framework for understanding tourists' choices of destination—by taking different approaches and applying them to different stages of the choice process (or the 'vacation sequence', as van Raaij and Francken 1984 call it). Mansfeld (1992) believes these approaches are following more normative steps in recent years—analysing first the motivational characteristics of the decision to take a trip, followed by the actual vacation sequence.

In Goodall and Ashworth's (1988) study of decision-making theory and theorists, they concluded that there are two main camps pitched against each other. One sees man as an 'economic–rational' being, choosing the alternative that optimises benefit, or gives the greatest utility given time and money constraints. The other views human decisions in terms of 'random utility'.

The personal need of individual human beings to understand and rationalise their surroundings, to establish a sense of order and, by the principle of 'consistency' (Cialdini 1988) to stand by the decisions made, supports the more rational, mathematical, and economically logical approach. However, it is more likely that, in making a decision to take a specific destination over another (or even to believe in one theoretical approach over another!), individuals have been influenced by both rational and irrational elements. Examining both elements from a research perspective will provide a more complete understanding of the machinations of the decision-making process and its consequences for tourism managers. This supports the 'second camp' mentioned above (the behavioural–probabilistic approach based on random utility) over the 'first camp' (the normative–rational approach). It is probable that individuals might never really understand how they reached a decision.

Cialdini (1988) uses the example of the racetrack to explain this principle. Tourism can just as easily be used in Cialdini's analogy. In the description that follows, the experience of a bettor laying a bet is described—with the tourism decision-making equivalents in brackets.

Like a microcosm of the wider decision-making world, a bettor has an array of alternatives. The bettor can examine the information available, but it is limited to form guides (the equivalent to brochures, newspapers, magazines, and so on in tourism) and some previous experience (in tourism, this equates with word-of-mouth, or having been to a destination before). In the thirty seconds before the bettor places the bet (equivalent to the weeks and months of deciding where to go on holiday) the bettor is edgy and lacking in confidence. Yet, as Cialdini says, within thirty seconds after making the bet (equivalent to choosing where to go), the bettor is significantly more confident. The need to justify decisions, and to act consistently—because society places a high value on consistency, and individuals know this—is very pressing. Leading up to the actual race (that is, in touristic terms, the time before the trip), the bettor tends to be much more committed to the decision, as if protecting it against criticism. In a similar way, a friend of the author defended her decision to continue a planned trip to Egypt (because she had paid and it was organised)—even after eighteen Greek tourists had been gunned down in front of their hotel in April 1996.

While the race is being run (the equivalent of the actual trip), confidence can oscillate. At one moment the horse is second, and the next it is last (perhaps the equivalents of the hotel being excellent, but the beach being filthy). After the race is run (that is, the trip is over), it has either lived up to built-up expectation and the bettor has had a win, or it has failed to meet expectations (equivalent to a tourist's evaluation of the destination choice).

This sequence of events, and the accompanying psychological reactions, can be presented in model form as well as in the above anecdotal form. An example of the treatment of the vacation sequence, as it pertains to push/pull factors, and as it is affected by the media, is given in Chapter 6.

Tourist Classifications

The recognition that there are different reasons for travel allows tourism organisations to optimise their time and effort in catering for their clients. The simple approach of classifying travellers into basic groups—such as 'Visiting Friends and Relatives' ('VFR') or 'Business and Leisure'—has been expanded by researchers who claim that the simplistic classification, although a convenient shorthand definition of segments in the market, is useless as a predictive tool. Several additions have been made to fill this perceived gap. These are shown in Table 3.1 (page 43).

It should be noted that, in the 'special interest' category, the British Tourist Authority's technical definition deliberately excludes 'boarding education and semi-permanent lodging'—which brings 'study' into question in this category. Apart from this disparity, the classification is a good one.

Table 3. 1 Segments in the mass travel market

Segment	Notes
Relaxation and physical recreation	includes nature lovers and beach-orientated people
Sightseeing and culture	includes the wanderlust tourist who might adopt either a 'nodal mode' (based at one touring centre) or prefer 'linear tour' (moving from hotel to hotel)
Visiting friends or relatives	self-explanatory
Special interest	includes study, sport, health, religion, and conventions

Source: Based on Holloway 1986, taken from Laws 1991

More Tourism Demand Approaches

Operational Typologies and Research

American Express (AMEX) commissioned research into tourist destination choice and came up with a system of 'benefit bundles'—which enabled AMEX to develop a new approach to advertising and sales. Goodrich (1979, cited in Laws 1991) lists the resultant classifications as shown in Table 3.2.

Table 3.2 Benefit bundle analysis

Type	Characteristics
Passive-entertainment types	middle aged; interests are urbane and passive; interests include shopping, relaxation, good cuisine, entertainment and climate; pleasant attitude by local people is important
Sports types	male dominated and sports orientated; value good accommodation, a range of sports facilities, and relaxation away from the children
Outdoor types	middle aged; interested in scenic beauty, historical and cultural aspects

Source: Adapted from Goodrich 1979, cited in Laws 1991

Other writers have used operational typologies or hypotheses in the study of travel motivation, and the relationship between work and leisure. Zuzanek and Mannell's four hypotheses (1983, cited in Ryan 1991a) delineate traveller intention, as shown in Table 3.3 (page 44).

Table 3.3 Travel motivation hypotheses

Hypothesis	Characteristics
The trade-off hypothesis	people choose between work and leisure time
The compensation hypothesis	holidays and leisure compensate for boredom or troubles of everyday life
The spin-off hypothesis	the nature of work produces not contrary, but similar, patterns of leisure activity
The neutralist hypothesis	there is no relationship between work and leisure

Source: Adapted from Zuzanek & Mannell 1983, cited in Ryan 1991a

McIntosh and Goeldner (1986) have argued that the mere anticipation of pleasure motivates travel purchases—perhaps linked to 'consistency and commitment' to one's decisions (see above). In their study, McIntosh and Goeldner listed four specific travel motivations:

- the desire to know more about other countries;
- the reduction of tension through physical activities;
- the desire to meet new people and to escape from routine; and
- the desire for recognition, attention, and appreciation.

The 'escape' motivation and the 'tension–release' motivation fall closely in line with the 'compensation hypothesis' of Table 3.3. The other motivations listed could, just as easily, be describing a scene in one's domestic environment—where it is even possible to simulate the feeling of being in other countries by dining in an exotic restaurant or seeing a film (all of which reduces the argument of McIntosh and Goeldner). Nevertheless, operational typologies do offer some valuable insight into tourist decision-making.

Psychographic Segmentation

Unlike most products on sale, the tourism product is a package offer of both the tangible and the intangible. It represents an opportunity for the purchaser to buy a dream, to escape from reality, and to acquire fulfilment. How the purchaser achieves this is part myth and part theory. Researchers care to believe more in the latter. The psychological determinants of demand are varied and potentially deep-seated within the individual. Cohen (1974), Crompton (1979), and Mathieson & Wall (1982) have all provided keys to some of the secrets within. Sorting the collection of possible motivations into patterns of behaviour is a much more difficult task. Think of the positioning of these variables as players in an Australian Rules football match. These players are placed in approximate positions on the field, but the game is played in a more-or-less random fashion—as those who have witnessed the game will testify. But, as in any game, however random it might seem, there is always a goal—literally and metaphorically. There is also a goal in the tourism game—ultimately to make a decision whether to go on holidays, and then to choose a destination.

Figure 3.1   Playing-field of travel motivations

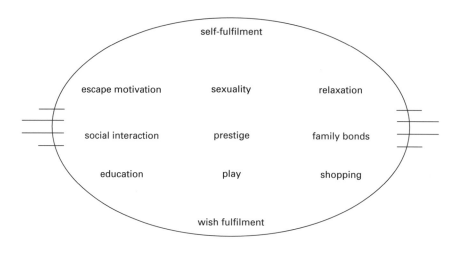

Source: Author's presentation

As Wells (1975, cited in Laws 1991) noted, the advantage of psycho-graphic information is that it 'can put flesh on demographic bones'—thus assisting marketers in their job. An example of this process (see Table 3.4, page 46) is used in the USA to sub-categorise the population into four general consumer groups based on values and lifestyles (VALS). This has received supporting commentaries from Mitchell (1981) and Kotler (1983), according to Laws (1991).

Sunlust and Wanderlust

These two groups of people differ in their motives—one seeking relaxation and the other seeking energy/activity. On occasions, writers have warned people off certain destinations by trying to appeal simultaneously to these different groups. However, it appears that the 'club formula', successfully used by Club Med for example, manages to combine the two—by offering something for everyone, and by offering this in different locations around the world (for the more wandering types).

This raises the issue of sports in tourism, which provides a bridge

Table 3.4 A VALS approach to tourism market segmentation

Type	Characteristics
Survivors	typically have shied away from activities that require high levels of physical energy; record the lowest participation in most travel-related categories
Belongers	central concern is to be accepted by others; more vacations are taken by all other VALS types combined than by this group; when they do travel, a strong likelihood that the trip will be by car
Achievers	success, leadership, and power are of central concern; exhibit better-than-average participation in several business and pleasure activities; in pleasure travel they are higher than average in hotel/motel stays, use of rental cars, and of travel agencies
Socially conscious	empathise with social concerns and place less emphasis on materialism; mirror the 'achievers' in their travel participating in higher-than-average travel by air, stays in hotel/motels, use of rental cars, and travel agencies

Source: Based on Blazey 1989, from Laws 1991

between the two modes—sedentary and activity. Standeven and De Knop (1999) talk about the relationship of tourism and sport in great detail—elements of which are discussed in Chapter 8.

Institutional Differences

Classification of tourists has also been based on the extent to which they prefer their trips to be organised, the need to identify with a specific location, time flexibility, and intrinsic versus extrinsic rewards—to name a few.

Cohen (1974) was the one of the earliest to categorise tourists by their level of independence. His classification was:

- *Organised mass tourist:* the least adventurous; remain within packaged tour confines or 'environmental bubbles'; make few decisions;
- *Individual mass tourist:* similar to above, but might hire a car and visit the 'sights';
- *Explorer:* arrange their own trip; like to see new things but still want home comforts; like to mix with locals and might speak the local language; and
- *Drifter:* shun contact with tourists and tourist complexes; prefer host community offerings; sometimes work in the country in labour-orientated jobs, affecting their contact with host community.

Other writers on this subject have reviewed and criticised Cohen's segmentation, claiming that it fails to comment on the reasons for travellers' adopting such behaviour. Pearce (1982) reviews and supplements the categories, adding fifteen types based on five role-related behaviour patterns. Wright and Witt (1990, cited in Ryan 1991a) also argue that multimotivational models better depict the situation. Plog (1990) suggests a continuum of tourists (from allocentric to psychocentric). This basically describes the range of behaviours in similar terms to Cohen's 'explorer' (allocentric), who seeks new destinations, and his 'organised mass tourist' (psychocentric), who is happier with like-minded tourist company. Iso-Ahola (1980, cited in Ryan 1991a) applied the push-and-pull factors to motivation for travel. Push factors are, simply put, the wish to get away (escape), whereas pull factors are the desire to see some other area (reward).

Escape–Reward Models

As mentioned above, Iso-Ahola (1980, cited in Ryan 1991a) argued that the drive to escape personal problems or routine situations interacts with the pull of anticipated pleasures. This interaction is presented in Figure 3.2.

Figure 3.2   Motivations of holidaymakers

Desire to leave environment behind	Seek Intrinsic Reward	
	Personal	Interpersonal
Personal	Ego-enhancement; escape responsibility	Strengthen kinship
Interpersonal	Status enhancement; prestige	New people, new places, play

Source: Iso-Ahola 1980, cited in Ryan 1991a

Focus on Research on Travel Motives

Australian Examples

As discussed above, people travel for reasons that are, perhaps, really known only to themselves. Nevertheless, for clarification purposes, the reasons can be grouped together to form general travel typologies based on travel behaviour.

The World Travel Organization (WTO) has broadly classified tourism to provide a framework for discussion, and to standardise data to facilitate comparison and planning. The broad classifications of travel type are shown in Table 3.5. These figures are a good indication (for tourism planners and information providers) of the primary reasons people visit their destination. It also illustrates the relative appeal of the destination in broad terms.

Table 3.5 Percentage visitation to selected destinations by purpose of travel

Travel type	Bermuda	Hawaii	Indonesia	Australia	Hong Kong	United Kingdom	Pakistan
Leisure, Rec. & Holidays	82.6%	79.4%	74.4%	62.3%	54.1%	43.2%	19.8%
Business & Professional	10.6%	11.4%	23.2%	13.7%	30.5%	26.6%	28.5%
Other (incl. VFR*, Health, Religious)	6.8%	9.2%	2.4%	24.0%	15.4%	30.2%	51.7%
Total Visits ('000s)	413	6326	3403	2996	19 154	8983	379

Note: *Visiting Friends and Relatives

Source: WTO 1997

As shown in Table 3.5, visitors are drawn to Australia principally for leisure, recreation, and holidays—but not overwhelmingly so (when compared with Bermuda and Hawaii). The reasons for visiting the UK appear to be the most evenly spread of the destinations offered in this example.

It is also interesting to evaluate the chief motivations for outbound travel from Australia. Table 3.6 (page 49) illustrates the top twenty reasons Australians choose to travel—the most popular reasons being to experience something new, and to see beautiful scenery.

Travel-motivation market research is an important source of statistics, and may be applied to commercial uses (such as a barometer for travel advertising), or to non-commercial uses (such as national tourism organisation statistics).

The Australian Tourism Commission (ATC) carries out, commissions, or uses substantial tourism research in a range of areas. This research comes from the Australian Bureau of Statistics, Bureau of Tourism Research, National Visitor Surveys, and the Tourism Forecasting Council (among others).

Data surveyed include:
• tourist arrivals and departures;
• visitor overnights in accommodation;
• tourism employment;

- transport modes;
- indigenous tourism projects and funding;
- environmental tourism studies;
- social and economic impact studies;
- training and education; and
- marketing strategies (selling and pricing, demand and supply inventories).

Table 3.6   Top 20 trip-driven reasons for Australian outbound travellers

	Reason for Travel or Attribute of Destination	Mean Rating (4 = very important to 1= not at all important)
1	Going to places not visited before	3.26
2	Outstanding scenery	3.16
3	Meeting new people	3.11
4	Opportunities to increase knowledge	3.10
5	Interesting rural countryside	3.10
6	Value for money	3.01
7	Personal safety	3.01
8	Arts & cultural attractions	2.98
9	Transportation (such as airlines)	2.97
10	Experiencing new lifestyles	2.97
11	Fun & entertainment	2.92
12	Standards of hygiene & cleanliness	2.89
13	Visiting friends & relatives	2.86
14	Historical, archaeological or military sites, buildings etc.	2.85
15	Relaxation holiday	2.85
16	Escape from the ordinary	2.85
17	Being together as a family	2.84
18	Inexpensive travel to destination	2.79
19	Best deal available	2.78
20	Availability of pre-trip/in-country tourist information	2.78

Source: WTO 1997

Research is carried out on a regional basis, on a state basis, for the whole nation, and worldwide.

The ATC applies this research as part of its mission, which is:

- to market and brand Australian tourism through promotional programs in more than forty countries;
- to increase the yield, dispersal, and volume of visitors to Australia;
- to lead and coordinate cooperative marketing programs within the domestic tourism industry and with participants abroad;
- to maximise opportunities presented by the Olympics, Paralympics [and other major events]; and
- to provide input into government and industry policy development.

ATC Tourism Speech Notes 1998

Summary of Motivation Theory

In recognition of the difficulties faced by researchers in agreeing on a unified theory of tourist motivation, the World Tourism Organization (WTO 1997) established an attribute-based list of the core requirements of a sound tourist-motivation theory. Table 3.7 explains and summarises this foundation for motivation theory.

Table 3.7   The core requirements of a sound theory of tourist motivation

Attribute	Description Theory must be:
The task of the theory	able to integrate existing tourist needs, recognise needs, and provide new orientation for future research
Appeal of the theory	appealing to specialist researchers, useful in tourism industry settings, and credible to marketers and consumers
Ease of communication	easy to explain to potential users and universal (not country-specific) in application
Ability to measure travel motivation	amenable to empirical study; ideas translatable into questions/responses for assessment
Multi-motive vs single-trait approach	aware that travellers might seek to satisfy several needs at once; theory must be able to model pattern of traveller needs, not just one need
Dynamic vs snapshot approach	aware that individuals and societies change; theory must be able to consider/model changes taking place in tourism
Extrinsic and intrinsic motivation	aware that travellers are variously motivated by intrinsic, self-satisfying goals and/or extrinsic, socially controlled rewards (for example, opinions of others)

Source: WTO 1997

Connecting Information and Tourist Perceptions and Decisions

Most of us know something about a place or person before we encounter the real thing. Expectations are rooted in a weave of preconceptions that are formed over the years. Tourism decisions might be based not so much upon the information that is aimed at potential tourists, but on how this information is perceived and assimilated into pre-existing belief structures. Information from social or commercial means can be moulded into an image (or media image) that sometimes intentionally alters preconceptions and, other times, reinforces pre-existing beliefs. The way commercial information is manipulated to influence complex tourist behavioural processes is shown in Figure 3.3.

Figure 3.3   Using commercial information to influence tourist decisions

Information aim + Communication means = Commercial Desire

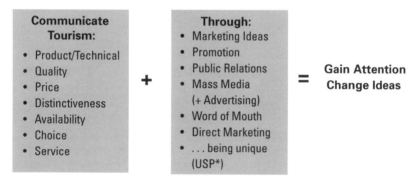

Note: *USP = unique selling point
Source: Author's presentation

The attributes of a tourism product or service can be communicated through direct means—such as the spoken or written word. These are referred to as 'significative stimuli'. Symbolic representations are also possible through the use of pictures or images. The ability to shape these images or words to 'fit' the market under normative conditions (that is, where the tourism product/destination is not suffering from negative publicity) is an important media function. (See Chapter 9 for more detail on negative publicity and the decision-making process.)

In advertising, for example, physical characteristics (such as size, colour, contrast, movement, intensity, and position) convey the various elements of the tourism service or destination (quality, price, availability, choice, distinctiveness) in order to gain attention and, ultimately, to increase sales. How the advertised and the non-advertised message is decoded by potential consumers is vitally important. Using commercial media does not guarantee that the link between information aims and commercial desires can be made—because human decision-making behaviour is dynamic and unpredictable. This is especially so when the travel decision involves health or safety concerns (as is often the case with international travel).

However, as the *Fast Facts* on traveller health/safety myths and truths will confirm, tourists frequently make misguided or presumptuous decisions—based on sensational or incorrect information.

Fast Facts on Traveller Health

Myths and Truths

One of the most commonly (but erroneously) held beliefs about travel is that there is a great risk of violent crime, terrorism, or injury in host nations. This fallacy is perhaps exacerbated by media images.

The most common crimes experienced by travellers are of a non-violent nature—such as bag-snatching, pick-pocketing, and theft from hotels and hostels. Health problems are more common, but 90 per cent of these are not serious.

McManus (1999) says that, from three million or more short-term overseas departures by Australians in 1998, only about 800 needed hospitalisation, and approximately 590 died while abroad—most from either natural causes or accidents. 'But a significant number of Australians venture to, or near, the world's trouble spots,' admitted McManus. Approximately 50 000 Australians visit Africa yearly, 70 000 go to the Middle East and North Africa, and 25 000 to Central and South America.

Professor Robert Steffen from the University of Zurich compiled an interesting list (from World Health Organization figures) of the monthly incidence of health problems experienced per 100 000 travellers to tropical destinations. The results showed that 80 per cent were minor health problems, with less than one per cent of the sample needing hospitalisation or evacuation, or dying abroad (see Table 3.8, page 53).

According to research, although health problems should probably be the biggest concern while abroad, health problems are not the greatest worry for most people. People worry more about burglary while they are away (90 per cent of the respondents), followed by illness and accidents (40 per cent), family safety (33 per cent), bad accommodation (26 per cent), bad weather (19 per cent), bad food (18 per cent), and work (6 per cent) (Pelton, Aral & Dulles 1997).

Table 3.8   Health problems experienced by travellers to tropical destinations

Health problem	Number of problems (per 100 000 travellers)	Health problems (per category as a % of total)
Experienced a health problem	55 000	55
Felt ill	25 000	25
Consulted a doctor	8 000	0.08
Stayed in bed	6 000	0.06
Unable to work on return	2 000	0.02
Hospitalised while abroad	400	0.004
Evacuated by air	60	0.0006
Died abroad	1	0.00001

Source: Pelton, Aral & Dulles 1997, citing Condé Nast Traveller figures

Conclusion

Because decision-making by tourists is not determined in isolation (but is based on a variety of psychological, social, and economic factors), defining and understanding decision-making is therefore difficult. There are many theories of tourist decision-making, but no single approach adequately explains all of the various elements at work. These theories include: operational typologies, sunlust–wanderlust, escape–reward, institutional preferences, and various tourist classifications.

The link between information and commercial media tourist perceptions, on the one hand, and decision-making, on the other, as introduced in this chapter, will be further developed in Part II, and in Chapter 9 of Part III.

Discussion Time

- There is a new generation of independent travellers who rely very much on detailed guide books. How would you categorise these travellers? What decision-making criteria would be important to these travellers? Would they be greatly influenced by commercial tourism information and, if so, what sort of information?
- In small groups, discuss your last travel experience. Think specifically about the basis upon which you made the decision to take this option. After this group discussion, arrange the decision-making

criteria that you have established into a table or figure. Explain the
content and logic of the figure to the other groups.
- Explain the importance of perception on travel decisions.

PART II

Information, Communication, and Tourist Decision-Making

4

Information Providers

Who are They and What are Their Sources?

It is Friday night, and a tourist couple in London is making plans for the weekend. The alternatives available to them are:

- to stay in London (read by the fire, and perhaps see a film on Saturday night); or
- to go away for the weekend (and perhaps have a picnic on the Sunday).

Which will it be? Aside from time, money and, possibly, the traffic, the natural thing to consider is the weather. Before making a decision, knowledge of the weekend weather forecast is vital. If it is going to be fine and sunny, a weekend picnic sounds lovely. If the forecast predicts rain and thunderstorms, a picnic does not sound very appealing at all. Based on this single independent variable, the plans might be completely changed.

Although this might be only one variable in a relatively simple weekend away, add to this the sorts of matters to be considered before even undertaking foreign travel:

- the 'foreignness' of a new country;
- reports of aerial disasters;
- exchange-rate fluctuations;
- visa requirements;
- health, hygiene, and immunisation worries;
- hotel safety;
- terrorist threats; and
- what to do with the family pet, the house, and the car while away.

This list covers only some of the potential concerns before travel to a distant country. Like the couple in London, who gather the appropriate information before making their decision (by checking the weather forecast), travel to foreign destinations requires an information search before making a commitment.

However, just as the mere checking of a weather forecast does not guarantee fine weather over the weekend, gathering information on foreign travel might not protect a tourist from change—which can often come rapidly and without warning.

Who can provide the information required by a potential tourist?

The sources and providers of tourist information are many and varied. Some of the better known are presented in Figure 4.1 (page 59). The overlap of some information providers with their sources reflects the often two-way nature of the information flow—as confirmed by a representative from the Office de Promotion du Tourisme (OPT) of Belgium, and by an information counsellor from the Australian embassy in Belgium, that they have occasion both to elicit and solicit information (personal interviews with the author 1996 and 1998).

Figure 4.1 is by no means exhaustive. There are other sources and providers of information—given special circumstances. In the case of consular information, this must sometimes be obtained from other sources further up or across the information chain.

For example:

- The Department of Foreign Affairs and Trade (based in Australia) sent out consular travel advice on travel to Iraq to its embassies (see Figure 4.2, page 60). (This is an example of vertical information flow from a source not directly mentioned in Figure 4.1.)
- The Australian Tourism Commission in London and Frankfurt sent information on the fire threat in Sydney in 1994. (This is an example

Figure 4.1   Information sources/providers for tourist
decision-making

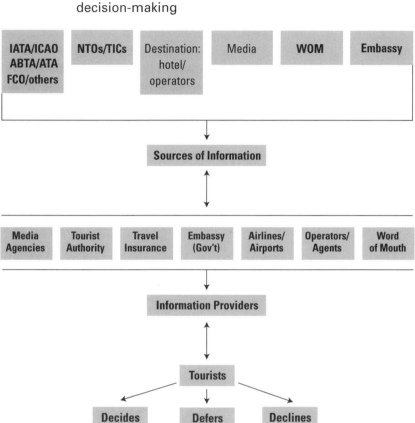

Legend: WOM Word-of-mouth; ICAO International Civil Aviation Organisation; IATA International
Air Traffic Association; FCO Foreign and Commonwealth Office (UK); ABTA Association of
British Travel Agents (UK); ATA Air Traffic Association (USA); Gov't Government; NTO National
Tourist Office/Organisation; TIC Tourist Information Centre ('Welcome Centre' in USA; Visitor
Centres)

Source: Author's presentation

of a horizontal flow from a source mentioned at the
same level in Figure 4.1.)

- The monitoring (upgrading and downscaling) of
  travel warnings from the Foreign & Commonwealth
  Office, London, regarding travel to Indonesia (see
  Focus).

Figure 4.2   Consular Travel Advice

**DEPARTMENT OF
FOREIGN AFFAIRS
AND TRADE   NEWS RELEASE**

D40   22 AUGUST 1995

Consular Travel Advice – IRAQ

The Department of Foreign Affairs and Trade has reviewed its Travel
Advice for Iraq issued on 22 August 1994 and reiterates that due to
the uncertain conditions in Iraq, Australians should defer non-
essential travel to that country.

The Department urges Australians intending to travel to Iraq for
essential reasons to keep abreast of developments through the media
and to register their presence in Iraq with the Australian Embassy in
Jordan, between 4th and 5th Circles, Zahran Street, Jabel Amman,
Amman. Telephone (962) (6) 673246 or 673247, Facsimile (962) (6)
673260. The Department can be consulted by telephone on (06)
261 9111.

Source: Australian Embassy, Brussels, Belgium 1995

Focus on Monitoring Travel Advice

Indonesia Example (20 May–11 June 1998)

Date (1998)	Travel Advice (key instructions)
20 May	We strongly advise against all travel to Indonesia . . . British nationals . . . advised to leave immediately.
20 May	[UPDATE] British nationals . . . advised to leave as soon as possible by normal commercial means . . . the security situation may deteriorate, particularly in Jakarta . . . Those in safer areas who decide to stay should remain indoors . . . There is less risk in Bali . . .
21 May	Because of the uncertain security situation, we strongly advise against all travel to Indonesia for the time being . . . Following . . . Soeharto's resignation . . . Jakarta and other major towns have been largely quiet. It is too early, however, to predict the eventual impact . . . British . . . are advised to stay close to home, avoid crowds and to follow events on television and radio.
22 May	. . . we continue to advise against all travel to Indonesia . . . including those who have left . . . Since the resignation . . . the atmosphere is more relaxed. There are fewer troops . . . Students and the Military jointly [police] the large crowds . . . It is too early to tell how acceptable President Habibi's new Cabinet will prove to be.
23 May	The situation in Indonesia is calmer but not yet stabilised . . . we recommend that only those with a pressing need should return . . . This advice will not be relaxed before 25 May. Jakarta is calm . . . Most shops and businesses are reopening. British [should] avoid the area around Parliament . . . It is too early to judge public reaction to President Habibi . . . Public demonstrations may continue and it would be prudent to avoid visiting university campuses . . . follow developments on television and radio.
26 May	The situation . . . is calmer. Those who left . . . may now consider returning but should take into account . . . the situation . . . remains unpredictable. For other travellers . . . only those with a pressing need should visit . . . the Embassy has, at present, no basis for advising against the resumption of visits to Bali . . . Jakarta is calm [but] . . . There are reports of small-scale looting [and] . . . increased risk of crime . . . British . . . in Indonesia [should] follow developments on television and radio . . . exercise caution . . . particularly by night [and] when taking a taxi . . . [use] . . . a reputable firm
29 May	We advise against all non-essential visits to Indonesia (except Bali). The situation . . . is calmer but has not yet stabilised. Residents who left . . . may now consider returning . . . There may be further political demonstrations . . . which could turn violent. Given the serious economic situation and food shortages, rioting may break out . . . [repeat of advice for resident British] . . . Bali has been relatively calm and tourist services are operating normally. We are no longer advising against travel to Bali.
11 June	We are no longer advising against travel to Indonesia . . . calmer following the change of government . . . but it has not yet stabilised . . . Visitors . . . and those residents returning should be aware that the situation remains unpredictable . . . demonstrations are likely to continue in Jakarta and other major cities . . . [repeat of advice for resident British] . . . Bali . . . operating normally.

Source: British Embassy Brussels, Press & Public Affairs Section 1998

The most important thing is that information can be obtained when it is needed—whether to allay tourist concern about PKK (Kurdistan Workers Party) terrorists in Turkey, or simply to confirm a flight.

Finding the right source is another question. If the difficulties confronted by the author in gathering facts for this book are any indication of the malaise of (sometimes conflicting) sources of information, this might not be as simple a task as it seems. Closer liaison between tourism participants would assist in weaving these loose threads into a single, harmonious fabric. A body to oversee this networking could also expedite the search for travel information. Despite good intentions, this might be very difficult to achieve because an information provider, like the information sought, is not always perfect and up-to-date. And centralising tourist information would be a difficult task. The World Tourism Organization's (WTO) grand scheme to link tourism databases around the world does, however, take up this challenge (see *Fast Facts*).

Fast Facts on the World Tourism Organization

Tourism Information Exchange Network

In recognition of the importance of tourist information and the fact that technological developments outstrip the ability of many people to keep up to date with the latest sources, the World Tourism Organization (WTO) decided to set up the WTO Tourism Information Exchange Network (TIENET) in the early 1990s. This is a grand scheme, but the WTO has to cope with fluidity of the vast sea of travel information. The information is dynamic, and moves and changes like a great ocean. When one source dries up another overflows.

The WTO realised that some preliminary action steps were required before its information network would be fully operational. It had to:
* reorganise the WTO Documentation Centre's Holdings and Archives;
* build a parallel bibliographic database system (to complement its existing statistical database), made up of:
  * 'Tourdoc': documents on general, technical, and economic aspects of tourism;
  * 'Tourleg': legal texts related to tourism (operated within the UNESCO Information Management Software Mini-Micro CDS/ISIS);
  * 'LRTA Microthesaurus': developed by CAB International as an indexing tool;
* work in collaboration with other institutions to create a multilingual thesaurus for information exchange within the TIENET;

- pave the way for the proposed network by publishing the World Directory of Documentation Resources and Systems for the Travel and Tourism Sector (May 1991, WTO). The directory contained 184 pages outlining the systems and databases integrated in the network (over 100 information systems in 71 countries).

Goeldner states that the advantages of a Tourism Information Systems (TIS) and personal computer use by tourism professionals are:

- the ability to restore control over information;
- placing of this control back in the hands of management;
- enabling managers/users to be more receptive to the possibilities provided by TIS;
- as a tool for management:
  - the hardware is a vehicle;
  - the databank a place to store and retrieve vast amounts of information;
  - the software and analytical packages allow retrieval, combination, comparison, and presentation of data; and
  - the communication package is the link between distant users and the system.

Goeldner 1995

Beni adds that the globalisation process engenders:

> ... democratic access ... by means of networks of PC's ... [enabling] intercommunication among producers, distributors, service renderers, travel traders, leisure and entertainment businesses, education ... [and] consumers.

Beni 1996

Figure 4.1 (page 59) represents a cross-section of some of the more important sources and providers of information to tourists. An attempt has been made to present tourism participants in a sequential format—not unlike van Raaij and Francken's (1984) 'vacation sequence', or Crompton and Ankomah's (1993) 'choice set propositions', which both attempt to explain tourist destination choice using grouped delimitation. As Crompton and Ankomah observe, the aim is:

> ... to assimilate and process information relating to the large number of alternative vacation destinations from which they can select.

Crompton & Ankomah 1993

However, there is a fundamental difference between Figure 4.1 and the above-mentioned formats. This difference is not necessarily to be found in the intention to clarify information overlap, but in the stage of the tourist's decision-making process being examined. Many studies have examined destination choice—reflecting the desire of hotel/resort operators and information end-users to better understand their market. Figure 4.1 presents the components which precede (or possibly even preclude) a tourist's decision to undergo the travel in the first place. In the diagram, some interaction between sources and providers of information is illustrated at the top. The flow from top to bottom ends when the tourist decides to go, or defers the trip to a later date, or declines the potential travel. These three alternatives ('decides', 'defers', or 'declines') can be termed the '3Ds'.

The holistic decision process for tourist purchases, of which Figure 4.1 explains the first level, is presented in Table 4.1.

Table 4.1 The decision process for tourism purchases

Decision	Process
Desire to travel	collect and evaluate information from relevant sources (see Figure 4.1)
Select holiday	on the basis of destinations of which the tourist is aware, decide on tour operator, price range, duration, travel companions, and so on
Prepare for holiday	purchase clothing, photographic materials, guide books, arrange immunisations, secure possessions, acquire visas and documentation, change money, and so on
Holiday experience	continued evaluation of the choice against expected level of satisfaction

Source: Based on Laws 1991

As illustrated in Table 4.1 the decision to travel can be a complicated one—often exacerbated by such problems as:

- information that is insufficient, conflicting, or wrong;
- a range of communication breakdowns;
- the often complex dynamics of group decision-making (families, friends); and
- conflicting travel motivations.

These issues, and others, will be discussed below.

Information Providers and Tourist Information Search

Defining Information Search

Moutinho defines information search as:

... an expressed need to consult various sources prior to making a purchase decision.

Mouthino 1987

Fodness and Murray (1997) identify three important factors in this search: motives, determinants and sources. McIntosh and Goeldner (1986) suggest that tourist planning is geared ostensibly towards enhancing the quality of the trip. Others have added that minimising the risk of something going wrong is also a strong influence on tourist information search. Snepenger, Collins and Snepenger (1992) also suggest that several elements might predetermine the information-search process—such as the composition of the travel group, past experience, the newness of the destination, and whether there will be friends or relatives at the location.

Additional elements should be included—such as the actual availability of information, timing and seasonal constraints (see Figure 4.3, page 67), the length of the pending trip, and the cost of the trip.

Tourist Information Provider's Perspective

Not all information providers regard the provision of tourist information as their most important function.

Sometimes information is provided directly to tourists (either for free or for a charge) but, at other times, it is distributed indirectly through the media or third parties (for free or for an indirect charge). Many information providers regard this part of their work as a secondary element of their overall objective—which might be to make profit (in the case of travel agents and operators), or might be national representation (in the case of consulates).

Providing information to tourists can, in some instances, be essential for safety or legal reasons. Travel insurance companies, some travel agents and operators, the International Air Traffic Association (IATA), the (US) Federal Aviation Administration (FAA), and consulates all have a moral or legal obligation to provide certain facts when approached by tourists for information. For example, the Royal Automobile Club of Victoria (RACV) obliges their agents to offer travel insurance when a travel sale is made—as a result of some highly publicised cases where travellers had no insurance and needed urgent medical help. Consulates might also sometimes feel obliged to issue unsolicited warnings to potential travellers about safety problems in certain destinations (if the situation is grave enough). The US State Department prefers to err on the side of conservatism when the safety of Americans citizens is involved. Because the USA is such a high-profile country, Americans do tend to be targeted for violence and crime on holidays, so the attitude of the State Department is understandable.

On the other hand, many tourist information providers see their primary role as information provider. These include:

- tourist information centres (TICs);
- welcome centres (in the USA);
- visitor centres (commercial information centres often attached to a tourist attraction);
- travel agents and operators (to a lesser extent);
- national tourist organisations; and
- publishers of specialised tourism magazines, journals, and papers.

Where the motivation for providing information to tourists is commercially driven, an understanding of the information-search behaviour of tourists would be very interesting and potentially useful. It might also be more relevant to government-operated tourist information facilities, as governments begin to reduce subsidies to these services in the future. This is why TICs in many developed tourist-receiving nations (Ireland, England, France, Australia, USA) are looking to become more financially autonomous by providing products (maps, books, souvenirs, restaurants, and so on) as well as services (information, 'book-a-bed-ahead', and so on). Some say that this increased commercial orientation in government information services competes unfairly with non-subsidised private tourism services, and that these commercial-styled TIC establishments might experience an identity crisis. This raises the question of whether objective information can be provided only in a non-financial exchange (De Groote & Nielsen 1998c). But this remains hypothetical in the current environment, as subsidisation is currently still the largest source of revenue for most TICs.

Tourist Information Seeker's Perspective

Increasingly, tourists are being segmented, using source-based approaches, according to their information-search behaviour. In other words, researchers are looking 'backwards' to see which information sources were used to plan a trip (Fodness & Murray 1997). It is also possible to use a 'forward' approach—starting with the possible causal factors and then segmenting people by their discriminate information search (looking at the actual sources of information and, perhaps, also the amount of effort a tourist puts into finding information). Making a distinction between 'passive' and 'active' information search is also important for tourism researchers, and for practitioners looking to identify ways of improving the flow of information.

Fodness and Murray provide two valuable classification tools for outlining tourism-information sources and traveller-information search. The first model, as shown in Figure 4.3 (page 67), subdivides information sources into four groups on a grid: personal vs impersonal, and commercial vs non-commercial. The second model, as illustrated in Figure 4.4, classifies traveller information search by pre-trip planning time and by the number of sources reviewed.

Figure 4.3   Information sources sub-classification

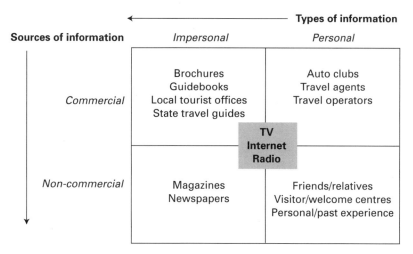

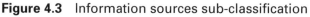

Source: Altered from Fodness & Murray 1997

In this Figure, television, the Internet, and radio have been superimposed over all categories of Fodness and Murray's model. Television can be commercial (tour-operator advertisement on commercial television) or non-commercial ('The Holiday Show' on BBC World). Television is generally impersonal but, in the future, digital technology on command will be a reality—allowing interaction between television and user. The Internet has both commercial and non-commercial applications, and is both personal (email exchanges) and impersonal (surfing anonymously around the worldwide web).

Figure 4.4   Pre-trip planning timescale and number of information sources considered

Pre-trip planning period	Number of sources considered	
	Fewer	*More*
Shorter	Routine Search	Time-limited search
Longer	Source-limited search	Extended search

Source: Fodness & Murray 1997

Communication and Information Problems in the Travel Industry

Intercity or Local Train?

Although the model of basic communication presented in Part I (see page 26) is theoretically sound, like a radio it requires some fine-tuning before the reception is at its best.

The passage of information can be viewed as two trains that ferry passengers, rather than messages, to an end destination. Both trains leave the departure point at the same time, but one is an express train and the other a local train. This can be compared with the model of 'reactive communication' as shown in Figure 4.5—which consists of a grapevine and a party line.

Figure 4.5   Reactive communication

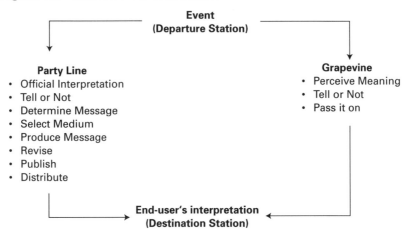

Source: Derived from Reilly 1990

Which train is the better? Or which path of communication is the more effective? The limitations of a local train are clear—it reaches the final destination much more slowly (like the party line, which must go through correct channels). The advantage of the express train is its speed, thus arriving faster at the destination (like the grapevine communication passage—nothing travels faster than a rumour!). On initial inspection, the choice of which channel is better seems obvious: faster is better. But we should look at this conclusion more closely.

There is an old saying that advises 'less haste; more speed'. The implication is that haste can lead to mistakes. It might be that someone's needs are better served by careful, more closely sanctioned communications—depending on the information and its importance. Compare this with the local train, which might be slow but, if the train traveller wants to get off at a stop between the departure and destination points, the local train is the better choice. In information terms, it provides a chance to revise the information. On the other hand, word-of-mouth and first impressions are often inextricably linked and difficult to overcome—taking precedence over the slower, more thoughtful analysis, despite potential faults. This is a psychological element—what Cialdini (1988) referred to as 'consistency'. People believe what they want to believe. For example, there is a tendency for people to believe what their neighbours say about the difficulties that girls might face travelling alone in Morocco—even in contrast to official travel agent warnings. Tourism professionals at the Office de Promotion du Tourisme (OPT), Brussels, and travel agents in Louvain (Belgium), confirmed this phenomenon in interviews with the author.

This illustrates that information obtained through different channels takes on different meanings, and potentially different levels of importance, depending on such factors as the situation at hand, the individual needs of the communicators, and the stops along the way—as in the case of the two trains.

We will now examine a few of these communication barriers (or 'train stops').

What Is in It for Me?

Before a reader or listener can absorb a lot of information, there must be a perceived benefit. People are essentially self-oriented. As Reilly (1990) states, someone planning to take a cruise will be interested in material relevant to cruises, but try getting them to read an advertisement on train trips to Paris or Scotland, and the strength of 'perceived benefit' becomes apparent.

This also raises the question of *relevance* in communication exchanges at all levels—individual, group, or mass. The essence of the word 'information' is that it be somehow informative—thus distinguishing true information from a mass of noise, visuals, or words. Take the example of tourists driving in a country where they do not speak the language. Road signs in written language along the way become redundant. However, the use of simple and clear symbols can be a paralinguistic detour around such communication 'roadblocks'. For example, the downward pointing triangle with a red border is generally accepted as a 'give-way' or 'yield' message at an intersection but, if this sign were in foreign words, the message might not be received.

Information in its purest form can come from any number of sources.

A good teacher, a salesperson, a travel agent, or even a friend, can be good communicators when they are able to make the subject interesting and relevant to the audience. The subject of travelling is a good subject for holding the attention of an audience. It is something that most people enjoy talking about and hearing about—although people do have their limits. If someone tries to show all of their travel photographs to friends who stayed at home, this becomes obvious! Finding individual or group relevance when presenting a subject, including a travel presentation, is important. The audience might need to be brought into the communication experience by, for example, asking a question of someone who is looking out the window, or asking a person planning to travel what price range they are interested in. Observing the audience and establishing their needs is, therefore, very important. This is a useful tactic for sales staff doing sales presentations. A little less of the 'presentation', and more of the sales 'discussion' should enable the customer to see the perceived benefit in continuing to listen to the sales representative and, hence, not blocking the message out.

Problems with Purpose and Clarity

There is a reason for this heading mentioning 'purpose' first. Without purpose, clarity is almost impossible to achieve. To convey a message properly to the audience, the sender must evaluate the goal. With a clear goal, attention can then be focused on the clarity of delivery of the message. Reilly (1990) has criticised the tourist industry's overuse of 'fuzzy commentary' about the attractions and beauty of a destination or, in his analogy, a ferry crossing when tourists might simply want to know the exact ferry schedule. Clarity is achieved when the sender understands the questions being asked. And, in the case of brochures and newsletters, the sender should avoid droll generic messages that are at risk of having a negative impact on tourists.

However, situational constraints do exist in advertising. For example, the safety record of an airline is not something that is easily 'doctored', or ever should be (according to Verchere 1995). In light of a string of heavily publicised incidents (for example, air fatalities, or terrorist risks in Israel, or bombs in the Paris metro, or gas in the Tokyo underground), a tourist promoter's 'purpose' is to allay fears of flying or travelling in general. This is shown in the advertisements presented in Figures 4.6 and 4.7 (pages 71, 72). Both advertisements succinctly and clearly convey the purpose of their message. The first is McDonnell Douglas' persuasive response to the May 1979 American Airlines DC-10 crash that was blamed on the manufacturer. In the aftermath of the accident, Ralph Nader, a consumer advocate, called for a boycott of the product. This could have adversely affected all airlines using the aircraft—not just the manufacturer. Something had to be done, and the advertisement in Figure 4.6 was the result. The second is KLM's response to terrorist threats, and to the subsequent warning to American travellers by the Reagan administration to avoid Greece, following evidence of poor security at the Greek international airport in 1986. The economic impact on the tourism industry was immense during this period. (This, and the role of the media, will be further discussed in Chapter 5, and in case studies in Part III.)

Figure 4.6 Counter to safety fears in DC-10 aircraft after fatality

Published with permission of Boeing

Figure 4.7   American tourists appeased about foreign travel

Courtesy Netherlands Board of Tourism

Advertisements such as these, that attempt to change consumer attitudes or assuage fear, can be quite powerful. There are some doubts as to the effectiveness of the same campaign if it were to be used in a period of relative peace and safety. The question of media impact is a difficult one and requires much more analysis than can be provided here (see Chapter 5 for greater detail). Terrorism does not appear to wield the influence it once did in the 1970s and 1980s—as confirmed by travel operators in discussion with the author about the revival of travel to Turkey and Egypt in the mid 1990s. So it is vital that the message be not only purposive and clear, but also timely and contextual.

Credibility

As noted in Part I, for communication to be effective, the sender must be viewed as credible. In many situations in the tourist industry this is, unfortunately, not so. An example of this credibility gap might be a hotel guest who encounters sour, unhappy reception people in a hotel that specifically promotes guest satisfaction and friendly service. To overcome this, some hotels have set up specific procedures for recruiting and training staff (see Tables 4.2 and 4.3)

Table 4.2   Sheraton hotels recruitment criteria (1990)

1	Pleasant personality, ready to smile and a pleasant way of speaking
2	Clean, neat appearance and good personal habits
3	Ability to understand instructions quickly, and to carry out duties quickly
4	A good memory, making it possible to remember the names of guests
5	Judgment to prevent disagreeable situations or, if they arise, ability to handle them
6	Open-mindedness, willingness to accept new ideas and methods
7	Desire to learn, ambition to do an outstanding job, desire to offer brilliant service and obviously enjoy doing so

Source: Courtesy Sheraton Employee Handbook 1990

Table 4.3   Sheraton guest satisfaction system (1990)

Smile	Every time you see a guest, smile and offer an appropriate hospitality comment
Be friendly	Speak to every guest in a friendly, enthusiastic and courteous tone and manner
Be responsive	Answer guest questions and responses quickly and efficiently, or take personal responsibility to get the answers
Be creative	Anticipate guest needs and resolve guest problems
Be professional	Demonstrate our professionalism with warmth, care and understanding
Be hospitable	Show each guest that you want them to come back to Sheraton

Source: Courtesy Sheraton News Release 1990

It is important to remember that a message is more than good intention—it must also be believable before an audience will be persuaded. And the credibility of the presenter is important. McGuire (1969, cited in Rajecki 1982) notes that the same amount of information is retained by an audience listening to a speech on pesticides, for example, presented by a famous chemist or a by school teacher. However, the difference lies in the believability—the renowned chemist has more credibility. This has important implications for the tourist industry with regard to their marketing campaigns, brochure presentation, and what the company is generally claiming. Thomas Cook, for example, would be more convincing to tourist consumers offering a worldwide guarantee on travel products than would an independent travel agent.

This credibility gap was put to a serious test in the McDonnell Douglas example (Figure 4.6, page 71). Importantly, the company was aware of the problem, and managed to do something about it. Various studies (McGuire 1969; Eagly & Himmelfarb 1978—both cited in Rajecki 1982) have shown the value of credibility in persuasion. This, in turn, is linked to perceived competence, expertise, status, intelligence, and so on.

Credibility must also be earned. Consumers expect companies to deliver what they promise, and usually a company will have only one chance to prove itself. If a tourism provider promises something, that company must then 'make good' on the promise—because consumers will not be fooled forever.

In the advertisement shown in Figure 4.8 (page 75), Southwest Airlines responded to Northwest Airline's claim to be 'Number 1' in customer satisfaction. Southwest chose humour to highlight the inaccuracy of Northwest's claim, and then went on to explain in more factual terms why they deserved to be called the best in customer satisfaction. The net result of such a 'gloves-off' marketing campaign was, presumably, that Northwest's credibility suffered after (apparently) false claims had been made. People might have been less inclined to believe future claims made by that company, thus affecting their overall image. Blind respect is not afforded in the travel consumer society where service and honesty are crucial.

Censorship, Freedom of Information, and Misinformation

Censorship is not limited to governments in undemocratic countries. Censorship can occur in the tourism industry. If a tour brochure deliberately fails to mention a minor detail about hotel surcharges, it is tantamount to censorship. Editors censor information in newspapers for legal and ethical reasons, or in acting responsibly in a particular situation—such as working with the authorities in the Iran hostage crisis in 1989.

Failure to inform a tourist of a detail can amount to censorship, but providing the wrong information, or deliberately misinforming the tourist, is equally as unacceptable.

The simple travel brochure, the window into almost every tourist

Figure 4.8   Southwest Airline's counter to (apparently) false claims by Northwest Airlines

Source: © 1992 Southwest Airlines Co.; all rights reserved; published with permission

operator, not only provides a great deal of information about the tours and destinations being offered, but also says much about the company itself—such as its policies on censorship and honesty. The brochures are symbols of the company, just as much as corporate logos are symbols of a company.

Figure 4.9 (page 76) shows the logo of a United Kingdom pay-per-view television channel that is dedicated to travel. Although simple in its design, the logo and subtext immediately convey an association with tourism. Inside the letter 'a' is a sun symbol and, in the 'e', is a star (or possibly a starfish to symbolise the sea). Because mass tourism has traditionally been associated with the 'sun and sea' holiday formula, the connection being made by the logo is transparent. The subtext ('TV that takes you there') implies that, by watching this channel, people will feel that they are on holidays. Although this is an effective logo, Landmark Travel Channel is re-branding its corporate image (and logo) to encompass new media developments. The channel is getting involved in digital interactive technology, whereby viewers are able to purchase holidays from a 'Holiday Shop' and search a travel database called 'Holiday Guide' for unbiased information and photographs by using the television remote control.

Figure 4.9   Travel TV logo

TV THAT TAKES YOU THERE

Source: Landmark Travel Channel 1998

Brochures should also provide full details about the destination, which would include whether the place has experienced crime on tourists or health risks, and whether security problems still exist. For example, incidents such as:

- the Hayward case, in which two British tourists were shot by muggers after becoming lost in Miami (Ryan 1991b);
- the risk of AIDS, cholera, hepatitis B, or plague—as reported in India in 1995 (*Sunday Times* 1995);
- the history of violence in Kenyan wildlife parks—such as the reporting of two French tourists shot in Meru National Park, three Germans injured in Ambolesi Park, and a Belgian shot on the nearby coastal road (*Africa Economic Digest* 1989).

These are a few examples of tourists facing security risks while travelling. It should be added, however, that fuller information in the brochure would also mean saying that the Kenyan government, for example, carried out a successful campaign against criminals and poachers in the parks after the above events took place.

Fuller information in brochures does pose some problems. It is essentially a sales document. Information that might be interpreted by future customers as negative—such as their anticipated leisure being at risk of interruption by Peruvian 'Shining Path' rebels—might not be the best advertisement for the operator. It goes against the business raison d'être—which is to make profit. How much the operator is willing to reveal about possible risks must be weighed up against the legal, ethical, and economic consequences. A representative from Owners Abroad in the United

Kingdom (UK), discussing risks in Cyprus at the time of the Gulf War, had this to say:

> ... we have to take a longer-term view, and short-term cost considerations cannot stand in the way of longer term risks to our reputation.
>
> Representative from Owners Abroad quoted in Ryan 1991b

Ryan qualifies this statement by observing:

> However, as in all cases, such judgement can only be exercised in the light of the information that is available, and the way in which that information is disseminated. There are two categories for giving out information: the first is employees in the industry itself; the second is the customers of whom there are at least two broad types; the independent traveller, and the tourist who is buying a package.
>
> Ryan 1991b

This raises another related problem. Despite good intentions by employees to provide greater detail, the situation in foreign destinations is often 'fluid', and brochures are printed up to eighteen months in advance of sales. This problem is exacerbated by the failure of operators to give updates to tourists—faced with potential scare-mongering and with a certain amount of responsibility to their principals on the ground.

Compare the following quotation from Chris Smith, Travel Manager for Ilkeston Co-operatives, with the 'Owners Abroad' quotation above:

> We maintain our Peru program, which is now much modified since its inception in 1985, because we do have a responsibility to those that helped us to develop it. By sticking to them in bad times as well as in the good, we hope that we are of benefit to them and, in the long term, to our customers. We hope that the situation will improve in the future and it will be remembered that we continued our connection and did not simply leave them.
>
> Cited by Ryan 1991b

In referring to 'bad times', Smith might have had in mind the many attacks on tourists in the region by 'Shining Path' guerrillas—such as on Edward Bartely, a British hitchhiker shot in 1989; Frank and Luva Korallus, a couple kidnapped and suspected killed in 1989; and two French tourists taken from a bus and shot in 1990.

On first inspection it does appear that the short term is being served by this particular operator, but Ryan (1991b) adds that the company kept a symbolic connection to Peru only. Tourists left in droves, and only a few hundred went there in ensuing months. This is a clear sign of tourists' desire for security, and that they will vote with their feet by not going to risky destinations. The decision is ultimately up to the client. At least this is how it is viewed by consular officials, travel insurers, and travel agents and operators—all of whom responded similarly to the present author's questions on responsibility for the end-decisions regarding potentially risky travel.

The Royal Automobile Club of Victoria (RACV) states that travel insurance premiums for higher-risk countries reflect the actuarial risk of covering a person intending to travel there. Home and Insurance, one of Britain's largest travel insurers, states that:

> Claims in respect of violent crime have risen dramatically in the last few years as people increasingly venture further away from European resorts.
>
> Cited in Ryan 1991b

How much of this is known by the increasingly more mobile 'mass tourists' (as per Cohen's 1974 classification—see Chapter 3)? Would they continue to be increasingly more independent and brave if they had such knowledge? Would they fly if all available information was made public to more than just a select few? Failing to provide information to travellers is sometimes a deliberate action, and sometimes a matter of omission. Either way, it amounts to a failure to communicate the real or potential threat to the travellers' safety—and is unacceptable.

One major example of this failure was recorded in the lead up to the PanAm flight 103 crash in Lockerbie, Scotland, in 1988. It was reported that threats had been made about the bomb to the authorities in the UK, and that German authorities had uncovered a terrorist cell in Germany, where they found bomb-making equipment and samples of the bomb that allegedly went off on PanAm 103. It is claimed that, for security reasons, this information was not passed on to the general public, nor to the passengers on the flight itself. High-level US government officials did not board the PanAm 103 flight on 21 December 1988. This suggests that travel information might also be distributed selectively—a dire possibility should there be truth behind it. (The implications of the Lockerbie disaster will be discussed in Part III.)

Verchere claims that:

> ... the airlines soft-pedal the comparative safety of their industry for fear of attracting too much consumer attention to a tricky and sometimes untidy part of the business
>
> Verchere 1995

Verchere also states that organisations such as the International Civil

Aviation Organisation (ICAO)—although having reporting and regulatory requirements for air safety and air accidents—admits that 'a certain number still go unreported' (Verchere 1995).

The view that more can be done in the way of safety measures—beyond rhetoric and ineffectual lists of so-called desired practices—is also held by Paul Wilkinson (1990), director of the Research Institute for the Study of Conflict and Terrorism (RISCT), who cites supporting commentary from such authors as Ryan (1991b) and Brenchley (1986).

What, then, can tour operators do to improve their communication with their customers? According to Ryan (1991b), they can:

- identify potential problems at locations in drawing up their initial programs—before issuing brochures;
- react to events after issuing brochures; and
- react to events when clients are actually at the location.

Full and appropriate information, and more effective communication of the information, is a solid measure towards responsible action. And this is not merely a moral issue—it also has legal implications. For example, the Small Claims Tribunal in Australia interprets brochures and statements made prior to a contract of sale as conditions of the 'offer and acceptance' of an officially binding contract.

Information Overload and Poor Communication Distribution

Telecommunications, multimedia computing and networks, interactive television, transnational reservation systems, and tourism information directories, do not represent Aldous Huxley's brave new world. Rather, taken together, they represent an active system of communications currently in operation in the tourism industry. With this complexity comes an accompanying clutter of information—as overlapping information competes for the attention of tourists. This complexity also makes the job of travel consultants all the more complicated and taxing—already difficult because of growing demands by their clientele. The greater the quantity and variety of incoming information, the greater the difficulties encountered by the human brain in processing it all and working out individual messages.

As tourism providers improve their ability to filter out useless information, they must also be mindful of the content and method of their own outgoing communications. Bearing in mind that that the travel industry is a complex network of contributors, and that effective communication between individuals can be flawed, there is a significant possibility of a breakdown in communication.

Figure 4.10 shows one of the more simple examples of the channels of travel distribution, and Figure 4.11 connects the communication process to the tourist flow system. Imagine large volumes of information passing between each of the segments illustrated in the diagram, add to this the pressure of time deadlines, customer demands, and general communication obstruction, and the margin for errors is radically increased.

Figure 4.10   Channels of travel distribution

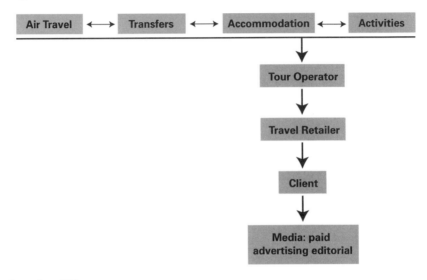

Source: Laws 1991

Figure 4.11   Communication in the tourism flow model

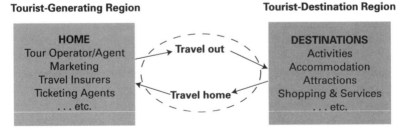

Source: Author's presentation

Do tourism providers advertise a holiday package on the radio or on television? If they use television, can they afford it, and will it reach the desired audience? What time slot is best? A cheaper alternative might be the Internet or print, but can they control the output and input of information, and will they reach the appropriate audience? And how should they deliver the message—humorously, seriously, shockingly, reassuringly, innovatively, and so on? (Figure 4.8 is a good example of the humorous approach, whereas Figures 4.6 and 4.7 present a reassuring message.) All of these questions and more must be asked when choosing the best medium for communicating tourist products.

Keeping in close contact with ground staff, destination principals, transfer staff, and so on, requires careful and efficient handling. The handling of customer complaints is also important. Does the tourist provider send a letter of regret, or telephone personally, offer a refund, or a sincere apology? Although content and components of the communication exchange are relevant, it is clear that the manner in which it is distributed is also very important.

As technology advances at a rapid pace, those tourism regions that harness modern technology increase their chances of prospering in a rapidly changing tourism environment.

Marketing and Information

Underlying the discussion about effective communication is the desire to provide the best possible tourist service. There is a strong economic rationale behind the complex ministering to customer likes and dislikes, the decisions they make, and the reasons behind these decisions. Purchasing decisions, like the information that precipitates them, are crucial to any company. Tourists effectively tell the company about themselves by their actions and words—adding to the body of knowledge that inevitably helps the company with its own decision-making regarding product and service offerings. The information process is, thus, a flow—a flow that begins before a company opens its doors for the first time, moves downwards, sideways, and even backwards, and is never-ending. When tourists return from a trip, certain information should be gleaned from their actions and comments, and this information should be used in planning for the future. Looking backwards enables tourist providers to anticipate what might happen in the future, and looking sideways enables them to scan other operators and opportunities.

This is where marketing managers take up the task—learning to manage demand through monitoring information and attempting to control it (although the perpetual nature of information means that controlling it is virtually impossible). Building expertise in the marketing of information and demand requires special skills and involves decision-making in many areas—including pricing, distribution, servicing, advertising, and product. Table 4.4. illustrates some of the possible responses to these different levels of demand.

Table 4.4 Levels of demand and management responses

Level	Response
Pre-Operations	no public knowledge of their company; gather information and present to customers (market research); establishment of product, prices, and distribution channels
Normal Operations	supplying services to near-capacity; monitor customers and competitors; continue campaign of product awareness through continually revised methods
Irregular Operations	demand flows inconsistent with supply (under-capacity or over-capacity); gather information re incongruities in location, market orientation, seasonality, standards and service shortfalls; study trends towards societal shifts in demand; examine costs of staying in or getting out
Full Capacity	ideal situation, but information concerning risks of lowering service must be monitored
Overrun	facilities, staff, residents, and other clients are overrun with unwelcome tourism; appropriate information and advice required; alter market orientation by increased prices or altering image using Cialdini's (1988) 'Social Proof' thesis (undesirable tourists identify with the social setting presented to them as acceptable to their self-image)

Source: adapted from Laws 1991

From this table, it is evident that, although information is available in abundance, knowing how to interpret and use it is a more assiduous task. This is the role of marketing specialists and advertising experts—who dedicate their time to analysing demand and what mechanisms best trigger demand for their particular tourist product or service. 'Outsourcing' through consultant companies is growing in popularity. Market research might provide some of the answers to the riddles of tourism demand, but there remain many questions about the effects of marketing and the use of the media to inform the public about tourist offerings. (See the Case Study in Chapter 9 for more information.)

Conclusions

Decision-making is complex in the real world of imperfect information. An understanding of the process of how tourists search for information is important for information providers and seekers.

There are various information and communication problems faced by the travel industry. These include:

- reactive versus normal communication;
- lack of perceived benefit by receivers;
- problems in purpose and message clarity;
- credibility gaps in senders;
- censorship and the questions of freedom of information and misinformation;
- information overload and how it leads to poor communication; and
- the marketing of information versus marketing information.

All of this causes problems inherent in measuring marketing and media effect. A fuller understanding of these communication problems gives tourism managers and students of tourism and communications some insight into how to handle their own communication behaviour and that of their customers. This should enhance the communication and management of individual tourist organisations, and thus ensure that the tourism industry as a whole functions more smoothly.

The next chapter will develop the subject of media effect in terms of travel industry decision-making, and the current research on the topic.

Discussion Time

- Form the group (best with eight members) into a circle. Choose one person from the group and recite a five-word sentence to them out of earshot of the rest the group (for example, 'Flight changes require written confirmation'). The person returns to the circle and attempts to whisper the same sentence verbatim in the ear of one of their neighbours. This person then tells the next person, and so on, until everyone in the group has heard the sentence. Ask the last person to write down the version of the sentence received. Compare the original with the final versions. With five words only, there might be little difference. Try the same exercise several times, using eight-, ten- and twelve-word sentences successively, and note the deterioration in accuracy from the original to the 'relayed' message. Ask individuals at various points along the communication or 'rumour' chain what sentence they heard—to detect where the message broke down. Now compare the efficacy of this approach to message transfer with simply posting a notice with the same information where it is visible to all intended recipients of the information.
- In small groups (of three to five members), design a communication network system appropriate to your institution or organisation, linking

decision-makers in the system to subordinate levels in the organisation, and eventually to end-users of the information. Present the result to other groups, explaining the reasons for each link. Be sure to think about possible breaks in the channels, and the reasons for these weaknesses. (Note: The group instructor might wish to analyse the communication network informally built into each group while they carry out this task—looking at leadership, followership, and passive audience roles within each group—and thus develop the group instructor's own network systems for the class. But beware of offending the sensibilities of group members.)

- Imagine that your institution or organisation has been accused by a tabloid newspaper of breaking a very important occupational health-and-safety regulation, and that the damage to public confidence in your establishment is estimated to be in millions of dollars. In small groups (not more than five members), nominate a company/institution type (your own or fictitious), invent the contravention of which you have been accused, and write a press release and advertising slogan to defend your organisation against the claim. Return to a full group and present each case.

5

Tourism and Media Effects

SYNOPSIS OF CHAPTER

- 'Media effects' and who is interested in them

- Whether the media do exert influence over audiences and society in general

- Some examples to understand the media-effects argument

- Some examples of a misunderstanding of media effects

- *Focus* on air safety and Swissair's 1998 accident

- *Fast Facts* on advertising efficacy through key research results

Are People Affected by the Mass Media?

People depend, to a greater or lesser degree, upon mass communication for much of the information and entertainment they receive. Although their immediate surroundings, their towns, and their districts, have longstanding information networks which worked adequately in the past, more and more people turn to the mass media to learn about the wider society. A conflict in Bosnia is no longer a mere civil war of no consequence to the world community as a whole. Reporting on wars—primitive in the Korean War, developing by the time of the Vietnam War, and developed to the point of being televised blow for blow in the Gulf War—has reflected the evolution of the global society. It could be argued that the very nature of the global society has its roots in the global mass media. But are people affected by the media? And, if so, in what way?

The short answer to this question is 'yes' and 'no', depending on the perspective from which it is viewed. This is a question that has been, and continues to be, the subject of debate and research. Critics of the media-effects argument have emanated from different fields of research, and have utilised different approaches to analyse the question. However, according to McLeod, Kosicki and Zhangdang (1991), there are certain common characteristics that all fields of research share:

- that their primary focus is on audiences;
- that *influence* is an integral component, whether it be from the viewpoint of changing behaviour or sustaining the status quo; and
- that the source of influence is attributed to a certain aspect, form, or content of the media-message system, the medium, or the individual message.

As these authors observe:

> Definition of the media-effects perspective is a task made difficult by the great diversity in theoretical styles, research questions and methods of gathering evidence and making inferences
>
> McLeod, Kosicki & Zhangdang 1991

McLeod, Kosicki and Zhangdang, in their own way, attempt to clarify the confusion of conflicting viewpoints on the subject of media effects. In what follows, we will attempt to present the case of media effects in much the same way as McLeod, Kosicki and Zhangdang—but using examples and statistics from tourism and other industries for clarification.

Understanding and Misunderstanding Media Effects

There are two sides to every story. Although authors and researchers will go to great lengths to establish scholarly critiques of other writers' media-effects research, there will always be believers in the business world, the tourist industry, and the public/governmental domain in general, who continue to believe in the power of the media. Examples of this can be seen in tourism advertising on television, in print, through catalogues, and in newsletters/releases. Politicians illustrate their belief in the mass media with their electoral campaigning on television, their live debates, and in the delivery of important safety warnings—as illustrated by the Reagan administration's warning to American citizens not to fly to Greece in the mid eighties because of terrorist dangers. Nevertheless, the question remains, why do some believe in media effects and others disbelieve?

Clues to Understanding

Informative Catastrophe (Audience Perception)

As previously noted, the mass media are used to deliver information on an array of topics of varying importance and urgency—from a newspaper advertisement for a telephone pizza-delivery service, to a statewide total fire ban warning on television. The pizza-delivery service can be used as an analogy for the communication process involved.

Choosing a medium is like selecting a pizza from a large menu. Once the type of pizza is chosen, the extras need to be selected. This is analogous to choosing the medium and choosing the message. A delay is expected between sending the message and receipt of feedback concerning the message. The reply, like the pizza, should arrive on your doorstep eventually (that is, feedback), but the quality of the product is sometimes poor and indiscernible. (Those who have eaten a cold, soggy delivered pizza should understand this analogy quite well!) Although every effort is invested in sending the right message, there is no guarantee of a desired response.

Lombardi (1990) discusses the role of the mass media in mass emergencies, creating a theoretical model of communication that is presented in Figure 5.1. Lombardi offers the example of the Chernobyl incident to establish his point, and to link the communication of this event through the mass media to certain manifest socioeconomic consequences.

Figure 5.1   A theoretical model of communication

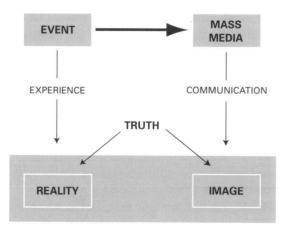

Source: Lombardi 1990

The essence of Lombardi's argument is that there are certain strategic characteristics concerning information broadcasted in the event of a disaster or catastrophe. The name given to this by Lombardi was 'the informative catastrophe'.

Referring to Figure 5.1, the event (for example, the Chernobyl disaster) and the media are on one level—implying that, without knowledge of the event's being transferred through a medium (not necessarily the mass media), the event might not have otherwise existed. This supports what Merrill, Lee and Fiendlander referred to as the 'fission effect':

> . . . an action plus the perception of this action gives us public opinion.
>
> Merrill, Lee & Fiendlander 1990

Moving down through some manifest experience, or the communication of the event, Lombardi (1990) claims that, in the absence of direct information spread, society attributes an abstract truthfulness to information emanating from the mass media. If there is no opportunity to experience the event or its after-effects first hand, to compare or sense the event personally, the sole truth becomes the broadcasted one (Gow & Otway 1990). This reflects on the handling of the media by authorities during a crisis situation—indirectly acknowledging the strength of its impact on society. If the public were to be 'fully informed', authorities sometimes fear panic, or potential public danger—showing that authorities accept an implicit relationship between the media and public reactions.

This was illustrated in the alleged cover-up by aviation and police authorities (including British and American security services, and even PanAm) preceding the Lockerbie PanAm 103 disaster. According to David Yallop (1995), although specific warnings had been made about a flight out of Frankfurt being attacked, only '. . . VIPs and a number of intelligence operatives were pulled off that plane'. Yallop was a British journalist who had interviewed Abu Nidal—an infamous Palestinian terrorist who had warned of retaliation bombings for the shooting down of an Iranian airbus by the US Navy in July 1988. The reason for not passing information on about the threats to this flight in particular, and the reason for the restriction of information about air safety issues in general, is clear—the authorities do not want to alert the general public. Similar comparisons can be made with the information withheld from the public during hostage crises—thus encouraging responsible journalism under extremely dangerous circumstances when people's lives are at stake.

In editorial comments, other journalists have sometimes been particularly scathing towards their own—such as McGuinness in response to the loss of two small carrier planes and the subsequent role of the Australian Civil Aviation Authority (CAA) and Bureau of Air Safety Investigation (BASI):

> . . . we have seen the standard irrational response to the issue from Government, Opposition and media that always follows such an air disaster.
>
> McGuinness 1994

It is thus evident that the public might take the information of an event—such as an aviation disaster, or Chernobyl—and apply an abstract level of truth to the matter in the absence of contradictory personal experience. Reactions to this information are manifest in various ways:

- sometimes affecting purchasing patterns (such as people choosing to not fly Air New Zealand after their reported fatal accident);
- invoking emotions, such as by the families of victims;
- affecting the emergency systems in charge of handling catastrophes; and even
- affecting the mass media themselves, who have the task of sorting out event details and deciding what to release and what to withhold.

But underlying the analysis of effects is the audience's response to the event. Because it is extremely difficult to measure accurately, this remains as the stumbling block to definitive research in the field.

McGuinness raises an interesting concluding point on human responses to news of (say) an air accident:

> The fundamental issue is, of course, that of risk analysis. Most people are not very good at comparing the risks of different kinds of activities and, in ordinary life, take far greater risks than they would be prepared to accept in what they think of as controlled situations
>
> McGuinness 1994

This infers that the veneer of public information is filtered to protect people from their own enlightenment, or perhaps that people involve themselves in risky situations unknowingly in the absence of full information. He adds that:

> Air travel is inherently unsafe, in that no matter what precautions are taken there are bound to be some accidents, and some of these will be fatal. Fatal accidents in air travel tend, when a large aircraft is involved, to be spectacular and peculiarly horrifying.
>
> McGuinness 1994

Focus on Air Safety and Traffic vs the Traveller:

Some Facts, Myths and an Evaluation of the SwissAir Flight 111 Accident

According to Maxa:

> Overall, the US airline industry has enjoyed an excellent safety record that, with the occasional blips, has generally improved since deregulation (in 1978).
>
> Maxa 1999

Maxa was referring to the (US) *Airline Deregulation Act 1978*—which transferred responsibility for airline activity to the Federal Aviation Administration (FAA) and the Department of Transport (DOT) to allow free market competition between airlines, allowing them to determine their own fare structures. This resulted in a 'shake-out' of the industry, lower air fares, and the formation of 'mega-carriers' (Walker 1999).

But others have not been as easily convinced as was Maxa. Critics of deregulation say that competitive pressures to cut costs have affected maintenance and new-parts programs to the point where, in the USA, aircraft age and safety has become a 'hot' topic. One company's average plane-age is 26 years—11 years more than the US average of 15 years. The three biggest carriers in the US are lower than the average—with their average planes being 12 years of age.

However, it should be noted that the number of US airline accidents (recorded in raw figures) shows no signs of worsening during the 1980s and 1990s (see Table 5.1).

Table 5.1   US airlines accident record 1985–95

Year	Accidents (per year)	Accidents (per 100 000 hours of flying)
1985	22	0.24
1986	24	0.23
1987	36	0.32
1988	29	0.25
1989	28	0.25
1990	24	0.20
1991	26	0.21
1992	18	0.12
1993	23	0.18
1994	23	0.17
1995	35	0.26

Source: FAA 1998

With the exception of 1995, airlines in America in the first half of the 1990s showed signs of improvement in terms of accidents per flight hour. The Federal Aviation Administration (FAA) predicts that, due to economic growth fuelling demand for air travel and cargo services, airlines in the USA alone will carry almost one billion passengers a year by 2010, compared with the 1998 figure of 643.3 million, and the 1999 estimate of 659.2 million passengers (Maxa 1999).

Despite predictions of increasingly crowded skies and overworked air traffic controllers, some commentators still believe concerns over airline safety are overrated when one considers that there were 40 676 deaths on American roads from 6.5 million accidents in 1994. Compared with 23 air accidents in the same year, air accident danger is very small. But the fear, although apparently irrational, continues. It is interesting to compare this with McGuinness' comments (see page 89) indicating that he believed that people should be more afraid.

This idea—that air travel is a 'time bomb waiting to go off'—is echoed by Usher. In an article entitled 'Flight or Fright' (subtitled 'Passengers can now lessen the chances of choosing airplanes with a bad record, but should they have to?') Usher puts the fear of flying into context.

> There is a 'Jaws Factor' to flying. The chances of death in a plane are not vastly greater than those of being chewed by a shark while swimming, but the terror of cruising through the clouds one moment and nose-diving earthwards the next is as primordial and petrifying as the nightmare of dorsal fins and triangular teeth.
>
> Usher 1997

The media in both cases must assume some, if not all, the responsibility for this over-exaggerated fear. Fortunately, in this Internet world, people are better able to distinguish fact from fiction when it comes to airline safety records. The FAA has a website giving airline safety records and detail about the planes in various fleets—as well as fact sheets on aviation accident records (see Table 5.2, p. 93).

Usher adds:

> The Flight Safety Foundation, based in Virginia [USA, calculates that]: a person who took a random commercial flight every day of the year would have to live for 26 000 years before being in a crash. A traveler is much more likely to die on the road to the airport . . . Deaths [associated with airlines], excluding those from hijackings, are around 1500 a year—with a record 1840 in 1996—compared with an average of about 1100 during the '80s. Given that traffic is increasing about 6.5% a year, if the ratio of fatal accidents to flights stays the same, the annual death toll will continue to rise.
>
> Usher 1997

As countries pursue more 'open-skies' policies, and as new airlines sprout up all over the world, there is a concern as to whether air safety standards are being properly observed. These standards are set out by various authorities—such as the International Air Traffic Association (IATA), Europe's Federal Agency for Air Travel (FAAT), and the US Federal Aviation Administration (FAA). In Europe, the Germans are known for their strict safety standards and increasingly discerning passengers. British pilots and engineers also have a good reputation for their technical abilities and workmanship, but D. Learmont, a former British Royal Air Force pilot and spokesman for Flight International, says:

> We want our cake and eat it; we want low-cost flying and to fly safely. [British tourists] will accept traveling on airlines from very weird parts of the world in order to have a fiver knocked off the price of the family holiday . . . Germans are different; they check out the airlines being offered.
>
> Learmont, quoted by Usher 1997

Usher supports Learmont's statement.

> Part of this German attitude stems from the crash of a Turkish charter plane off the Dominican Republic in February last year . . . Germany has been setting the pace for European safety: the government ordered increased inspections, which have led to a rise in the number of defects found, and to the removal of one operator's licence.
>
> Usher 1997

The FAAT's planned group called Air Eurosafe, '. . . is an attempt by various European countries to help underdeveloped nations lift safety standards to First World levels' (Usher 1997). Australia's national carrier, Qantas, and Switzerland's national carrier, Swissair, share the top places in airline safety per flying hour (Pelton, Aral & Dulles 1997). Swissair's position on this ranking might have been affected by the Flight 111 crash outside Halifax in Canada (September 1998). Qantas holds top place for having had no fatalities in-flight in its long flying history.

Swissair Flight 111

Swissair Flight 111 crashed on 3 September 1998 in the area of Peggy's Cove (near Halifax), Nova Scotia, Canada. There were no survivors from 215 passengers and 14 crew.

Airline fatalities receive inordinate media coverage—especially when it involves a reputable airline, and especially if the crash occurs in or around a developed nation where the world's media can gain easier access to the crash site for those all-important 'carnage' shots. Grieving families, stressed airline staff and directors, press conferences, and expert after expert offering unsubstantiated theories on what might have happened—all this is becoming the standard fare following such tragic events.

Table 5.2   FAA fact sheet on aviation accident statistics (1987–96)

US Carrier Fatal Accident	%	Total Number	Foreign Carrier Fatal Accidents	%	Total Number
Loss of control	32%	11	Loss of control	28%	38
Other/unknown	18%	6	Controlled flight into terrain (CFIT)	26%	36
Controlled flight into terrain (CFIT)	12%	4	Other	10%	14
Runway incursions	12%	4	Landing	7%	9
Ice/snow	9%	3	Hijack	6%	8
In-flight fire	6%	2	Fuel exhaustion	5%	7
Windshear	3%	1	Ice/snow	4%	5
Landing	3%	1	Sabotage	4%	5
Sabotage	3%	1	Runway incursions	3%	4
Hijack	3%	1	In-flight fire	3%	4
Midair collision	0	0	Windshear	2%	3
Fuel exhaustion	0	0	Midair collision	1%	2
Rejected takeoff	0	0	Rejected takeoff	1%	1
Total	100%	34		100%	136

Source: FAA 1998

The handling of the Swissair crash by its chief executive officer (CEO) and public-relations people was professionally and admirably done. Relevant statistical and engineering information (type and flight history of the aeroplane) was quickly released. All the information was posted on the Internet and could be accessed through several channels—such as the websites of Swissair and Boeing (the latter having a vested interest in allaying doubts about the make of aircraft involved in the accident).

According to Boeing, the aeroplane involved in the accident was delivered to Swissair in August 1991. It was therefore a relatively new plane. It had accumulated over 6400 flights and 35 000 flight hours. The aeroplane was a McDonnell Douglas-11 (MD-11). Boeing noted:

This is the second hull-loss accident involving an MD-11 in the nearly 8 years since the airplane type entered commercial service . . . 178 MD-11's [in the] world fleet have proven themselves in terms of safety, reliability and performance.

Boeing 1998

The press releases from Swissair's CEO, Jeffrey Katz, achieved a balance of genuine remorse for the families of the victims and reassurance of the public that Swissair had not lapsed in the quality of their planes. The 'Swiss-made' tag normally symbolises something of good quality—the Swiss being known for their engineering diligence and excellence. The aim was for Swissair to exercise immediate damage control—as it did—to remove any suggestion that Swissair might be a dangerous carrier. Their exemplary record before the incident helped to minimise the damage to their image. Katz was quoted as saying the day after the crash:

> As you can understand, the mood among the family members is sombre. We will continue to stay hard at work to provide assistance, support and information to them during this very difficult time.
>
> Katz quoted in Swissair 1998

Katz followed this immediately with:

> . . . the HB-IWF MD-11 aircraft involved in the accident . . . maintenance records show that all FAA directives were fully complied with. I can confirm this was a well-maintained and airworthy aircraft.
>
> Katz quoted in Swissair 1998

It will be interesting to review Swissair's passenger figures over the coming years, and to compare them with figures before the accident. It is probable that the turnaround will be quite fast. Following the accident, media attention directed at Swissair died down very quickly. Compared with the attention received by PanAm after the Lockerbie crash (which, it has been argued, led to PanAm's eventual demise), Swissair appears to have 'got off' rather lightly so far.

It does seem that the media play a vital role in determining the gravity of the impact—both financial and psychological—that such a major crisis has on an airline. Figures 5.2 and 5.3 (pages 95, 96) provide an analysis of Swissair's media-management approach.

Figure 5.2 Swissair Flight 111 Crash—Public-relations and Media Management

Date and Phase of Campaign	Number of Internet Press Releases
Fire Brigade Phase	
3 September 1998 (crash day)	4
4 September 1998	2
5 September 1998	2
6 September 1998	2
7 September 1998	2
8 September 1998	0
9 September 1998	6
10 September 1998	3
11 September 1998	0
12 September 1998	3
Clean-up Phase	
13 September 1998	0
14 September 1998	1
15 September 1998	1
16 September 1998	1
17 September 1998	1
18 September 1998	1
Fallout Phase	
19 September to 7 October 1998	0
Update & Wait Phase	
8 October 1998	1
9 October to 14 October 1998	0
15 October 1998	1
16 October to 28 October 1998	0
29 October 1998	1
Fingers Crossed Phase	
30 October to 19 November 1998	0
Update & Abate Phase	
20 November 1998	1
21 November to 22 November 1998	0
23 November 1998	1
Final Greenlight Phase	
24 November 1998 for years	?

Source: Compiled by the author using Swissair 1998

Figure 5.3   Evolution of press releases after Swissair Flight 111 crash

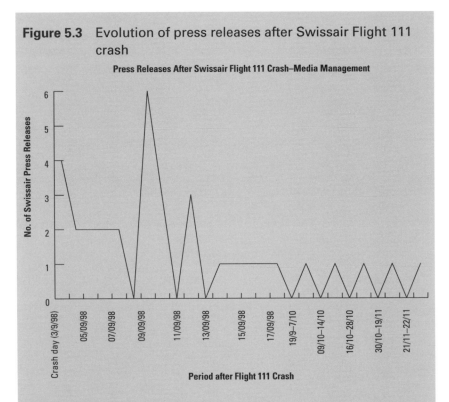

Source: Compiled by the author using Swissair 1998

Between the day of the crash (3 September 1998) and 23 November, Swissair published (on the Internet) 32 press releases in English, 34 in German and 34 in French. It is arguable that the volume of press releases issued by Swissair corresponded fairly closely with the expected or real media attention that the disaster received.

Figure 5.2 (page 95) shows an interesting public-relations pattern—which the present author has divided into certain phases.

Initially, the output of press releases was very high as Swissair wanted to be seen to be doing everything possible in providing full information and assistance. This stage in the public-relations process—which might be termed the 'fire brigade' (damage control) media stage—waned after about 10 days

The next media stage ('clean-up') then began. This term symbolises the actual crash clean-up and the putting out of media 'spot fires'—dealing with any new revelations before they were leaked, and being seen not to have forgotten the disaster too quickly.

The 'fallout' media stage was a period when Swissair did not issue press releases—perhaps waiting to assess the immediate aftermath, and to take stock of the situation.

'Update & wait' refers to the advance issuing of new information that came to light, followed by intermittent waiting periods to gauge reactions.

Another waiting period followed. This is termed 'fingers crossed'—enough time after the disaster to measure the losses of sales, and to assess confidence in the company.

As more information came to light, the next stage—the 'update & abate' stage—expresses the release of any new information as necessary, while observing an underlying desire to let the event begin to abate in the public's mind.

The 'final greenlight' stage is when the media had more or less let the event drop. It was no longer newsworthy in the absence of dramatic new information. The company still faced longer-term revelations (in the form of official inquiries and recommendations)—but these were likely to be well into the future.

Figure 5.3 (page 96) presents the evolution of Swissair press releases in the months after the crash of SR111. An important press release, which effectively marked the end of the damage-control stages, was the announcement (18 September 1998) of the setting-up of a post-emergency organisation (PEO), which is to remain in place for up to two years.

Philippe Bruggisser, SwissAir Group CEO, also stated that:

> ... investigations such as this are long-term in nature and that, in future, Swissair will only comment on the facts of the matter, refusing to discuss speculation.
>
> Swissair Press Releases, 18 September 1998

After this press release, the graph shows an on-and-off pattern—demonstrating that the crash had not been forgotten, but having the effect of allowing the matter to fade in the public's attention. (The public-relations approach to handling information and the media after a disaster is also discussed in Chapter 9.)

Airlines and high-profile companies recognise the importance of taking the facts and arguments to the media before the media have the chance to imprint a potentially devastating image of their company on the psyche of the viewing public. The use of the Internet to relay information to the public has also added a sense of immediacy to the event—a source of information perceived as factual and authoritative, but not sterile and faceless.

Swissair's handling of the Flight 111 crisis clearly showed a company that planned to survive the industry and media fallout—and not experience the fate of PanAm, which suffered badly, and perhaps ultimately failed, as a result of the Lockerbie incident (see Chapter 7).

Influence (Social Proof)

Behavioural scientists have taken the principle of social proof, and have applied it to various situations—both in an effort to substantiate their findings, and to test them in as many different contingencies as is scientifically efficacious. One such test was conducted in a survey that gathered information on 'copycat' suicide and murder tendencies following front-page news of similar incidents in newspapers.

The principle of social proof holds that people look to those around them for cues as to how they should behave. Cialdini (1988) cites the infamous Jonestown massacre as a classic example of social proof—in which cult followers proceeded in an orderly fashion towards a tub of poison and committed mass suicide. In the absence of contradictory information, isolated in the jungle of Guyana (South America), the southern Californian victims looked to each other for cues and supporting behavioural modes. This has been explained in terms of the 'Werther effect' described in Goethe's *Die Leiden des jungen Werthers* ('The Sorrows of Young Werther', 1774). Young German readers of the book copied Werther's suicide— leading to the banning of the book for its potential effect on youth.

Phillips (1980, cited in Cialdini 1988) conducted an astonishing study on this effect, using the case of suicides reported in newspapers. This study has implications on the media-effects debate, because the results of the research display manifest reactions to media content and presentation:

> . . . it has been shown (Phillips 1979) that immediately following certain kinds of highly publicised suicide stories, the number of people who die in commercial airline crashes increases by 1000% . . .
>
> This evidence raises an important ethical issue. The suicides that followed these stories are *excess* deaths. After the initial spurt, the suicide rates do not drop below traditional levels, but only return to those levels. Statistics like these might well give pause to newspaper editors inclined to sensationalise suicide accounts as those accounts are likely to lead to the deaths of scores of people. More recent data indicate that in addition to newspaper editors, television broadcasters have cause for concern about the effects of the suicide stories they present. Whether they appear as news reports, information features or fictional movies, these stories create an immediate cluster of self-inflicted deaths, with impressionable, imitation-prone teenagers being the most frequent victims (Bollen & Phillips 1982; Gould & Schaffer 1986; Phillips & Carsensen 1986).
>
> In a later study (Phillips 1980), Phillips further added that social proof applied to automobile fatalities in that they also had a tendency to 'shoot up'.
>
> Cialdini 1988

The graphs in Figures 5.4. and 5.5 (pages 99, 100) demonstrate the results of Phillips' study. Remarkably, adding to the strength of this media-effects argument, Phillips' study revealed that fatal crashes increased dramatically only in those regions where the story was publicised, and that the wider the publicity given the original suicide story the greater was the resultant increase in crashes.

Figure 5.4   Difference between observed and usual monthly suicides

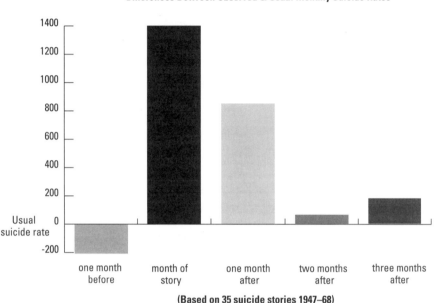

Differences Between Observed & Usual Monthly Suicide Rates

(Based on 35 suicide stories 1947–68)

Source: Phillips, cited in Cialdini 1988

This research raises the question not only of manifest effect but, for potential users of the mass media in the travel industry, it also raises the question of the psychological theories proposed by Phillips in explaining this phenomenon.

One theory was based on 'audience bereavement'—that is, that the readers went through a process of sadness for the loss and the victims, and subsequently became distracted in their job and caused accidents in automobiles and aircraft. Another theory supposed that the drivers and pilots experienced stress and depression caused by the awful headlines, and that maintenance staff might have been too depressed to perform their tasks properly, causing increased machinery flaws and accidents.

Neither of these theories held much weight, according to Phillips. Cialdini reports that Phillips looked further into the problem for a possible solution:

Figure 5.5 Comparison of increases in fatalities between different transport modes before, during, and after a news story breaks

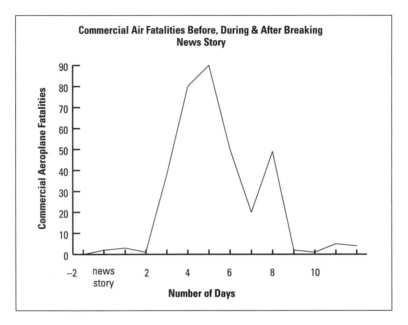

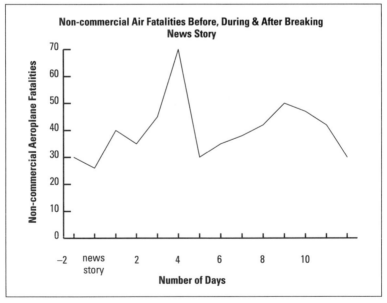

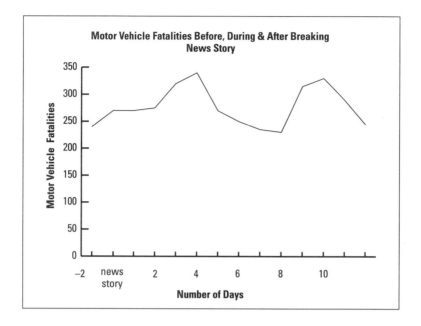

Source: Phillips, cited in Cialdini 1988

Newspaper stories reporting suicide victims who died alone produce an increase in frequency of single-fatality wrecks only, whereas stories reporting suicide-plus-murder incidents produce an increase in multiple-fatality wrecks . . . it is fantastically specific.

Cialdini 1988

These results are too specific to be explained by the more general 'people are depressed and pay less attention to their jobs' theories. Phillips attributes the principle of social proof to the phenomenon where people commit suicides that copycat an event reported on the front page of a newspaper:

. . . the principle of social proof is behind the phenomenon of like people committing copycat suicides in the event of highly publicised front-page suicides.

Phillips, quoted by Cialdini 1988

Figure 5.4 shows that the difference between observed and usual monthly suicide rates surrounding the publication of 35 suicide stories between 1947 and 1968 is substantial. The lowering of suicides in months after the suicide stories shows that the increase immediately after the publicity could not be explained as being merely an upward trend.

These results are mirrored by the graphs of commercial air fatalities and motor vehicle fatalities (Figure 5.5) under similar testing circumstances—before, on, and after the date of the suicide stories. There is less fluctuation in non-commercial fatalities. No explanation is offered for this by Phillips or Cialdini.

An interesting follow-up research project would be to study any reported increase in insurance purchased for travel subsequent to media coverage of a travel accident—where the insurance, or lack thereof, featured as worldwide news. Such a case was reported in Athens, where a young Australian woman was badly burnt in a car accident and, having no insurance, was refused treatment. The world press featured the story and the result was favourable for the woman. Members of the public rallied together in a fund to help pay for her medical charges. This, in itself, represents a positive direct public response to media reports. When asked by the present author whether this had an impact on the level of insurance taken after the incident, the response of RACV Travel Insurers (Australia), was:

> By law, travel agents now must offer insurance to all passengers they book. They accept or decline. It must be stated on the travel document that they declined it . . . [although] generally no [we haven't noticed an increase], but we do push it. It's a business.
>
> Interviews Royal Automobile Club of Victoria 1995

The above comment refers to a law requiring that travel insurance be offered to the consumer at the point of sale. Thus, although the public propensity to buy travel insurance had not (apparently) been affected immediately after the incident, the public had been indirectly affected—because the government reacted to it by enacting this law which, inevitably, does affect all members of society.

Phillips' research (cited in Cialdini 1988) might also have important impact on the decisions of airline passengers—causing them to reconsider the assumptions people hold about the airline industry's safety and controllability. This harkens back to McGuinness' (1994) assertion that people take 'far greater risks than they would be prepared to accept in what they think of as controlled situations'

Phillips' research also has implications for tourism providers, and for their understanding of the role that the media plays in their business—especially regarding public perception of air safety. That providers are concerned to allay fear of flying was shown in Figures 4.6 and 4.7 (pages 71, 72)—in which advertising of safety and credibility was made in response to media coverage of (and consequent public concerns over) terrorist problems in Europe, and supposed DC-10 design faults. Such concern was also shown in the Swissair case (page 92).

Role of the Media in Stable, Secure, and Safe Tourism

Underlying the development of tourism throughout the world has been an equivalent development in information and the knowledge-based society (Ritchie 1990). It is important for the '. . . Tourism Industry to examine how the travel behaviour of individuals in a knowledge-based society' affects managers and operators in the development of tourism policy and strategic planning, and in their future use of, and response to, tourist media.

This can be looked at from three different perspectives:

- the quest for stability in terms of economic wellbeing;
- the quest for security in travel destination choice; and
- the quest for safe tourism practices.

In each case the mass media have a certain role to play. Tourist information providers might benefit from an understanding of these relationships.

Economic Wellbeing

According to Ritchie (1990), the world has experienced decades of economic growth and relative security. Yet, despite advancements in technology and managerial control, the 1990s proved to be economically challenging. Economic wellbeing through a guaranteed career path appears to be a luxury on which fewer and fewer people can rely. People have been forced to take responsibility for their own career development—able to rely no longer on the 'first-in-last-out' principle previously obtaining in companies. Nevertheless, the tourism industry worldwide has provided a great opportunity for career changes and employment ventures—as shown in Figures 5.6 and 5.7 (pages 105, 106). It could also be argued that tourism's unfettered growth is related to improvements in communication technology and distribution. Through improved flow, economies of scale and competition have generally brought tourism prices down for the average traveller. Furthermore, the average traveller expects better value for money than ever before:

> Australian travellers have never had it so good. Domestic package holidays are cheaper than five years ago—reflecting big fare falls since domestic deregulation in 1990. Apart from a few destinations, such as Hawaii, overseas travel is an all-time bargain. In 1972, Qantas introduced a round-trip, economy-class flight to London for [A]$750, or 7.4 weeks pay for the average Australian male at the time. Today, cut-price return tickets to London cost less than $1800—about 2.6 weeks pay—and one Asian airline is promoting a fare for less than $1500.
>
> Needham 1996

Airfare reductions around the world can also be attributed to the use of yield-management techniques by airlines and other tourism businesses, and to improvements in communication and distribution systems in the computer age.

Despite the availability of bargain airfares, and more choice than ever, people are still very careful how they spend their money. With inflation eating away at disposable income, or reduced income due to unemployment, it seems logical that a luxury purchase such as travel would be the first thing to be crossed off the list. But this is not so. Tourism and travel statistics include a range of travel options—from a costly packaged tour to the Middle East to a cheap driving holiday visiting friends and relatives. The number of trips taken to various individual destinations might decrease, but the overall picture shows that demand shifts to other destinations or cheaper travel alternatives. Turkey, Greece, and Egypt felt the effects of changes in holiday patterns (by British tourists especially) in the early 1990s.

The issue of why there was an aggregate reduction in outbound holidays from the United Kingdom offered from 11.6 million in 1989 to 9.28 million in 1990 was of some concern and was discussed at a Tourism Society seminar, reported on by Raitt in 1990 (cited in Laws 1991). It appeared that short breaks within the UK, taken more frequently, grew in popularity over the period.

Essentially, individual travel choices are sensitive to price and prevailing economic conditions at a micro-level. Knowles (1990) cites the oil crisis in the mid 1970s as an example—US tourist traffic flowing to European destinations decreased from 3.8 million in 1973 to 3.1 million by 1975. On the other hand, as noted earlier and shown in Table 1.1 (International Tourist Arrivals), on a macro-economic level, tourism is more economically resilient, having experienced negative growth only once (between 1981 and 1982) since comprehensive records began in the 1950s.

Mass-media portrayals of factories closing down, workers being laid off at car-assembly plants, and statistics of unemployment and inflation rising simultaneously, give the average person a poor impression of the economy as a whole. If Phillips' study (page 98) bears any substance, the effect that such news might have on its audience could, indeed, be manifold. For instance, it might reflect the changes in tourist spending patterns experienced in the early 1990s to Turkey and Greece. However, according to Knowles:

> ... as past experience has shown, the public awareness—whether of positive or negative conditions—takes some time to grow, with a constant time lag between conditions and perceptions.
>
> Knowles 1990

Figure 5.6 Evolution of the proportion of tourism employment to
total employment worldwide

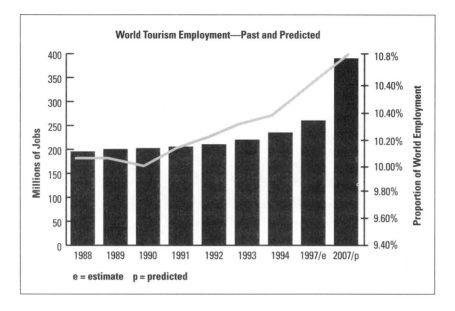

Source: author's chart using data from World Travel & Tourism Council 1997

Thus it is possible that the results of changes in the spending patterns in the 1990s might not be truly felt or understood for several years. This means that, if the news of an economic downturn reached society now, it might take some time before it has an impact— from Knowles' viewpoint. However, Knowles' point of view implicitly refutes the impact study by Phillips, and other figures showing drops in tourist arrivals to specific destinations (for example, due to war).

Perhaps the *nature* of the news presented in the mass media is at question—rather than the *effect* it has on the audience. Unemployment figures might not be as strongly felt as news of a murder-suicide, or a war in Croatia. It might reflect myriad individual thoughts and tastes outside the realms of scientific testing.

Travel Choices and Security

Ritchie says:

> In the area of the physical, as opposed to the economic, security, we have known for some time that real or perceived physical danger is certain to diminish the prospects for a given destination or firm.

Ritchie 1990

Figure 5.7   Evolution of the proportion of tourism employment to total employment in European Union

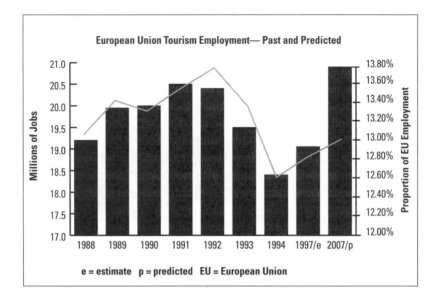

Source: author's chart using data from World Travel & Tourism Council 1997

This has been illustrated on many occasions in the research literature, and has been demonstrated in recent years in Croatia, India, Turkey, Indonesia, Sudan, and Sri Lanka—indeed, in virtually any destination where news has reached the public of possible dangers. The Australian cricket team chose to forfeit their first match in Sri Lanka in the 1996 cricket World Cup, rather than risk playing in Colombo—in the face of perceived dangers posed by the Tamil Tigers. Based on mass-media images, the Australian team perceived a real threat—whereas the other teams in the World Cup (except West Indies) chose to ignore the media representations of possible dangers, and placed their faith in Sri Lankan assurances that it was safe for them to play.

There is also a further complication. The potential for risks to traveller security increase as they become '. . . more interested in enriching their lives with experience rather than hands-off entertainment' (Ritchie 1990). This description implies that travellers are seeking more adventure travel, more distant destinations, and greater thrills. It might be useful to understand the psychology behind human security needs—as well as examining some of the recent examples of tourist risks and responses (see also Terrorism and Tourism, page 145 Part III).

The subject of tourists' aversions to risk was raised by McGuinness (page 89) and is connected to motivation studies. However, according to Pearce and Stringer (1990), 'In social psychology, the area of tourism study is undermanned'. Hence, there has been little in the way of research to confirm or deny the hypothesis that tourists are inclined to make their destination choices using security as a criterion. Tourism professionals suggest that security issues are more influential in determining a tourist's decision not to go, or to defer their trip.

Table 5.3 is a list of the important aspects to be considered in leisure tourism decisions.

Table 5.3   Aspects of leisure tourism decisions

Length	Frequency	Cost	Distance	Risk
Day trip	high	low	local	low
Overnight	moderate	low	short	moderate
Week	low	varies	medium	higher
Main holiday	annual	high	no constraint	higher

Source: Adapted from Laws 1991; 'risk' column added by present author

In Table 5.3, the addition of the fifth column (variable risk) to a table of leisure tourism decisions assumes that greater emphasis should be placed on security and risk factors—a position supported by:

- travel insurance companies (RACV, Royal Tours, Interviews, 1995);
- Ritchie (1990), who adds that the following recommendations should be considered:
    - responses to crime: organised travel and/or receptive visitor services that shelter travellers from crime; destinations that eliminate crime will be preferred (Ritchie 1990);
    - response to health and safety: specialised products and services that protect the health of the traveller and/or facilitate access to reliable medical services in foreign environments will have a competitive advantage (Ritchie 1990).
- travel agents and operators (Interviews 1995–96) who confirmed the effect of risk concerns on tourist travel planning:
    - *Office de Promotion du Tourisme (OPT)*, Belgium: 'There was [concern] before—when there were terrorists in Europe. It didn't make any difference if it was Italy or here [Belgium]. But now? No. The image is affected for a time because we [in Belgium] don't have an image most of the time. We're small. In the States

they don't perceive a difference between us';

- *Travel agent*: 'That's another influence [apart from price]. For political problems, we are very careful. For instance, Egypt. We didn't sell Egypt for maybe two to three years; then, at the beginning of September, there was a sudden increase in demand. We had a lot of bookings. And then three weeks ago there was another incident with people in a train . . . It's difficult to judge what to do . . . the same could be said of Paris [which experienced] some terrorism . . . people have to decide for themselves if it's risky or not. We say no only on the advice of the Minister, [but, even so] . . . we haven't sold [trips to] Paris since June or July [1995]'.

- *Airline*: 'Air New Zealand went through an unfortunate situation when it crashed an aircraft in the Antarctic, which had a huge affect on the company . . . [people] will fly, but they'll fly another airline'.

All taken from interviews with the present author 1995–96

Given the reality of safety as a factor in tourism decision-making, what are some of the potential disruptions to tourist flows?

Table 5.4 Factors disrupting tourism flows

Duration	Causes of disruption (examples in brackets)
Short-term	strikes and industrial disputes (Paris, Belgium 1995); storms, water shortages (Indonesian floods 1996, Australian drought 1990–95); transport accidents (PanAm 103 air crash 1988); crime (theft of wallet or passport); operator bankruptcy, cancellations (Jetabout in 1980s)
Medium-term	fluctuating exchange rate (US$ low in late 1980s); differential inflation rates (travellers from developing countries to Europe); political unrest (student riots in Indonesia 1998); health concerns (gastroenteritis)
Long-term	war (Bosnia/Kosovo 1990s); tax burdens (Sweden before joining EU); religious extremism (Algeria, Afghanistan); health concerns (malaria, yellow fever); harsh political regimes (Burma/Myanmar)

Source: updated from Laws 1991 and Pethiyagoda 1996

Safe Tourism Practices

The moral values of the tourist present an interesting angle from which to view media effects in tourism. These moral values often reflect the shifting values of society towards what might be termed 'socially undesirable' tourism. This could, theoretically, lead to a downturn in certain areas—as a result of what has been described as 'guilt-edged tourism' (King 1995). This describes socially conscious tourism—conscious of environmental effects, human rights records, and so on.

The role of the mass media in this is very important. As noted previously (page 87), according to Lombardi's (1990) theory (of information outside one's immediate realm of senses being relayed with an abstract level of truth through the mass media), individuals rely heavily on the media for information on the political actions of other countries. The idea of 'guilt-edged tourism' is that tourists—based on information gleaned from tourist authorities and the media—make a conscious decision to defer or decline a proposed trip on the basis of their personal moral values. This scenario is presented in the following:

> Political correctness will be firmly back on the travel agenda in 1996. The military regime in Myanmar [Burma] is promoting 1996 as 'Visit Myanmar Year', but many commentators are calling for a tourist boycott in protest of the Government's appalling human-rights record. However, others argue an influx of tourists for new ventures like the Orient Express-owned 'Road to Mandalay' cruise ship may force the Government to clean up its act.
>
> King 1995

This call for action to protest against the human rights record of a particular destination can be compared with the Reagan administration's publication of a boycott of Greece by American tourists in light of poor safety standards during the 1986–87 terrorist threats in Europe. The use of the media in this is vital, and is more important than word-of-mouth. Word-of-mouth does not have the weight of authority behind it. When security is at stake, people will favour a formal ('partyline') channel in their decision to defer or decline. In contrast, people tend to favour word-of-mouth in making decisions to go. Generally, people are innately cautious.

This has important ramifications for tour operators who must decide how to promote their destinations in the event of a safety or security complaint about their principal destinations. A formal ratification of tourism practices in a destination country (confirming their safety) carries a great deal of weight. The examples of the KLM and McDonnell Douglas advertisements (see pages 71, 72) illustrate the value of 'credible' sources in reassuring the public.

Tourism is an increasingly difficult business to control—as more and more people travel. People who might be ill equipped for the rigours of travel abroad find themselves in foreign surrounds. Glossy brochures have painted an almost surreal picture of perfection, and many people therefore have very high expectations. A UK newspaper reported on a tourist, returned from Cyprus, who said that he had looked forward to his holiday all year, and that it was ruined by an injury received when the roof of the games room in his hotel collapsed on him (Ungoed-Thomas 1998). The same article touched on an interesting new theme—that tourists are holding the tour operators responsible for illness, injury, or simple dissatisfaction with the purchased holiday. The opening lines to the article went as follows:

> Sun, sand and stress are the ingredients of an increasing number of package holidays . . . thousands of irate tourists suing for compensation.
>
> Ungoed-Thomas 1998

For example, more than 300 tourists are seeking a payout in a joint action against tour operator, Sunworld, claiming that they suffered salmonella poisoning from their hotel in Majorca. Why sue the tour operator, and not the Spanish hotel? It is probably a question of who has the deepest pocket, but it is a very worrying trend for tour operators who, in all due diligence, could never foresee every possible health, safety and security contingency. According to Ungoed-Thomas:

> . . . tourists have become increasingly fastidious and willing to press their grievances. The catalyst [is] . . . a European Union directive in 1992 [regarding] package travel regulations, which made tour operators responsible for every part of their holidays.
>
> Ungoed-Thomas 1998

Brenda Wall formed the lobby group 'Holiday Travelwatch' after she realised that her case—a landmark High Court action following a case of food poisoning on a Caribbean package tour with First Choice—was not the only one on this issue.

> Wall estimates in the past year she has taken more than 20 000 complaints from holiday makers and hundreds of those are now seeking legal advice for group actions.
>
> Ungoed-Thomas 1998

This suggests a deterioration in holiday standards. On the other hand, Jeremy Skidmore, editor of *Travel Weekly*, believes that holiday standards have improved in the last decade, but that 'people's expectations have risen more'. (Ungoed-Thomas 1998). Graham Lancaster from the Federation of

Tour Operators echoes this point, noting that 'it isn't a travel industry trend, it's more to do with society' (Ungoed-Thomas 1998). It would seem that it is not just the host destination that needs to worry about satisfying increasingly experienced and demanding tourists.

Self-Perpetuating Mass Media

In explaining media content, Davison, Boylan and Yu (1976) list the formulators of content as being media owners, journalists, government (directly and indirectly), and the audience itself.

To be successful, the media must be able to sell to the public the information that they are offering. Success means staying in business. The imperative to maintain viewers or circulation can also be interpreted as a 'media effect'. People buy a newspaper because they like to read, and their choice of newspaper is based on cost and content. Newspapers understand this, and decide on their content with this in mind.

In attempting to understand this relationship between media content and media effect, the media poll their audiences.

> Our media system operates on the premise that the audience is the customer and those who own and use the system are salesmen . . . By constantly being polled, the audience determines the type of programming that is offered by television and radio.
>
> Davison, Boylan & Yu 1976

Newspapers and magazines learn about consumer desires by their circulation figures.

Knowing which medium is the most effective in reaching the customers is paramount for tourism providers. In interviews with the present author, providers suggested that television was believed to most effective, followed by print (particularly colour print). Once a medium is chosen, the question of content becomes important. Content must be viewed by tourism operators primarily in terms of the audience's appreciation—that is, information for the purpose of selling. Research is fundamental to this end. An empirical example of this type of research is provided in *Fast Facts* on page 112.

Division of newspaper readers or television viewers into categories on the basis of occupational status is an example of the sort of market research that is very helpful—as shown in Table 5.5 (page 112).

Table 5.5 Market breakdown of readers/viewers by occupational status

Group	Description
AB	upper middle- and middle-class (managerial, professional)
C1	lower middle-class (clerical, supervisory)
C2	skilled working-class (skilled manual)
DE	working-class (semi-skilled, unskilled manual; subsistence)

Source: Carter 1971

Advertising a new destination or promoting a tourist product makes use of this sort of classification. Take the example of a luxury cruise around the Caribbean, or a holiday to a five-star resort along the Great Barrier Reef. Tourist providers of this sort of product obviously would aim at the AB or C1 groups—or perhaps, the individuals within each group with more disposable income.

Database providers sell tailormade access to their database. An example would be an airline and a credit card company. These might share their customer database to make a frequent-flyer profile that can be used for future direct marketing.

People sometimes receive promotional material from companies that they have never heard of—a good example of database-sharing or selling-off. Such practices are viewed unfavourably by some people who detest 'junkmail'. For this reason, many organisations that store personal details ask people to tick a box—allowing the organisation to use this information commercially.

Fast Facts on Travel Advertising

Does Anyone Pay Attention to Travel Advertising?

According to research conducted on behalf of the *Wall Street Journal* (Dow Jones & Company Inc.), people do read advertising and can recall it.

Beta Research Corporation in New York conducted the *Wall Street Journal* 'Europe Travel Survey' (between February 1997 and August 1997). A questionnaire was mailed to 2000 *Wall Street Journal* subscribers—with a 35.7% return rate netting a sample of 694. Data were collected on air travel and ratings, hotel usage and ratings, car rental, communications, television viewing, credit-card ownership, and demographics. Countries surveyed were all European Union countries, plus Switzerland and Norway. The respondents were 90% male, with an average age of 47.7 years, and 75% being in senior management positions.

For the purposes of our study, interesting results included the following:

Airlines Advertising Readership

- 81.4% of respondents read airline advertising (5.8% always, 15.3% regularly, 60.4% sometimes);
- 15.7% never read airline advertising;
- 2.9% no answer.

Interest In Airline Advertising

- 62.3% of respondents were interested in destinations served by the airline;
- 58.6% were interested in ticket prices/special offers;
- 35.6% were interested in departure schedules/frequency;
- 32.9% were interested in frequent-flyer incentives;
- 31.7% were interested in types of aircraft operated;
- 25.5% were interested in quality of airline personnel;
- 24.2% were interested in reservations, check-in, ground services;
- 15.0% were interested in in-flight food/beverage selection;
- 14.6% were interested in other features of in-flight service.

Source: *Wall Street Journal* 1998

Mass Tourism and the Mass Media

The earliest recorded instance of mass tourism occurred in 1841 when Thomas Cook organised a train journey from Leicester to Loughborough (Laws 1991). The tour was a success, attracting a substantial group. Cook later ran a weekend trip from Leicester to Liverpool, this time printing a brochure of the event (*A Handbook of the Trip to Liverpool*) in his own print shop. Again successful, he ventured farther afield and planned excursions and visits within the trip. He is reported to have said:

> The main object of the conducted tour, apart from being able to calculate the exact cost before starting, is to enhance the enjoyment by relieving the traveller of all the petty troubles and annoyances of the journey.
>
> Laws 1991

With great foresight, Cook recognised the importance of the connection between the medium of communication, in this case the printed word, and the information it could purvey. It is one of the earliest examples of the relationship between tourism and the media.

Thomas Cook was thus the pioneer of tour wholesaling, and has subsequently become one of the biggest tour wholesalers in the world (Moutinho 1987). The company has also branched out into retail, affording greater opportunities to distribute its tourism products and its information services. Evidence of Thomas Cook's rise was shown in an advertisement of the first 'Great Exhibition of the Works of Industry of All Nations, 1851', which promoted the exhibition across distances never heard of previously:

> Railways were . . . well-established features in the countryside, and Thomas Cook (having several years before began running trips at bargain prices) now capitalised on the success of the exhibition and begun advertising trains. Parties of industrial and agricultural labourers were able to come from all parts.
>
> Goddard 1995

Thus, from a simple brochure to full advertisements of the world industrial exhibition within ten years, Thomas Cook's evolution continued to run parallel with the evolution of the early mass media and early mass marketing. He capitalised on the increased awareness of travel opportunities made possible by improved education and literacy, and the improving technology of the print mass media.

From humble beginnings, tourism has grown to the point where it is expected to gross US$2.75 trillion by 2010, and be the biggest industry in the world—according to the World Travel and Tourism Council (Ritchie 1990).

The development of tourism journals from 1950 provides interesting insight into the development of tourism studies as a social science (Table 5.6, page 115).

Some of these journals include: *The Tourist Review, Annals of Tourism, Journal of Travel Research, International Tourism Quarterly, Tourism Management, Anatolia, Asia Pacific Journal of Tourism Research, Australian Journal of Hospitality Management, Tourism Culture & Communication (Australia), Journal of International Hospitality, Leisure & Tourism Management, Travel & Tourism Analyst (Economist Intelligence Unit), Progress in Tourism & Hospitality Research, Journal of Vacation Marketing, Pacific Tourism Review (NZ), The Tourist Review (AIEST), Journal of Travel & Tourism Marketing, Journal of Tourism Studies (Australia), Festival Management & Event Tourism*, and *Journal of Eco-tourism Development.*

Apart from the academic tourism journals, there is also a plethora of travel magazines, newsletters, organised tour catalogues, specialty magazines (catering to the more boutique travel interests of tourists), and general enthusiast literature.

Table 5.6 Development of media use 1950–84

Period	Total Number of Tourism Journals	Total number of Tourism Articles
1950–54	1	6
1955–59	7	15
1960–64	16	36
1965–69	46	82
1970–74	117	224
1975–79	99	258
1980–84	120	379
Overall 1950–84	292*	1000

* Does not add up because of overlap of years

Source: Theuns 1992

The growth in tourism literature has been mirrored by a huge growth in tourism operators. Many of these have merged into larger conglomerates.

This is discussed in the *Focus* on technology issues in tourism in Chapter 6 (page 131). Beni (1996) attributes much of the 'massification' of tourism enterprises to information technology developments.

> This recent challenge set by computerized telecommunications within the globalization process has been forcing companies in the travel trade to merge.
>
> Beni 1996

This is illustrated by the British travel industry where the 'Three Bigs' in the UK are Thomson, Airtours, and First Choice. These companies own a host of tour operations, travel agencies, and airlines in the UK—and as far abroad as Australia. For example, Thomson own Thomson Holidays, Austravel, and Ausbound—to name only three of their expanding tour operations. They also own a travel agency chain (Lunn Poly) and an airline (Britannia Airways). In late 1997, Airtours owned four tour operations, two travel agency chains, and an airline. At the same time, First Choice owned five tour operations, two travel agency chains, and one airline (*Sunday Times* 1997c).

In addition, the desire to maintain a competitive edge with innovative, high-quality products encourages strategic alliances within the industry. Paradoxically perhaps, it is difficult to believe that 'mega-enterprises' would be able to innovate as quickly, and with the same market responsiveness, as a smaller start-up organisation.

Media Viewing and Holiday Decisions

Crucial to the media-effect argument in a tourism context is the need to understand media-viewing behaviour. Attempts have been made to correlate media effects and media phenomena—in order to aid the tourist industry in its use of the media. This is a difficult task because there are numerous variables involved in both fields of study—tourism and the media. What is required is to take a single event and analyse it in terms of media-viewing behaviour, and its implications on tourism.

Such research was conducted after the (US) Yellowstone National Park fires of 1988. The park is a tourist attraction of world repute. The research was conducted by Snepenger and Karahan (1991) and investigated the level of media viewing by the public after the fires, correlating media-viewing behaviour with demographic variables, park-visitation practices, and environmental attitudes.

Data were gathered through interviews on and off the site. Of the approximately 1500 useable surveys completed, only one per cent of respondents did not watch or read anything about the fires; 5.5 per cent watched or read a little; the majority watched or read something (35.6 per cent) or almost everything (41.1 per cent); whereas almost 17 per cent of the sample indicated that they watched or read everything they could about the fires. Using standardised regression coefficients, the strongest correlate with media-viewing behaviour was the level of visitation to Yellowstone prior to the fires. Older people tended to watch and read more about the fires than younger ones.

Snepenger, Collins and Snepenger (1992) established that the level of interest in the event was high, and that the level of individual commitment to media offerings (whether it be a product, service, or destination) is a strong predictor of the level of information search.

Finally, the research highlighted that natural disasters such as fires and floods catch public interest. This might possibly be expanded to include non-natural disasters—such as air disasters, terrorist activities, and other such interruptions to tourist flows. But this is yet to be properly founded. What has been established is that 'awareness and interest' are key factors in making a vacation decision. Yellowstone National Park has experienced increased visitation since the fires (Snepenger & Karahan 1991).

It has also been suggested that other areas that have experienced a catastrophe recorded increased visitation after the event. The example offered was Mount Saint Helens, which erupted in the 1980s (Snepenger & Karahan 1991).

Clearly, this research provides valuable information to information providers and tourist operators in examining the after-effects of a disaster in a tourist destination. The data definitely support conclusions regarding natural phenomena and might, perhaps, be extrapolated to non-natural disasters. This offers insight into the aftermath of a natural disaster, and might provide clues as to how to plan the re-emergence of a tourist destination so afflicted. In making a financial decision regarding whether the destination can survive the damage (both in physical terms and reputation), the manager might be more confident to proceed with reparations in light of research indicating potential increased visitation after the event.

Hamilton Island, off the east coast of northern Australia, is an example of this. Following frontpage headlines and television news of a fire at the resort, the owner, an Australian entrepreneur, said in an interview that he could not bear to think about starting all over again—from both a financial and an emotional point of view. He might not have allowed for the valuable promotional potential that the fire had given the resort. He chose to rebuild, while perhaps not fully aware of the media impact of the disaster—but he gambled on success. Taking the results of Snepenger and Karahan 1991 (of a strong connection between tourist visitations and awareness of the destination due to the disaster), the managers at Hamilton Island might have embarked on the reconstruction with greater confidence.

As in most arguments, there are two sides to the coin. Although the evidence provided tends to favour the media-effects rationale, there has been much criticism levied at the research methods that claim to support these favourable arguments. These criticisms need to be examined to provide a proper balance.

Reasons for Misunderstanding

It is natural to assume, with the huge volume of information available from the mass media, that people will absorb it and learn from it. The first half of this chapter has attempted to show that sometimes this is true—even if it is difficult to prove scientifically.

In the second part of this chapter, the other side of the coin will be examined. Media campaigns do not always achieve the desired result.

The United Nations Campaign

There are various reasons for wanting to raise public awareness—such as publicity for a tourist destination, or a new product launch, or a forthcoming conference, or an election, or a fair, and so on. After World War II, there were campaigns to increase support for the United Nations Organisation (UNO, or UN). A number of publicity groups initiated a promotional campaign for the UN in Cincinnati (USA) to raise awareness of the organisation and its mission.

The program was well financed and organised, and lasted for six months. It aimed to immerse the public thoroughly in UN messages and paraphernalia, using the following means:

- mass media—newspapers and radio spots (as many as 150 spot announcements each week);
- schools;
- religious groups;
- advertisers;
- slogans ('Peace begins with the United Nations—the United Nations begins with you');
- display cards and posters;
- signs on buses; and
- matchbooks and blotters featuring the UN logo.

Remarkably, following a survey conducted by the National Opinion Research Centre in the University of Chicago, it was shown that the campaign had very little effect on the level of information retained by Cincinnati residents (Davison, Boylan & Yu 1976). It was found that, prior to the campaign, approximately 30 per cent of the population was almost totally ignorant of the UN and its purpose and, in a survey done after the campaign, this figure hardly changed at all.

What happened? There is a number of possibilities that could explain this phenomenon—at least in part.

Theoretically, context and relevance might play a part in explaining the poor retention of the UN's message by Cincinnati residents. Although the United States played a major role in the second half of World War II, the involvement was limited to those men and women enlisted in the armed forces. The American public at large had only remote knowledge of the horror of war going on in Europe and Asia—with the single exception of the bombing of Hawaii by the Japanese in 1941. Their information was from an 'informed catastrophe' perspective (Lombardi, page 87) and, as such, lacked real-life experience. For the average American in Cincinnati, the level of interest was less than it would have been if a greater percentage of the respondents had had first-hand experience of the atrocities of war—and thus be more appreciative of the UN's message of peace. It would be interesting (if possible) to see a breakdown of the survey respondents to see whether war veterans had a better retention of the UN information campaign.

It is apparent that more than awareness is necessary—relevance is also important. In the case of the Yellowstone fires, people who had visited

Yellowstone before sought out more information on the fires. In the case of the UN campaign, impact might have been inhibited by a of a lack of relevance—at least in the perception of the people being surveyed.

Another possible reason for the failure of the UN campaign to register an impact could be 'saturation'. The UN's message might have been over-publicised. Perhaps, rather than having the message reinforced by further information, people might have no longer paid attention to the information—due to overload.

It is also possible that, in the aftermath of the war, people were so intent on rebuilding their lives and the economy that their attention was distracted away from media messages like that of the UN.

These are only untested theories, but they could perhaps go some way to explaining the campaign's failure.

Critics and Critiques of Media-Effects Research

Believers in the media-effects argument tend to do so based on pragmatism rather than scientific ratification:

> Most media managers see academic media research as too abstract to be useful and too negative to be considered seriously for its policy implications.
>
> McLeod, Kosicki & Zhandang 1991

However, from an academic point of view, many criticisms have been directed at the research approaches, and at the oversimplified and sometimes distorted assertions made. McLeod, Kosicki and Zhandang presented three broad areas of critique:

- critical studies critique;
- cultural studies critique; and
- behavioural science critique.

Critical Studies Critique

This critique sees media-effect research as being confined by its reliance on a learning theory that is limited to the two variables—stimulus and effect. This criticism suggests that such an approach is overly restrictive in studying just the one effect—persuasion—to the denial of other effects (such as influence, inference, awareness, and so on).

This also reflects on the nature of the message and its sender-oriented content. Media-effects research has received criticism based on its dependency on corporate media and government funding which, it is argued, affects the legitimacy and efficacy of the results. According to Golding and Murdock:

As a consequence of its limitations, media-effects research fails to explore the cumulative, delayed, long-term, and unintended effects

Golding & Murdock 1978, cited in McLeod, Kosicki & Zhandang 1991

Cultural Studies Critique

This critique notes the following criticisms of media-effects research:

- that it uses inappropriate terminology and causal apparatus in speaking about variables and effects;
- that it focuses too much on observable properties and empirical sciences;
- that it focuses too much on isolated individuals, thus overlooking cultural variations in how people view the media;
- that there is an undervaluation of the audience's ability to extract meaning from the media, seeing the audience as simpletons; and
- that it is seen as overly message-driven and fails to identify, due to over-quantification, the qualitative distinctions in messages, meaning, and audience reception.

McLeod, Kosicki & Zhangdang 1991

Behavioural Science Critique

This criticism revolves around the disparity between the empirical results of effects research and the concept of 'powerful media' (McGuire 1986, cited in McLeod, Kosicki & Zhangdang 1991). This criticism is directed at the media practitioners—that is, advertising companies—who self-servingly and (not surprisingly) claim strong media impact for business reasons. But the criticism is (perhaps surprisingly) also directed at academic researchers—who must publish and are loath to present null results. In both cases, it could be argued that there is an underlying vested interest in definitive (rather than negative or null) results.

In addition, there is criticism of the ambiguity resulting from non-experimental methods that fail to specify exactly what aspect of a media message has an effect, and to what degree (McLeod, Kosicki & Zhandang 1991). There has also been criticism that research has been overly 'media-centric', mixing more general conceptions of media production with specific concepts (Reeves 1989, cited in McLeod, Kosicki & Zhandang 1991), and that research has been vague in its construction and methodology; weak in design, and lacking proper statistical procedures.

Behavioural scientists see these critiques as confirmation of the marginality of media-effects research as a form of proper scientific research.

With regard to advertisers, tourist operators, and business managers, these criticisms more than likely fall on deaf ears. Mass media appear to have a pervasive and integral role in the distribution of information, and this is the commonly accepted perception among most professionals within the tourism industry and the business world in general.

When asked by the present author, professionals in various fields of tourism (airlines, agents, national tourist organisations, and travel insurers) all conceded that the mass media (especially television) played an important role in their businesses. This appears to be a 'given'—unquestioned by tourism professionals. Certain conclusions are drawn about media impact—based on customer response to media offerings. Very little is done in the way of scientific substantiation of this media–customer relationship. It is usually not seen as necessary.

However, some do see the need for more information—such as a marketing manager for Suzy Waffles in Belgium (Interviews 1996) who stated that more market information is always needed but that it is just too expensive to gather through normal channels. This leads to the sponsoring of research by large corporations and governments, who possess the needed resources. But this money, it is argued, might bear a hidden cost—that results need to reflect the sponsor's vested interest. Airlines (such as KLM and British Airways), credit card companies (such as American Express), and tour operators (such as Jetset and Thomas Cook), to name a few examples, have been known to invest in commissioned research for various purposes.

Some valuable academic work has been done under the banner of corporate sponsorship, and should not be depreciated by criticism of research bias.

Despite these exceptions, there is always the risk that unsubstantiated research can lead to erroneous tourism decision-making that has definite affects on profits, and that can jeopardise the safety, enjoyment, and satisfaction of tourists themselves.

Further Comments on Effects

Study of media effects has a long history, dating from before what has often been accepted as the beginning of media-effects concerns—the Lazarsfeld studies of voting and campaigning at Columbia University in the 1940s (cited in McLeod, Kosicki and Zhangdang 1991). It can be traced back to the pre-empiricals, where observers such as Dewey (1927) and Weber (1910) — both cited in McLeod, Kosicki and Zhangdang (1991)— commented on media effects well before radio or television could be accused of exerting an influence. At that time, print was under scrutiny and reform was being advocated by media observers. Effects research now deals with a growing cross-section of investigative subjects beyond the previously dominant 'persuasion and attitude' based studies of Lazarsfeld.

Researchers later concentrated on ideas such as media effects being limited to the reinforcing of pre-existing views and assisting the undecided to move towards their demographic predispositions (McLeod, Kosicki & Zhandang 1991). Early research pointed towards a minimalist perspective on media effects, which later translated into theories of 'possible' stronger effects under the guiding hands of Lang and Lang (1959), Key (1961), Blumler (1964), and Halloran (1964)—according to McLeod, Kosicki and Zhandang (1991).

Interest in media effects is now very high, spurred on by television and the Internet, and by public concerns over portrayals of violence and sex in film. Governments are forced by societal expectation to further investigate this field. For example, the UK government investigated the film 'Natural Born Killers', by Oliver Stone—which was accused of causing 'copycat' murder behaviour in a limited number of its audience in the USA. The investigation might or might not have been definitive in attaching blame to the film, but the public pressure was substantial enough to cause the film to be banned from screening in British cinemas—so great is the strength of perceived effect, despite academic question marks.

A similar UK government inquiry took place in a case involving two young boys who allegedly kidnapped, tortured, and killed a baby. Attention was given to the violent films that were found in the family homes, within easy viewing of the alleged offenders. Again the real-life circumstances were presented in such a way as to override any criticisms of media-effects research efficacy.

As a final comment on the media-effects (mis)understanding, McLeod and Reeves (1980)—cited in McLeod, Kosicki and Zhangdang (1991)—suggested a list of media-effects dimensions which, although not exhaustive, offers deeper insight into current media-effects thinking. This is shown in Table 5.7 (page 123).

Conclusion

Table 5.7 provides a brief summary of the current thinking on media effects and research into the topic. Media effects might be myth or reality, and one's attitude depends on one's perspective.

A solid infrastructure—incorporating advertisers, government bodies, business in general, and tourism in particular—has been erected in the apparently firm belief that media effects is a reality, whereas research and critiques lend substance to the contrary view.

Ultimately, the truth lies in the intention behind the belief. Tourism

Table 5.7 Summary of media effects possibilities

Micro vs Macro	Discusses taking the study of micro (specific) effect analysis, historically common, and aggregating the influences to represent a macro relationship. States that a simplistic aggregation like this can lead to a 'knowledge gap', which means, although the media might succeed in conveying information to a population, it might do so in differing degrees to various status groups (Tichenor et al. 1970; Robinson 1972).
Alteration vs Stabilisation	Discusses the predominance of change as a media-effects criterion in research because it's easier to observe. Lazarsfeld's research, although questionable in its findings, is an example here. Some research into stable effects has been done in immunising against persuasive messages (McGuire 1964; Tannenbaum 1967).
Cumulative vs Non-cumulative	Discusses differences in media-effects research among influences that accumulate over time compared with single message changes. Television has given rise to ongoing research in this area with possible effects credentials.
Long-term vs Short-term	Explains that experiments show reasonable, although relatively short-term, effects following exposure to a message, but dissipate with time unless additional exposure takes place—that is, the message is strong (perhaps violent, sexual impression) or there is a cumulative effect (such as above) which sustains the effect, although potentially in a dormant state.
Attitudinal vs Cognitive vs Behavioural	Discusses the early effects research centred on attitude change, moving on to 'learning' effects of the media, viewing it as a source of information (more relevant to tourism and media than other approaches), and as a packager of mass information into a cognitive reality and the behavioural responses to this information (from an organisational point of view, a tour operator may make decisions based on the media effects research results or perceived impact of actions/traveller motives).
Media Content and Use	Considered focal in media-effects research, content and form of media messages is analysed for its often subtle psychological effects; from discrete stimuli to more tangible physiological effects (such as erotic stimuli and sexual responses). Content is also considered to be close to the heart of continued media success, related to circulation in newspapers and ratings on television, for example.

Source: Adapted from McLeod & Reeves 1980—cited in McLeod, Kosicki & Zhangdang 1991

participants invest a great deal of time, money, and energy under the presumption that their application of the media and its presumed promotional impact is purposive. In general, when business and survival is at stake, the normal human reaction would be to err on the side of conservatism—justifying action (investing in promotion through the mass media) as opposed to inaction. The latter would imply waiting for the customer to come to them—raising the question of how strong is word of mouth, and is it enough?

Nevertheless, an important conclusion can be drawn regarding research into mass-media effects on information-retention in the audience—'there is no direct relationship between exposure to information and learning of information' (Carter 1971). Even repeated exposure to a message does not guarantee that it will be remembered. On the other hand, according to Carter, the mass media have the ability to significantly increase information retention about a given subject—providing that the information is of use, or if it is concurrent with existing attitudes. This is particularly important for the tourism industry when contemplating investing time, money, and energy into marketing—based on an understanding that more and more people are undertaking travel each year. However, it might also offer a word of caution to operators looking at converting non-travellers into travellers— travel could be inconsistent with their existing attitude.

The final decision on whether media effects is relevant to tourism is up to the tourist participants themselves, from their viewpoint as information providers (see Chapter 4). When tour sales appear to increase in response to a television advertising campaign, there is little doubt for the tour operator concerned about the power of the media. Knowing just how a potential tourist responds to the information on offer is, however, another question—one that will be examined in the following chapter discussing media and potential tourist decision-making behaviour.

Discussion Time

- Discuss and note down the possible impact of the Internet (and other technological changes in communications) on the media-effects debate.
- Divide the room into two opposing groups. One will argue in favour of media effects, the other against. Select a person from each group to act as impartial adjudicators, who must (in a separate room from the debaters) summarise the arguments and agree on a balanced report at the end of the debate.

6

Media Effects and Tourist Decision-Making

SYNOPSIS OF CHAPTER

- The role of information in travel behaviour

- The sequence effect of push/pull factors and information on tourist decision-making

- Communication techniques to inform or influence

- *Focus* on how new media technology affects tourism and destination choices

- *Fast Facts* on Lonely Planet's website and website endearment research

How Do Tourists Decide?

Television plays a crucial role in the tourism information process. Virtually since the inception of commercial television, researchers have attempted to determine how many advertisements the average person is exposed to. Media Dynamics has estimated that the average adult in the United States is exposed to approximately 247 advertisements a day—not including the many billboards and signs to which they are exposed (*Fortune* 1996). Taken together, these advertisements mean that consumers are faced with a daunting array of alternatives. The decision to take one holiday over myriad available destinations is just one of the many consumer decisions and opportunities presented.

As a subject of academic research, tourist decision-making represents an equally challenging task. The following questions must be asked in order to determine the role of the media and motivation in travel behaviour.

- What motivates people to travel?
- Can the travel stimulus be controlled or influenced?

- Is there a direct relationship between the stimulus and the information presented through the mass media or any other medium?
- Does this information lead to a specific destination choice?

To find practical answers to these questions would no doubt assist travel planners and information providers in making their decisions regarding information selection and distribution. Models of the various elements have been created to map the sequence of events and decision processes dealt with by potential tourists.

Role of Information in Travel Behaviour

The various decision stages undertaken by potential tourists take them from a point where, once a decision is made to take a trip of some kind, the remaining decision process is channelled through information-gathering stages, to an elimination of alternatives and, finally, to the actual choice.

Many models have included a communication loop by adding a feedback stage for holiday/destination evaluation to take place. As a tool, such models are invaluable if understood by the tourism practitioner. Therein lies a problem, as many such models are rather complicated—intended more for their academic credentials than as a working tool for tourism planners, management, or information providers and students. A simpler example of one such model is presented in Figure 6.1.

From Motivation to Information-Gathering Stages (Media Scanning)

The sequence in Figure 6.1 (page 127) commences with the motivation to travel. This has been shown as either a 'push' or a 'pull' factor. This means that in the routine of daily life, the need to get away, 'pushes' a person to investigate travel alternatives. Alternatively, the lure or 'pull' of foreign locations (or the appeal of media presentations) draws people's attention and stimulates them to investigate travel alternatives. Indeed, it might be a combination of the two. There are certain destination-specific motivations and person-specific motivations inherent in this process. Nevertheless, the net result is that the person seeks further information on travel alternatives.

Manfredo (1989) says that 'travel information as such has not been accorded thorough attention in the academic tourism literature'. The interrelationship between information providers and sources, and the interplay between these and the tourist's eventual decision to 'defer', 'decline', or 'decide' upon a travel experience has been illustrated in Figure 4.1 (page 59). The information-search process depicted in Figure 4.1. is represented in the middle section of Figure 6.1—from 'Information Sources' to 'Establish Alternatives' down the vacation sequence to the

Figure 6.1   Sequence effect of push-and-pull motivations and information on tourist vacation decision-making

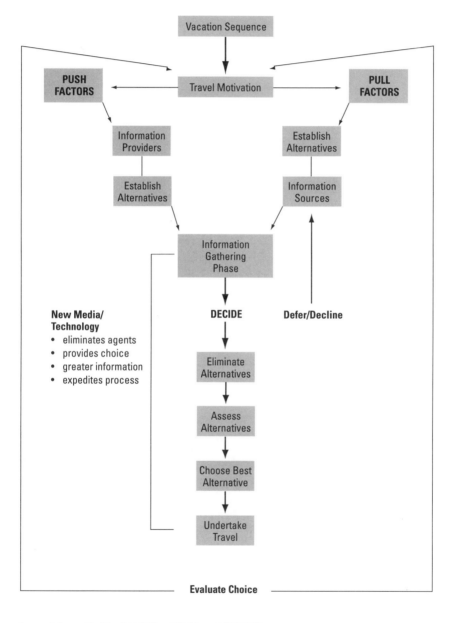

Source: Influenced by Mansfeld 1992, and Mathieson & Wall 1982

'DECIDE, Defer/Decline' point. There is an assumed motivation to travel, or at least a stimulus to gather information on possible trips. The stimulus might be from a television advertisement, or a holiday program aired on television or radio, or a brochure, or any other source of information 'pulling' the person.

Interviews with the Royal Automobile Club of Victoria (RACV) revealed that the effectiveness of holiday programs on television can be very marked. Following a regular weekend travel program each week, the RACV received a significant increase in enquiries about the featured destination.

The US Travel and Tourism Administration (USTTA) conducted research in four of its more important markets to know more about the sources used by potential tourists in planning a trip to the USA (see Table 6.1).

Table 6.1 Sources used to plan a trip to the USA

Sources	Japan	UK	Germany	France
Travel agent	50%	59%	70%	48%
Brochures/pamphlets	55%	44%	51%	37%
Family/friends	26%	39%	44%	25%
Airline	5%	6%	13%	8%
Tour operator	19%	12%	28%	7%
Read articles	16%	19%	15%	15%
Books/library	40%	19%	17%	12%

Source: US Travel & Tourism Administration

In most decisions this information-gathering stage will be purposive, at least to establish 'go or not go' criteria. It is important to tourism planners to know the tourist's decision criteria in reaching this point. Theorists have different views on the value of different kinds of information. For example, Mansfeld (1992) cites earlier research conducted by Nolan in 1976 on tourist information search, which stated that formal sources of information were ranked lowest in credibility, but highest in quantity sought or available to the seeker. (Note that Nolan ignores various printed material—for example, brochures, in his study. Nolan also states that official sources ranked highest on all accounts—cited in Mansfeld 1992.)

Mansfeld (1992) cites, from research he conducted in 1982, that tourists from the UK relied heavily on more informal commercial information—

rather than relying on travel agents and official sources. However, this appears to contradict the aforementioned USTTA assertions that British tourists consult travel agents in the majority of cases for trips to the USA. Mansfeld (1992) also cites, from van Raaij and Francken's (1984) research, that guidebooks and organisations play a minor role, whereas informal and social information is more often sought and consulted.

Again, this is not entirely confirmed by the USTTA results, but holds a degree of truth for the German respondents (44 per cent consulted) and, to a lesser degree, for the UK respondents (39 per cent). Van Raaij and Francken's research was published in 1984 and therefore does not take into consideration the proliferation of travel book publishing in the late 1980s and 1990s—thus potentially underestimating the modern traveller's increasing reliance on guidebooks and related autonomous travel material (see The Lonely Planet *Fast Facts*, page 138).

For a decision that involves potentially large sums of money, scarce time and inherent risks associated with the unknown (frustration, delays, cultural/linguistic differences), credibility as well as security become very important. Mill and Morrison (1985) add that travel agents (a perceived credible source) are, according to surveys done by the United States Travel Services, a declining source of information—with the significant exception of trips to more remote (perhaps higher risk) destinations. In these cases, people return to the source of perceived expertise in a traditional risk-averse manner.

These results concur with the comments drawn from tourism professionals in interviews with the present author. When asked for the main source of information for their clients, tourism professionals mentioned television first, and then word-of-mouth. When asked if the sources differed in the case of tourists contemplating a questionable destination—whether it be a security, financial, or other doubt—the authorised information sources were viewed as more credible. (This is further discussed in Chapter 9.)

Don Holt (Interviews 1995), former airport manager for Air New Zealand, stated that travel agents and operators were usually as informed as the national sources. But Holt added that he, as a tourism professional, would deal direct with tourist authorities (such as International Air Traffic Association) on important security issues in his own travel—such as whether to fly to Croatia in 1994, for example. But he admitted that the average person would not be aware of this source. This response thus distinguishes media effect in a person within the industry (who is perceived to have more insight and greater knowledge) from that of the average traveller. This relates back to the degree of knowledge, already established attitudes, and the 'knowledge gap' developed by Tichenor et al. (1970)—

as cited by McLeod, Kosicki and Zhangdang (1991), and previously discussed (see Table 5.7, page 123).

The key to information-gathering, when the sources of information vary in credibility, is to determine the decision criteria of the target market (that is, the tourists). Such criteria include push/pull, cost/fun, safety/thrill-seeker, and so on. Research done by Sirakaya and McLellan (1997) confirms this. Among a sample of 181 college students, respondents rated the following as the six most important factors affecting destination choice:

- local hospitality and services;
- trip costs and convenience;
- perception of safe and secure environment;
- change in daily environment;
- sporting activities/events; and
- entertainment and drinking.

Differences were detected between male and female respondents.

A comprehensive selection of information should be made available—a selection that matches the information demand with the information supply. This, it is hoped, should maximise the use and effect of the mass media for tourism purposes.

How to deal with the proliferation of informal (word-of-mouth) information, which might contradict the intended message of tourism managers is another matter. The evaluation of the product phase in the tourism model provides some insight into tourist impressions of a destination. But further investigation is required to understand how such feedback could be used to encourage or curb the flow of negative informal information. It is suggested that it would very nearly be an impossible task.

The model of 'Reactive Communication' (Figure 4.5, page 68) outlines the short communication chain of events in 'grapevine' or word-of-mouth information passage—which makes identification and isolation of source very difficult to ascertain and, in turn, alter. Prevention of bad press, monitoring of public relations and press coverage, and satisfying tourists while they are on holidays, are all possible ways of minimising bad publicity. But stopping or controlling it once it is in motion is a more difficult task. (See also Chapter 9 for the public-relations implications of negative informal information and the impact of tourist expectations and outcomes.)

Communication Techniques to Inform or Influence

Several communications strategies are applied in the travel and tourism industry to inform and/or influence tourist decision-making. Advertising agencies and professionals in the business refer to marketing communications as 'above the line' and 'below the line'. The former is advertising in various forms of the mass media where the agency or individual earns a commission. The latter includes activities such as direct mail, public relations, and sales promotion—for which a fee is agreed upon and charged up front.

Influencing potential tourists is most effectively achieved using the principle of 'AIDA' (Youell 1995). 'AIDA' stands for:

- *Attention:* attracted to the particular tourism product (for example, in a newspaper advertisement, a bold heading draws attention);
- *Interest:* maintaining interest in the advertisement by using clear, concise, and relevant language and images;
- *Desire:* influence potential buying patterns by offering incentives or initiating a drive to purchase the tourism product; and
- *Action:* information or gimmick to transform the potential buyer into an actual buyer (for example, a coupon to be filled out, a map or directions to the tourist property being promoted).

Selecting the appropriate medium is also very important—given budget limitations, target-market specifications, shorter decision-making paths (due to faster newer media technology) and, frequently, untested desired outcomes. Radio, television, newspapers, magazines and, increasingly, the Internet, can usually provide a 'ratecard', which outlines their respective coverage or circulation (audience that they reach), as well as detailed 'lifestyle' demographies of their audiences. Advice will also normally be given on the best format to use in advertising the particular product, as well as the issues of 'timing' and advertising 'frequency'.

In-house market research is advisable such that a tourist organisation can pass this information onto the advertising agency or promotions company—who should be able to do a demographic match-up between the target market and the likely market to be reached. Referring back to Figure 6.1 (page 127), an advertisement launch or promotions campaign should 'touch' a potential tourist from the Information Gathering Stage downward—until a vacation choice has been made.

Focus on New Media/Technology Effects

Effects on Tourist Information & Media Scanning

Information Technology (IT) plays an increasingly important role in tourism marketing, distribution, promotion, and coordination (Buhalis 1996). Indeed, the tourism and travel industry is considered to be one of the largest users of IT (Sheldon 1994, cited in Rimmington & Kozak 1997).

IT is becoming a vital link in the dissemination of information, and in the process of tourists searching for information upon which to base decision-making.

Travel and tourism is a global industry, and the advances in IT have been of enormous benefit to the industry. Some of the uses have included:

- providing a visitor to a tourist information centre with an instant report on bed availability in the desired destination;
- showing full-colour virtual catalogues;
- providing on-screen booking services;
- offering on-screen customer support;
- facilitating payment for airline tickets, leisure products and so on.

There are, of course, many other applications, but this brief list gives some idea of how the tourism industry has been revolutionised by advances in IT.

For the future, we might expect to see a cashless, paperless society in which purchases are made instantly and directly from the supplier—whether that be an operator or the destination itself. The traditional travel agency will have to re-evaluate and re-invent itself to fit into the future tourism distribution network. This repositioning could look something like the arrangement illustrated in Figure 6.2 (page 133).

Central Reservation Systems (CRSs)—for example, Systemone, Sabre, Worldspan, Gulliver, Apollo—have been the traditional link between the travel industry and customers via agents or middlemen. Such systems are at risk of becoming redundant should more and more customers choose to book directly with airlines and hotels. The first generation of CRSs (Rimmington & Kozak 1997) has confronted this possibility with their plan to institute a second generation of Internet-enhanced CRSs. Apollo and Sabre plan to distribute directly via their own websites.

The Internet is at the heart of this IT tourism revolution. For many 'technophiles', the opportunities to promote and distribute tourism products are immense. For others who are less technically inclined, the Internet is a marketing tool that sits uncomfortably with both suppliers and consumers of tourism products and services. The Internet has the potential to market, globally, a destination or product at a minimal cost—thus enabling small-to-medium-sized enterprises to compete with larger competitors. 'Technophobes' might squander this great opportunity while they wait for more definite proof of the power of Internet marketing and information distribution. This proof is on the way. A survey of Internet users has already been done (1996) on the use of the Internet in the tourism industry—with the following results:

- 68.7% of Internet users accessed the net from 'home';
- 89.9% used the Internet 'to get information';
- 71.5% used 'Travelweb' as a gateway to the Internet;
- 69.5% sought 'holiday' information on the Internet;

Figure 6.2   New tourism distribution and information channels in IT society

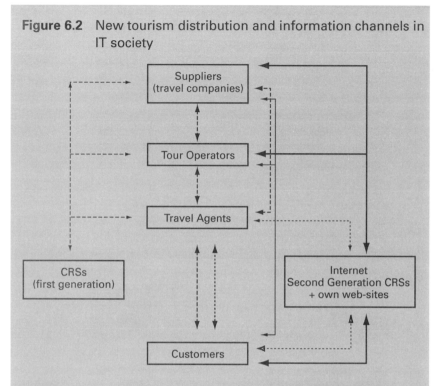

Source: Rimmington & Kozak 1997

- 36.7% sought particular 'destination' information on the Internet; and
- 55.7% sought the ambiguously labelled 'worldwide' as their most preferred destination

  from Rimmington & Kozak 1997

More comprehensive research was carried out in two phases by the Internet Advertising Bureau (IAB) and published in October 1998. From an estimated potential audience of a million persons, IAB managed to contact 16 758 respondents in Phase II of their survey. The chief purpose of the IAB advertising effectiveness study was to assess whether online advertising affects the following parameters:

- advertising awareness;
- brand awareness;
- product attribute communication; and
- purchase intent.

Although it was not exclusively directed at the tourism industry, the results of this investigation are still very interesting for tourism. This research also has important 'media-effects' implications (see Chapter 5). The results are described below.

IAB Internet Advertising Effectiveness Research Findings

- Consumer acceptance of online advertising is comparable to traditional media: 60–70% of the sample were 'in favour of or strongly in favour of' web, television, and print advertising, but were less supportive of radio advertising.
- Online advertising can dramatically increase advertisement awareness after only one exposure. Respondents were asked if they recalled seeing an advertisement on a particular website in the past seven days: 34% initially did recall the advertisement; and, when shown an additional exposure, awareness increased to 44.1% (at a 95% confidence level).
- Web advertising boosts awareness of advertised brands. Of the 12 banners tested, 8 showed positive increases in brand awareness of an average of 5% (from 61% to 64%) with a confidence level of 95%.
- Online advertising provides significant brand communication power: 5 of the 12 brand banners shown demonstrated clear positive changes (90% confidence), and 1 showed a polarisation of positive–negative attitudes, with a positive net effect on purchase intent.
- Online advertising has the potential to increase sales: 9 of the 12 brands tested showed positive increases in consumer loyalty, which increased 4% overall across the 12 brands.
- Online advertising is more likely to be noticed than television advertising: Millward Brown International's FORCE (First Opportunity to see Reaction Created by the Execution) measures a medium's ability to enable an advertisement to be noticed first. Out of 19 banners tested by Millward Brown Interactive, the average scores are shown in Figure 6.3.

Figure 6.3 Comparison of FORCE score effectiveness among different media

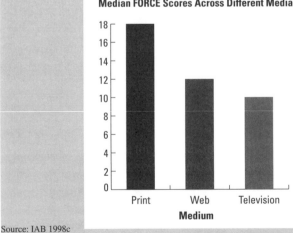

Source: IAB 1998c

Conclusions of the IAB Advertising Effectiveness Study

Online advertising using banners is a powerful medium of communication with consumers. It has a proven capacity to increase brand awareness, and therefore has the potential to influence tourists' information search and eventual decision-making. The researchers are strong advocates of online advertising efficacy:

> . . . any advertiser looking to build their brand and increase their sales should utilize online advertising alongside traditional media.
>
> IAB 1998

Such confidence in the medium means that tourism will inevitably be a part of this IT wonder force. Of course, IAB might have a vested interest in the power of their chosen field of research. More research from non-commercial interests would be welcomed.

Bennett and Radburn sound a word of warning when they observe that the:

> . . . sheer size and complexity of this extended range of choice is the factor which limits its availability, i.e. The opportunity set available . . . via IT systems is too broad for consumers to handle the information and make holiday choices
>
> Bennett & Radburn 1991

They add that it might be up to industry to structure consumer choice to help with the process of filtering destination opportunities. This is one way that travel agents could reinvent themselves as specialised consultants.

The Internet: an Overview

Despite contradictory opinions on IT and tourism, there is enough evidence to convince even the most doubtful that all businesses can gain something from communications technology. Figures 6.4 and 6.5 provide an overview of business-to-business IT solutions.

Figure 6.4   Applications of Internet and Intranet

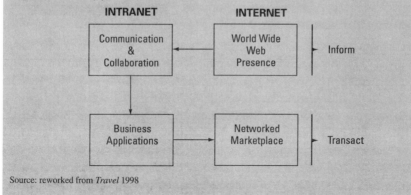

Source: reworked from *Travel* 1998

Figure 6.5 Communication systems: action and benefits

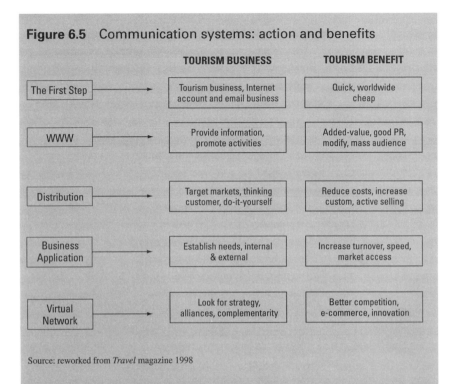

	TOURISM BUSINESS	TOURISM BENEFIT
The First Step	Tourism business, Internet account and email business	Quick, worldwide cheap
WWW	Provide information, promote activities	Added-value, good PR, modify, mass audience
Distribution	Target markets, thinking customer, do-it-yourself	Reduce costs, increase custom, active selling
Business Application	Establish needs, internal & external	Increase turnover, speed, market access
Virtual Network	Look for strategy, alliances, complementarity	Better competition, e-commerce, innovation

Source: reworked from *Travel* magazine 1998

It is only a matter of time before virtually all forward-thinking tourism participants are involved in IT. Total penetration of IT into the mainstream tourism industry might be some time off, but access to information and more outward market orientation are the first steps in the right direction. Beni explains:

> We are experiencing a phase of extreme and in-depth transition. What is valid today and consumed today will be obsolete tomorrow . . . [globalisation offers] pointers to show the directions these changes are to take.
>
> Beni 1996

Destination Choice Stages

Once the potential tourist is confident that the information is good enough to take a trip, the decision sequence moves down to the evaluation stages.

In Figure 6.1 (page 127), this begins at the stage of eliminating destination alternatives. Many detailed studies have been completed that elaborate on 'decision sets' and 'choice set' criteria (see, for example, Crompton 1992). For the sake of simplicity, this can be explained as a tourist seeking a final decision, acting to eliminate those destinations that are completely unacceptable and, from the subset of remaining alternatives, evaluating and perhaps eliminating each with some decision criteria in mind—in order to come up with the final choice.

Promotional material and media representations are still relevant at this stage of the decision process. More research is needed in this area to examine how promotional material and information-gathering affect the final destination choice *after* the decision to go has been made. For example, if there were a news report of the bombing of a bus in Tel Aviv days prior to someone planning to go there, would it force the person to revise their plans?

Hypothetical questions were posed by the present author to travel professionals on perceived threats and travel plans being altered after the decision process is presumed to be closed. One travel agent reported that, during the bombings in the Paris metro in late 1995, she did not sell any trips to Paris. People did not want to go. Most travel professionals reported that such news does have an effect, but that the extent of the impact varies from situation to situation—and is therefore difficult to assess. Consider the example of research performed by US Travel Data Center in the wake of the two air incidents:

- 15 June 1985: TWA flight 814 from Athens was hijacked to Beirut with one American being killed and 46 taken hostage by Shia militia;

- 23 June 1985: Air India flight exploded en route over Atlantic killing 325 passengers and crew.

The results of the survey indicated that, of the 6.5 million Americans who had reservations to fly abroad, 850 000 cancelled, and a further 220 000 changed plans to a domestic trip (Ryan 1991b). Europe had altered in the minds of American travellers who had already made their decision but, in the interim between planning and departure, 16 per cent had changed their plans due to additional information presented in the media. Although, in this example, the additional information (probably emanating from both formal and informal channels) led to a changing of commonly held attitudes about Europe being safe for Americans to travel, it is unclear how much this tells us about the relationships among the media, the events, and tourism. A similar set of facts might lead to a totally different response tomorrow. The tourist industry is left to decipher the information. (This question is examined in Part III of the present volume—which relates the risk of terrorist events to the triangular relationship among the media, an event, and tourism.)

Fast Facts on Lonely Planet Online

Can 'Visiting' WWW Homepages Endear Cyber Visitors to Tourism Businesses or Places?

Since 1994, Lonely Planet has been using the WWW to inform and update readers of their very popular guidebooks. Not only are their books the best-selling travel books in Australia and, arguably, the world (see Table 6.2), but their Internet site was receiving, in August 1998, an astounding 20 million 'hits' a month (a 'hit' is recorded every time someone visits the site).

Table 6.2 Dymock's 'Top 10 Bestseller' travel books in 1998

Rank	Title
1	Frances Maye's *Under the Sun*
2	Lonely Planet's *Western Europe Guide*
3	Bryson's *A Walk in the Woods*
4	Lonely Planet's *Bali and Lombok Guide*
5	Lonely Planet's *Britain Guide*
6	Bryson's *Notes From a Small Island*
7	*Lets Go Europe Guide*
8	Lonely Planet's *Australia Guide*
9	Lonely Planet's *Thailand*
10	Lonely Planet's *New Zealand*

Source: *Age* 1998

Lonely Planet's website contains condensed information from an estimated 200 destinations, handy links to other travel websites, recommendations, interactive map production, scenic photographs, travel updates for many of their books, and more. The site has seven main parts:
- destinations: travel profiles of destinations;
- postcards: reports from travellers;
- on the road: 'pictographic' pieces from around the world;
- detours: off-the-beaten-track destinations;
- health: complete checklist; and
- propaganda: commercial publications and paraphernalia.
The website address (URL) is: <www.lonelyplanet.com>.

Sources: Lonely Planet 1998; Youell 1996

Internet Homepage Endearment

In their study of Scottish tourism, Cano and Prentice (1998) elaborate on whether Internet homepage endearment translates into '. . . affective bonding to tourism businesses or destinations' through electronic visiting.

This is an interesting proposition in terms of Lonely Planet's website—because the affective bonding of tourism consumers to Lonely Planet might be not unlike the loyalty seen between tourist and destination. Lonely Planet's guidebooks become a part of the travel experience—which might also account for the popularity of the electronic visiting experience. It is uncertain whether this is a substitute behaviour where the 'real thing' (actually visiting a place in person) is not possible. The ability to encourage repeat visiting and positive recommendations electronically, or through word-of-mouth, is the essence of endearment, and carries great commercial potential. But, can electronic endearment be controlled?

Little has been written on this subject. Prentice, Witt and Wydenbach (1994) stress that informal personal interaction and conversation are important in this process. Clearly, electronic visiting challenges this view and raises the question as to how 'equivalent communication' (Cano & Prentice 1998) through the Internet can simulate the endearment process. It can be argued that the Internet is a conversational, multidirectional medium: that is, that commercial entities represent more than a product/service provider, but also serve as information providers to Internet users.

Cano and Prentice call this the 'communication concept', whereby tourism businesses facilitate and reward interaction through the 'entire consumption experience', and that a code of ethics, or 'netiquette', prevents abuses of this relationship taking place. For example, Lonely Planet provides a forum for exchange through their 'postcards' and 'thorn tree' sections to cater for transient travellers in need of information, or in need of a place to post notices. This builds up a confidence–loyalty relationship that might translate into commercial transactions through book sales at some stage. The blend of commercial and non-commercial is reassuring to travellers, and Lonely Planet's 'street credibility' enhances endearment to the website.

This example tends to confirm that 'cyber-visiting' endears visitors to a tourism business and, perhaps indirectly, to tourist destinations places as well (through their books—the 'travellers' bibles').

Conclusion

It appears that, although certain determinants affecting the tourist decision-making process can be identified—such as the different sources and the perceived credibility of information provided—much of the information-gathering process itself depends on situational constraints that are not as predictable. Basic tourism characteristics are influenced by different conditions—such as the weather; the real quality of service, product, and accommodation; and host attitudes and safety levels. And, although these factors are sometimes unknown at the time that tourists make their decisions, online tourist information has altered the way that a modern tourist plans a trip. The WWW has taken tourism information from the traditional one-way or one-sided distribution pattern to a multidirectional, multifaceted affair. Tourism planners and information providers try to match the information offer with the requirements of tourists—on the understanding that it is a dynamic industry with numerous limitations and variables impinging upon it. For academics, and for students of tourism and communications, it is an interesting area for further study.

Although tourism theory in this area is fraught with unproven assumptions and contradictory evidence, it seems that the tourism industry must fall back on previously reliable formulae and their faith in holidaymakers as rational human beings who are capable of evaluating travel decisions.

Discussion Time

- Divide the full group into two groups. These two groups are to form two imaginary 'focus groups'. Group 1 is working for a major tour operator. In recent months, advance bookings to their most important Asian destination have plummeted. Fear of political instability following economic crisis has caused massive cancellations of pre-booked trips. The job of the focus group is to develop a strategy to guide the company through these tough times, and to build company strength and morale. You should perhaps set down an evaluation matrix to examine the critical issues affecting the tour operator before discussing and creating your communication strategy (see example below). Group 2 is a group of government advisors working for the struggling Asian destination mentioned above. This government is concerned about what information is reaching its markets in the West, and what impact this is having on their image and tourist arrivals. Again using an evaluation matrix, group 2 should prepare its strategy to cope with this problem. Both groups have the same time to prepare (several days could be allowed). Once prepared, each group can present to the other its assessment of the situation, and its strategies to cope with that situation.

Evaluation Matrix Example

Group 1

Concern	Evaluation of Impact				Focus Group Response			
	No Impact	Minor Impact	Serious Impact	Comment	Mission	Action	Response	Comment
Marketing								
Sales								
PR								
Budget								
Management								
Retail								
Distribution								
HRM								
Demand								
Other								

Group 2

Concern	Evaluation of Impact				Focus Group Response			
	No Impact	Minor Impact	Serious Impact	Comment	Mission	Action	Response	Comment
Information Presented								
Effect on Image								
Destination's Economy								
Promotional Budget								
Tourism Policy								
Supply Factors								
Other								

Part III

Case Studies

7

Case Study I
The Effects of Terrorism on Tourism
(Do the Media Play a Role?)

SYNOPSIS OF CHAPTER

- The nature of terrorism, and how it is communicated in a tourism environment

- Causes and trends in terrorism

- The two sides of terrorism—approval and disapproval

- Israel's tourism under duress

- Northern Ireland; a tourism barometer for terrorism

- *Focus* on traveller's opinions 4–6 months after Lockerbie

- *Fast Facts* on dangerous places for travel throughout the world

- Conclusions on the triangular links among tourism, terrorism, and the media

What is Terrorism?

The term 'terrorism', like the acts implied by the term, is very difficult to pinpoint precisely. Terrorism in its various forms has become more prominent since the 1960s—with international incidents having increased tenfold since 1968, and having affected approximately half of the countries in the world (Wilkinson 1990). In the late 1980s and early 1990s, the word 'terrorism' became something of a catchphrase applied randomly to all sorts of violent acts (including acts of reprisal) of a political nature. An example of this is politicians' accusing their opponents of 'acting like terrorists'. This loose use of the term adds to the difficulty of definition—perhaps magnified by the mass media's portrayal of terrorism.

The US State Department Code Section 265(d) defines terrorism as:

> . . . premeditated, politically motivated violence perpetrated against non-combatant targets by subnational groups or clandestine agents . . . intended to influence an audience.
>
> US State Dept 1998

According to the RAND organisation (the name is a contraction of 'research and development'), which maintains detailed records of terrorist activities and trends, terrorism should be identified by the nature of the act, and not by the identity of its perpetrators or the nature of their causes. The RAND sees terrorism as involving a violent act with a motive, a mode, a perpetrator, and wide-reaching effects.

Wilkinson (1990) describes terrorism as containing certain ingredients, or having certain major characteristics:

- it is premeditated, aiming to incite extreme fear (terror);
- its target audience is wider than those immediately affected by it;
- attacks are characteristically random and symbolic—frequently involving civilians;
- the violence is viewed by society as outside social norms and therefore an 'outrage'; and
- the terrorist act is an attempt to influence political behaviour, to force issues, make demands, provoke reaction (or overreaction), to act as a catalyst for a more general aim, or to publicise a cause.

The RAND's advice—to identify terrorism purely by the nature of the act—is perhaps taken too literally by the world's mass media. According to the rules of newsworthiness, the horrors of the act, the visible carnage, and the loss of life through the act, make for more interesting viewing and bigger ratings. But the focus here is more on 'the act' than the 'nature' of the act.

People are more concerned about the outrage than the hazards (Peltu 1990, cited by Gow & Otway 1990). This implies the formation of an unhealthy relationship between the mass media and society, examining terrorism and risk information in 'human interest' terms rather than an analytical and informational approach.

In the RAND's *Chronology of International Terrorism*, is the following list of tactics used to achieve this terror:

- kidnapping;
- bombing;

- attacks on installations;
- airline and other transportation hijacking and bombings;
- barricading and hostage taking;
- assassinations and shootings; and
- incidents involving significant threats or conspiracies.

Hoffman & Gardela 1986

What Do We Know About Terrorism?

The RAND publishes a valuable summary of terrorist behaviour throughout the world. Terrorism is analysed from different angles, including:

- incidents with fatalities;
- breakdown by tactic, target, and region;
- most frequently targeted nationalities;
- breakdown of perpetrators by nation, target, tactic; and
- trends in international terrorism over certain periods.

The US State Department and several other organisations also produce similar information—which can be accessed quickly and simply through the Internet by use of the key words 'Terrorism Incidents'. Figure 7.1 (page 148) shows the evolution of terrorism incidents from 1979.

More use could be made of the academic and scientific knowledge available on terrorism. And it could be put to better use by tourism principals—particularly as it pertains to the media. Before the widespread use of the Internet, up-to-date information of this kind was more difficult to obtain. The average person, however, is more passive in the information search, and tends to learn about terrorism through the public media. The information is, therefore, subject to editorial whim. Travel professionals, particularly travel agents functioning semi-autonomously (that is, affiliated to a bigger agency group but responsible for their own customer decisions and much of the information given to customers), report that they scan the mass media for much of the information which they then pass on to tourists.

The mass media thus have a twofold entry into the travelling person's psyche—directly through print and broadcast, and indirectly through agents and tourism-information providers. It is very important that the information relating terrorism to tourism be up-to-date, objective, consistent, and legitimate. This is made more difficult when it is recognised that a terrorist act is intended to cause mayhem and confusion—that is, to rock the status quo. Terrorist groups of the late 1990s overstepped boundaries to attract an increasingly fickle and demanding mass media. For example, following the kidnapping of United Nations delegates in Angola in January 1999, Richard Yallop (from Care Australia) stated that international aid workers ' . . . once considered inviolate, neutral and untouchable' are no longer safe from the terrorist (quoted in McManus 1999).

Figure 7.1   Trends in international terrorism

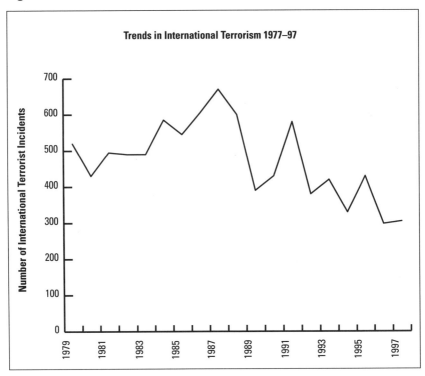

Note: Violent acts between Palestinians (1984–88) were included in US government statistics, but later revisions to the treatment of intra-Palestinian incidents have led to their removal.

Source: US State Department 1997

The graph illustrates the volatility of terrorism over the last twenty years of the twentieth century. For example, from its peak in 1987, terrorism decreased in the late 1980s, only to reach its 1990s peak in 1991 (attributable largely to the Gulf War). By the mid 1990s, terrorism had found something of an equilibrium.

Possible Causes of Increased Terrorist Activity

Attempts have been made to find a reason for the increased terrorist activity during the 1980s. Wilkinson (1990) offered the following list of possible causes of increased terrorist activity:

- deep and bitter ethnic, religious, and ideological conflicts;

- new and relatively fragile political and economic systems experiencing vital challenges to their legitimacy and authority;
- destabilisation following the global nuclear imbalance, leading to low-risk, affordable, proxy-style war (seen as terrorism);
- growth in new technology, which facilitates terrorism through mass communications (seeking wider audiences) and ease of access to weaponry; and, importantly
- terrorism being positively reinforced by relatively high success in achieving short-term tactical goals.

Many of the terrorist incidents summarised in Figure 7.1 (see also Table 7.4, page 158) continue in varying degrees. Terrorism has been shown in many cases to be a long, protracted process. The longer the terrorist activity continues, the more damage it causes—not only in human lives, but also in economics, trade, resource depletion, and tourism.

Beirut is a good example of a destination that was, before terrorist activities took a grip on the city, a well-frequented tourist spot on the Mediterranean. Visitors to Beirut are in little danger of terrorist activity in the late 1990s:

> . . . the days of hostage-taking are long gone . . . [but] tourist facilities will take a while to recover
>
> Barraclough 1996

Tamil Tiger bombings in Sri Lanka led to boycotting by the Australian and West Indian cricket teams in the 1996 World Cup (February–March 1996)—which provided the terrorist rebels with valuable international media coverage. The bombings, therefore, had the desired effect of frightening foreign involvement away—in this case sports tourism, as well as trade and potential investment.

Effects of Terrorism on Tourism

Physical threat (whether real or perceived) or serious disturbance to one's plans, are sufficient to reduce the prospects of a tourist destination or a tourist firm. Tourism is a fickle industry at the best of times—being subject to fluctuations in demand from season to season.

Tourism managers often respond to terrorism with stoicism—armed with little more than faith and hope that terrorist acts in a region in which they have a vested interest are sporadic enough not to deter tourists for any length of time. The return of tourism to Turkey (after terrorist threats damaged the industry in the early 1990s) is an example of the 'wait-and-see' mentality, backed by strategic public-relations activities aimed at minimising the damage (see also Chapter 9). National tourist offices around the world go to great lengths to promote their respective countries as being safe for tourism. But, as shown with the Indian plague scare in 1995, and terrorist threats by Kurdish rebel groups in Turkey in more recent times, the ability to counteract these events is severely hindered by the combined strength of negative media images and informal (grapevine) propaganda. Handling negative media events through public relations and destination marketing is a recognised way of treating the problem (see Chapter 9).

In some cases, the effects of individual terrorist acts were relatively short-term—with tourism and airline passengers picking up within months of the incident. The North American market acts swiftly to condemn a destination or carrier as unsafe, but resumption of business after the perceived threat subsides can be just as swift. Traffic to Europe from the US in 1987 (following terrorist threats, particularly in Greece), and in 1990–91 (due to Gulf War complications), resumed within a reasonably short time.

However, a company or destination might not always be able to pick up the tourism pieces after terrorism has struck—such as PanAm after the Lockerbie incident in December 1988. The airport manager for Air New Zealand (Melbourne), Don Holt, in answer to a question about whether people would fly if they felt unsafe (such as in the case of an aircraft loss), replied as follows:

> Look at PanAm and Lockerbie. You couldn't imagine such a disaster. It went to the wall and it was one of the finest airlines in the world. They were pioneers in airline services.
>
> Don Holt, Interviews, 1995

Tourism management's response must also accommodate the possibility of protracted terrorist activity—linked to a wider cause that might continue in the longer term. Fears are reinforced by continuing intermittent terrorist acts—such as in Israel in March 1996, and also in Northern Ireland after seventeen months of peace and improving prospects with the 1998 peace agreement. There are also proxy effects on tourism from such terrorist acts as the IRA bombings in London in March 1996.

Correspondence on this subject was carried in the London *Independent Weekend* in 1996—in the context of a discussion on the steady rise in prices in London hotels. A reader asked whether the recent bombing campaign had frightened people off. The response from the newspaper editor was:

> Yes, I'm afraid it has . . . Hoteliers were looking forward to a boom summer, but the bombing campaign has changed all that . . . [the hotels] rely on US visitors [who are] particularly sensitive to acts of terrorism

. . . many hoteliers have already received cancellations and expect more.

'Inside Track', 1996

The public view of terrorism is vital in this analysis. Tourists vote with their feet in cases where there is a perceived threat to their safety. This is a concern for governments and tourism operators alike. For example, the Egyptian authorities were alarmed with the immediate cancellation of eighty rooms in the luxury Mena House Hotel—opposite the pyramid of Cheops—following the terrorist attack that killed eighteen Greek tourists and wounded seventeen (MacLeod 1996). This followed a fluctuating period for Egyptian tourism—as verified by European travel agents. The 1993–94 tourist season saw numbers fall from 3.3 million to 2.5 million. After a security crackdown, as a result of which Egypt claimed to have brought the terror under control, numbers returned to 3.1 million—bringing in a valuable US$2.3 billion.

What might be of interest to tourism managers is to know how tourists view terrorism, and their impressions after a terrorist attack such as those described above.

Public Perception of Terrorism

It is important for tourist providers to know, in more detail, the actual fears of tourists. For example, more information could be gleaned from US tourists about their perception of the various 1996 bombings in Israel, Northern Ireland, and London. London hoteliers would benefit from greater knowledge of the perception of the US market to possible terrorist threat. Hoteliers might, for example, be able to promote certain safety elements if they understood exactly what the US tourists were afraid of. Research of this type has been done. Nevertheless, more recent and specific tourist-related research would be helpful.

Disapproval of Terrorism

To what extent does variation in public opinion reflect experience in each country with terrorism, and to what extent does it come from differences in media portrayals of terrorism?

For example, there appears to have been, in more recent times, a reversal of the media 'good guy/bad guy' image portrayed for both the Palestinian Liberation Organisation and the Irish Republican Army's political representatives, Sinn Féin, following more positive media coverage of these groups in 1997 and 1998. The media's tendency to polarise opinion is part intention and part convention. Its more newsworthy to have a good guy and a bad guy. The problem is, as society and the media grow more sophisticated, perceptions are no longer black and white. A good

Table 7.1 Disapproval of terrorism

Public Surveyed	Net Approval (% approving minus % disapproving)
Northern Ireland	−82
Great Britain	−72
Spain	−69
Denmark	−64
Italy	−63
West Germany	−61
Japan	−55
Irish Republic	−53
France	−53
Belgium	−43
Netherlands	−38
Argentina	−51
Chile	−37
Uruguay	−32
Ecuador	−22
Brazil	−19
Peru	+1
Venezuela	+9
Colombia	+31

Source: Index of International Public Opinion 1994

example of this is the way US President Bill Clinton's image survived the negative 1998 media coverage of his private life.

What remains clear from Table 7.1 is that those countries where terrorism has claimed the most victims rate higher on the disapproval scale. The relatively tolerant attitudes of the Belgian and Dutch publics is interesting—perhaps a reflection of the more liberal press in those countries. Undeniably, more research is needed on public attitudes towards terrorism and how the media in different countries portray terrorism—because the tourist public cannot be excluded from the public at large (Hewitt 1992, cited in Paletz & Schmid 1992).

As previously noted, the abstract truth of the event, as portrayed by the media becomes the real (perceived) truth for tourists in the event of no contradictory personal or dominant source information. The individual interprets information and asserts a differing level of significance to it—depending on his or her own value system. As illustrated in interviews with the author, some professionals in the tourism industry feel that word-of-mouth is a stronger medium, whereas others feel that official sources are more important. It appears that the more difficult tourist decisions (those involving higher risks) tend to rely on credible (formal source) information—despite the general trend away from using travel agents. This is more likely for decisions involving the 'defer' and 'decline' options from the '3Ds' ('Decide/Defer/Decline') illustrated in Figures 4.1. & 7.1 (pages 59 and 148, respectively). On the other hand, the more conventional the tourist decision, the lesser the tendency to rely on formal sources—with more reliance on informal, grapevine, unsolicited information. This is more likely for decisions involving the 'decide' (to go) option from the '3Ds'. (See also Chapter 9).

This has implications for how tourism managers should organise their anti-terrorism promotional campaign—while acknowledging the difficulties in controlling word-of-mouth communication. In a sense, if the terrorists are using propaganda to achieve their ends, tourism can be used as a propaganda tool to counter the terrorist offensive. However, fear is a strong ally of the terrorist, and fear is very difficult to douse with superlatives about the safety of a destination.

Social-proof techniques might prove useful in this case. For example, by painting an image in the media of happy and safe American travellers in London, the US public might be able to imagine themselves as secure. Experts have been used as successful purveyors of 'authority' and 'credibility'. People want to subjugate their decision-making onto a higher authority (for example, tourist authorities, government) and when people see these experts stating that it is safe to fly in a McDonnell Douglas plane, or to go to London, it has a positive impact. This would be a costly exercise, however, and must be rationalised by a justified need—such as severe tourism losses due to inaction. KLM, British Airways, and McDonnell Douglas have all invested in such campaigns at various stages in the 1970s and 1980s when demand was severely affected by bad press.

The first goal of information providers, therefore, is to present the confident face of the industry (negating the 'Defer/Decline' tendency in risky choices), thus bringing the tourist into the 'Decide' (to go) category. From there, informal commercial information (such as the advertisements suggested above) might then take over to sway the traveller to continue with the planned trip. However, some would argue that commercial information is transparently biased and, under uncertain conditions, potential travellers would seek unbiased third-party sources of information or confirmation (see Figure 9.5, page 223).

Favourable Image of Terrorism

Terrorism need not be seen in entirely black-and-white terms. It is just as possible that some members of the general public view it in terms of an underlying struggle that terrorist acts might circumvent.

Table 7.2   Favourable image of terrorists

Year	Organisation	As viewed in	Favourable Percentage*
1983	IRA	Great Britain	3
1979	IRA	Canada	10
1983	PLO	Great Britain	12
1979	PLO	Canada	14

*'Favourable Percentage' refers to those considering the organisation to be 'freedom fighters'

Source: Index of International Public Opinion 1994

The above represents but a sample of the potential variations in public viewpoints towards terrorism. Perhaps a good example to take a little further is the case of English interpretations of Irish nationalist (terrorist) acts.

In England, information about Northern Ireland, its history and culture, is scant and, perhaps, biased. More often than not the English public have little direct experience of the conflict—with the exception of intermittent bombings in British cities, such as the ones experienced in March 1996. Ireland has not been included in the English educational curriculum. Non-violent groups who try to inform the public on Irish independence issues are small and under-financed.

> British people are, therefore, almost entirely dependent on the mass media
> for news and interpretations of events in Ireland.
>
> Curtis 1984

Thus, although 86–97 per cent of individuals (Table 7.2) see terrorist groups in unfavourable terms, their interpretation of terrorist acts is jaded by fear and distrust—which must surely affect their travelling decisions.

Although not entirely scientific, the present author's personal anecdotal experience is interesting in this respect. Before meeting citizens from

Belfast and visiting their homes in 1992—and thus being able to hear their version of the independence struggles with the British—the present author held the majority British view (as revealed in surveys), and genuinely feared visiting Northern Ireland. After seeing matters in a different light, untainted by mass media coverage of the issues, personal fear of Belfast subsided, leading to return tourist visits to a city then generally regarded as dangerous.

It is also interesting to note the relatively more accommodating perception of terrorism by the Canadian public. An interesting comparison could be made between the Canadian response to terrorism and that of the US—which is less accepting. Perhaps further investigation on how much more often US companies and citizens (compared with Canadians) are made specific terrorist targets, might shed light on why people from the US tend to be more sensitive to terrorism.

Terrorism as a Problem

More often than not, terrorism is seen in terms of the violence and destruction that surrounds it. This is reflected in Table 7.3.

Table 7.3 Terrorism as a problem

Surveys conducted in	Most important problem	Percentage	Deaths from terrorism
Northern Ireland 1982	terrorism	34	2269
Spain 1979–82	terrorism/public order	22	455
Italy 1972–79	public order	16	227
Israel 1977	security	29	196
Great Britain 1971–72	Northern Ireland	13	155
France 1985–87	terrorism	5	124
Germany 1976	public order	8	25
Uruguay 1968–69	disorder/subversion	4	14

Source: Compiled from numerous sources by Hewitt 1992 (cited in Paletz & Schmid 1992)

Terrorists seek to attract attention, and they target both 'enemy' public and uncommitted bystanders—including apolitical tourists. Usually it is terrorist violence itself that is the issue for the public—rather than the terrorists' cause. During the height of terrorist activity (from the 1960s until the mid 1980s), researchers asked respondents what they felt was the most important problem facing their countries. Table 7.3 shows the percentage that selected terrorism or a related topic (Hewitt 1992). The results show a positive relationship with the number of deaths resulting from terrorism.

As far as tourism and travel are concerned, many tourists are rather myopic—interested in their travel plans, and how security and terrorism will affect them. There is evidence to suggest that travellers' rationalise their security fears. For example, Holt (Interviews 1995) stated that, 'Air New Zealand went through an unfortunate situation when we crashed an aircraft in the Antarctic, which had a huge effect on the company'. In answer to a question as to whether events such as this lead people to stop flying, Holt continued, 'They will fly, but they'll fly another airline'.

There is evidence to the contrary—which indicates that tourists perceive a very real threat following terrorist attacks or media presentation events. According to a Gallup Poll conducted by *Newsweek* magazine in April 1986, 79 per cent of Americans said that they would reject an opportunity to travel overseas because of the threat of terrorism. A survey of 205 travel agents found that approximately 48 per cent of their cancellations were related to terrorism in 1986 (Lehrman 1986, cited in Sonmez & Graefe 1998).

Cancellations can also be due to war or political crises. For example, in Dubrovnik:

> In the best pre-war year, Dubrovnik attracted six million 'overnights' [individual nights spent by visitors]. This year [1995] the total will be around 300 000, down by 95 per cent That's tourism as war.
>
> Morison 1995

The industry's response to the 1980s terrorism campaign was dramatic. Responses included:

- media campaigns encouraging Americans to return to Europe (see the KLM advertisement in Figure 4.7, page 72);
- price incentives shown in lower airfares, and 'two-for-one' tickets;
- free round-trip companion tickets;
- free car rental packages (British Airways and KLM, for example);
- cruise ships changing their routes;
- hotels offering discounts of 25–50 per cent.

Wall 1996, cited in Sonmez & Graefe 1996

Terrorism's Communication Through a Tourist Medium

It was Karber who first put forward the communications aspect in conceptualising terrorism, stating that:

. . . as a symbolic act, terrorism can be analysed much like other mediums of communication.

Karber 1971, cited in Sonmez & Burnett 1997

Karber's statement can be neatly superimposed onto the basic communication flow figure as shown in Figure 7.2. The process acts in more or less the same fashion as the communication model—including the associated roadblocks to effective communication.

Figure 7.2   Terrorism represented as a 'basic communication'

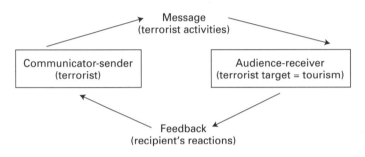

Source: Author's presentation

To further illustrate the relationship between the terrorist's 'communication' (through terrorist actions) and the tourism industry, a list of publicised terrorist activities involving tourist is shown in Table 7.4 (page 158).

Focus on Lockerbie

What Did Travellers Think 4–6 Months Later?

This is an important question for airlines and for tourist principals in general.

In research conducted by *Interavia Business & Technology* (a trade publication) and IFAPA (International Foundation of Airline Passengers' Association), of 4800 frequent flyers from ten countries (see Table 7.5, page 160):

- 62% saw no need for change to aviation security despite Lockerbie;
- 84% were willing to pay extra for improved security; and
- 62% were prepared to check-in early to allow extra security checks to be made.

Wilkinson (1989) cautions against making too much of these results. He believes that the timing of the survey was significant in the results—taken within six months of the infamous Lockerbie disaster which, although not

Table 7.4 Terrorism communicated through tourist targets

Date	Country	Incident
1993		
4 February	Egypt	fire bomb thrown at Sth Korean tour bus near Cairo
26 February	USA	car bomb explodes below New York World Trade Centre—6 dead, 1000 injured
8 June	Egypt	bomb explodes near Giza pyramids—2 dead, 12 injured (6 Britons)
27 June	Turkey	PKK (Kurdish Workers Party) uses hand grenades in Mediterranean resort area—12 foreigners injured, 16 Turks
5 July	Turkey	8 incidents (Jul.–Oct.), PKK kidnapped and later released 19 tourists
7 July	Peru	2 European travellers found dead—Sendero Luminoso terrorists suspected
25 October	Nigeria	dissidents hijack Nigerian Airways 310 in Lagos—150 passengers
25 October	Peru	car-bomb explosion in car park near Lima international airport—1 dead, 20 injured
27 December	Egypt	shots at tour bus—7 Austrians and 8 Egyptians wounded
1994		
19 February	Egypt	passenger train fired upon—2 wounded (1 Pole; 1 Thai)
4 March	Egypt	shots at Nile cruise boat—wounding German tourist
9–13 March	UK	IRA mortar attacks on Heathrow International Airport—no casualties
27 April	South Africa	car bomb explosion at Jan Smuts Airport Johannesburg—16 injured
26 July	Cambodia	Khmer Rouge attack train in Kompong Trach—kidnap Australian, Frenchman and Briton
8 August	Turkey	PKK kidnap & later release 2 Finish tourists for having no 'entry visa to Kurdistan'
24 December	Algeria	armed Islamic Group hijack Air France flight to Marseilles—7 dead (3 hostages, 4 terrorists)
1995		
12 January	Egypt	Al-Gama'at al-Islamiyya members suspected of shooting at tourist-carrying passenger train—6 wounded (including 2 Argentine tourists)
15 January	Cambodia	US tourist and guide killed by Khmer Rouge

23 May	Peru	Sendero Luminoso (Shining Path) plants 50-kg car-bomb in front of Maria Angola Hotel—3 dead, 30 injured
4–8 July	India	6 tourists taken hostage in Kashmir—1 escaped, 1 decapitated, others unknown
13 July	Turkey	PKK abduct (and later release) Japanese tourist
9 October	USA	Sons of Gestapo derail an Amtrack train in Arizona—1 dead, 98 injured
1996		
18 April	Egypt	gunmen attack Greek tour bus in front of Cairo Hotel—18 dead
17 July	USA	TWA800 flight explodes, killing 230—thought to be terrorism but attribution later reversed
22 July	Pakistan	Lahore International Airport bombed—4 dead, 68 wounded
22 July	USA	pipe bomb found on tarmac of Chicago Airport
26 July	Spain	Iberian Airlines 6621 en route to Havana hijacked—none hurt
3 August	USA	pipe bomb explosion at Centennial Olympic Park, Atlanta—2 dead, 111 injured

Source: Sonmez & Graefe 1998, using US State Department data

the first aviation crash (or even the biggest in terms of fatalities), dominated Western media because of its accessibility to the media (being close to a European centre). Wilkinson also states that this restricted class of passengers—'frequent flyers'—might have had an unusually high sensitivity level to security issues and that a broader cross-section of passengers might have yielded more meaningful results.

Wilkinson's criticism of the survey sample is interesting. One can argue this question of the validity of the survey sample from a number of perspectives.

- Wilkinson might be correct in suggesting that people who fly more frequently are over-sensitive to security issues compared with people for whom this is an infrequent concern.
- On the other hand, 'frequent flyers' might be a *better* sample because they have greater knowledge of security procedures and therefore might be better placed to make meaningful comment than inexperienced (and perhaps more anxious) people who do not really understand what is currently being done.
- Then again, 'frequent flyers' might even become 'desensitised' to security issues by over-exposure.

It is difficult to be certain how the selection of the sample might have affected the results.

Table 7.5   What Passengers Think 4–6 Months After Lockerbie

In general are you satisfied with security procedures at the airports you fly from?

Country	E	CH	F	SC	NL	GB	D	I	GR	USA	All
Yes	49%	55%	50%	55%	67%	46%	61%	46%	46%	40%	52%
No	51%	45%	50%	45%	33%	54%	39%	54%	54%	60%	48%

Are you more satisfied or less satisfied than you were a year ago?

Country	E	CH	F	SC	NL	GB	D	I	GR	USA	All
More	18%	18%	24%	20%	20%	31%	21%	25%	46%	17%	23%
Same	68%	71%	59%	65%	62%	49%	66%	69%	49%	65%	62%
Less	14%	11%	17%	15%	18%	20%	13%	6%	5%	18%	15%

Would you be willing to pay a nominal security levy on your ticket for a special fund administered through the International Civil Aviation Organisation (ICAO) to develop high-tech detection equipment, improve training, monitor airport security procedures and generally upgrade security in all of the world's airports in a way which will not slow down passage through controls?

Country	E	CH	F	SC	NL	GB	D	I	GR	USA	All
Yes	86%	82%	82%	87%	76%	90%	77%	91%	83%	79%	84%
No	14%	18%	18%	13%	24%	10%	23%	9%	17%	21%	16%

If yes, how much extra would you be willing to pay per flight?

Country	E	CH	F	SC	NL	GB	D	I	GR	USA	All
$1–4	20%	21%	25%	18%	15%	18%	21%	13%	22%	30%	21%
$5–9	34%	36%	39%	36%	29%	38%	41%	42%	32%	30%	37%
$10+	32%	25%	18%	33%	32%	34%	15%	36%	29%	19%	26%

Some airlines require passengers to check in well before normal check-in time to perform extra security checks. By how much extra time would you be willing to check in early?

Country	E	CH	F	SC	NL	GB	D	I	GR	USA	All
None	27%	36%	41%	44%	47%	36%	48%	30%	32%	16%	38%
To 1 hr	68%	52%	48%	50%	44%	43%	45%	57%	44%	64%	49%
1–2 hrs	5%	11%	10%	5%	9%	19%	7%	11%	24%	15%	12%
+2 hrs	–	1%	1%	1%	–	2%	–	2%	–	5%	1%

Would you be inconvenienced if there is a ban on electronic goods that you can carry by air, such as radios, calculators, tape players and computers?

Country	E	CH	F	SC	NL	GB	D	I	GR	USA	All
Yes	52%	53%	51%	55%	47%	53%	47%	49%	59%	45%	51%
No	48%	47%	49%	45%	53%	47%	53%	51%	41%	55%	49%

Number of replies

Country	E	CH	F	SC	NL	GB	D	I	GR	USA	All
No. of replies	44	119	151	211	86	197	155	53	41	128	1220*

Notes:

1. Key to country abbreviations: CH (Switzerland); F (France); SC (Scandinavia); NL (Netherlands); E (Spain); GB (Great Britain); D (West Germany); I (Ireland); GR (Greece); USA (United States of America).

2. *Total number of replies (1220) is greater than grand total of individual countries due to late replies not being allocated.

Source: Courtesy *Interavia*, cited in Wilkinson 1989

As Holt (Interviews 1995) stated, people will continue to fly despite news of air fatalities, 'but they'll fly another airline'. This supports Wilkinson's (1989) belief that, 'As memories of Lockerbie fade one might expect to see a dramatic decline in concern about aviation security'.

This prophecy was entirely correct, and is echoed by other writers in relation to governmental and organisational responses to air safety and terrorist threats. For example, McWhinney offers a critique of the basic sanctions-based approach to the enforcement of the Tokyo, Hague, and the Montreal conventions (in which important conventions for international aviation safety and procedures were laid down):

Faced with the snail's pace of inter-governmental cooperation and the giant gulf between the existing outdated and extremely limited provisions of the Tokyo, Hague and Montreal Conventions and what is actually required to enhance international aviation security, one is tempted to despair.

McWhinney 1987

There is a major problem with complete compliance by all airports and airlines to a world standard, beyond punitive sanctions. As Wilkinson notes:

. . . the majority of states would be unwilling to concede any sovereignty over such matters to an international body.

Wilkinson 1989

The International Civil Aviation Organisation (ICAO) and the International Air Traffic Association (IATA) have both put forward proposals throughout the years to streamline security procedures, but have had little success in implementing their plans.

Tourism Responses and Responsibilities in Relation to Terrorism

The chances of being killed as a result of terrorist activity are very small. Even during the peak years of terrorism (in the mid 1980s), of the 6.5 million Americans travelling abroad (in 1985), only 6000 were reported as dying overseas—this figure including natural death. In the same year, only seventeen Americans died as a direct result of terrorism. Compared with the 43 000 Americans who died on the roads, and the 20 000 murders in the same period, the fear of terrorism appears to be overrated (cited from Ryan 1991b).

Nevertheless, travel insurance companies recognise the actuarial risks when insuring travellers going to countries with a history of terrorist activity. The premiums are generally higher to reflect the greater risk. It should also be noted that premiums for the USA are mostly in the highest bracket (McAlister, Interviews 1995).

Why then, do people (particularly US citizens) fear terrorism so much? There is no single answer to this question. Tourism managers need to recognise that the fear is irrational. The information received on terrorism is mostly through one mass medium or another and is, therefore, distant and often patchy and inconsistent. Faced with this dilemma, tourists are forced to make decisions regarding their safety. Consumer decision-making processes are complex, and are made more difficult to analyse in a tourism context due to the nature of tourist products and services, which are diverse and frequently intangible. This, consequently, also makes them subjective. Add to this the intricacies of terrorist behaviour, and the potential effects on tourism, and the result is what many tourism operators had to face on occasions in the last twenty years of the twentieth century.

Tourism principals need to identify the link between media coverage and terrorists' usage of it. Information is the key to this. Tourists can properly distinguish information relating to threats to their safety from terrorist activity only if the information is complete—accepting that risks to tourists in foreign countries can change rapidly. Tourism principals might be tempted to withhold information from tourists about potential terrorist threats for fear that it will affect business. It is ignorant to think that consumers in today's mass-media society do not have at least some knowledge of the product or tourist destination. Tourism principals need to build trust and offer the sort of assurances and knowledge that the increasingly more sophisticated tourist requires. Small untruths, although seemingly harmless, can become a symbol of the relationship between tourism professional and tourist.

Although full and honest information about potential threats to tourists from terrorism can damage business, any tourist who continues to remain open-minded enough to ask questions about a destination deserves to be given complete and up-to-date information to allow the tourist to assess the risk of travel. This includes 'positive' information such as that above:

- the low likelihood, while abroad, of being killed by a terrorist;
- the attitude by individuals in some nations toward terrorists (some seeing them as freedom fighters rather than murderers); and
- that tourists rarely have been targeted directly by terrorist groups.

Full information need not be all negative. Withholding information at the point of sale will more than likely cause distrust, and is against the laws of contract in some countries. Assurances by the appropriate tourist authority (national tourist authority, tour operator/agent, airlines, IATA, and so on) will probably be acceptable to the tourist looking to affirm a belief in the safety of a particular destination—as is sometimes the case with adventure-seeking/independent travellers who deny the public consensus regarding the danger of a particular destination.

Fast Facts: Index of Dangerous Places (1997–99)

Where?	Why?	How bad?	Australians?
Afghanistan	war against Russia (1979–89) followed by civil fighting between warring factions such as Tajik and Pahktun fundamentalists; the strict Islamic Taliban leadership work to stabilise the country, but face harsh human rights criticism	+++++(HOT)	*
Algeria	Muslim fundamentals (FIS) target Westerners after 1992 election loss	+++++(HOT)	*
Albania	civil unrest after government-endorsed pyramid plan collapsed	†(WARM)	*
Angola	civil war between UNITA and MPLA over diamond and oil rights; hijackings; landmines	++++(HOT)	
Argentina	border feuds with Chile and Paraguay	†(COLD)	–
Armenia	energy and sovereignty disputes in Nagorno-Karabakh (see also Azerbaijan)	+(COLD)	–
Azerbaijan	border dispute with Armenia over land	*(COLD)	–
Bangladesh	natural dangers (flooding); economic pressure; rebels (Shanti Bahini)	+(TEPID)	–
Bolivia	drugs, poverty, terrorist (CNPZ) activity focus on US citizens	+(TEPID)	–
Bosnia-Herzegovina	complex ethnic civil war and border dispute in the Balkans	++(WARM)	–
Burundi	conflict between minority Tutsis and majority Hutus (CNDD); poverty	*****(HOT)	–
Brazil	violent and non-violent crime in major cities	++(WARM)	–
Cambodia	legacy of despotic rule (Khmer Rouge, NADK); fear of the West; restricted tourism	++(WARM)	*
Colombia	drugs, violent crime, terrorists (FARC, ELN, DFC,EPL/D); poverty	+++++(HOT)	–
China	poor human rights; communist shadow; Tibet question	+(TEPID)	–
Chechnya	independence rebels fighting Russian troops; kidnapping; crime	+++(WARM)	–
Cyprus	dispute over territory between Turkish and Greek Cypriots (UN border control)	+(TEPID)	–

Dem. Rep. of Congo	civil ethnic unrest; political disruption	+++(WARM)	*
Djibouti	civil dispute between the Afas and Issas, French observing troops and FRUD	++(WARM)	–
Ecuador	border dispute between Peru and Ecuador over land repatriation	+(WARM)	–
El Salvador	increased crime following 10-year civil war; focus (not exclusively) on US citizens	++(COLD)	–
Egypt	isolated Muslim fundamentalist attack on tourism (train, hotel, at the Pyramids)	++(COLD)	*
Eritrea	border dispute (strategic positioning for Red Sea access) with Ethiopia, bombings	+++(WARM)	*
Ethiopia	brief border struggle with previously friendly neighbours; bombings	+++(WARM)	*
Georgia	corruption, small rebel groups after difficult separation from Russia	+(WARM)	–
Guatemala	crime against tourists; clashes between wealthy 'Mistos' and poor Indians	++(TEPID)	–
Haiti	US-backed action to reinstate ex-president; corruption; instability	+++(WARM)	–
India (1)	terrorism in Kashmir (JKLF, Hizbul Mujahedin, ULFA, APHC; others)	++++(HOT)	–
India (2)	corruption; travel difficulty; tourist scams	†(TEPID)	–
Indonesia	Dispute over East Timor; economic hardship; political strife	++(WARM)	*
Iran	Muslim fundamentalism; ethnic mistreatment; limited tourist contact	++(WARM)	–
Iraq	economic hardship; disputes with UN; political dictatorship	+++(WARM)	*
Israel	land-rights disputes with PLO; border disputes; souring peace agreement	+++(WARM)	–
Kenya	crime; dissident groups; unstable political outlook	++(WARM)	–
Laos	border dispute with Thailand; economic imbalance	++(TEPID)	–
Lebanon (1)	north (safe), rebuilding after war	++(TEPID)	–
Lebanon (2)	south (unsafe), home of Hezbollah	++++(HOT)	–
Liberia	prolonged civil war; limited international access; unruly outlook	++++(HOT)	–

Malaysia	generally orderly; pirates in surrounding seas; mild political unrest	+(WARM)	–
Mali	tribal; rebel dispute	++(WARM)	–
Mexico (1)	restricted threat of possible harm in Chiapas region	+++(TEPID)	*
Mexico (2)	Mexico City at night (some danger in taxis, bus travelling)	+(TEPID)	*
Morocco	difficult for female travellers; petty crime; scam/hustling	++(WARM)	–
Mozambique	night travel dangerous; carjackings; landmines	++(HOT)	*
Myanmar (Burma)	human rights offences; political oppression; tourism boycott	+++(WARM)	–
Papua New Guinea	gangs frequent Port Moresby; theft; rape; murder	++(WARM)	*
Nigeria	violent crime, theft (especially between airport and Lagos)	++(TEPID)	*
North Korea	not presently open to tourism	–	–
Northern Island	peace moves; limited terrorist activity	++(TEPID)	–
Pakistan	terrorism in Karachi; border dispute with India; scams; shootings; anti-US sentiment	+++(HOT)	–
Philippines	fighting on scattered islands— Muslims vs Christians, government vs communists	+(TEPID)	*
Peru (1)	Shining Path Rebels previously focused terrorism on tourists	++++(WARM)	*
Peru (2)	resort areas (Arequipa, Cuzco, Ica) not dangerous bar theft and robbery	†(TEPID)	*
Russia	unpredictable; corrupt; difficult to enter; political & economic hardship	+++(WARM)	*
Rwanda	genocide; infrastructure fractured; unstable politically (RPF, Augustin Bizimugu)	++++(WARM)	*
Senegal	fighting between separatists and government; instability; landmines	+++(HOT)	*
Sierra Leone	civil war: govt with mercenary support (Executive Outcomes) and RUF	++++(HOT)	–
Somalia	civil and religious unrest (north vs south); no central government; poverty	++++(HOT)	–

Spain	ETA separatist group terrorist activities in northern Spain, no tourism ties	†(COLD)	–
Sri Lanka	Tamil Tiger rebel groups in north; infrequent terrorism in south	++(WARM)	*
Sudan	20-year ongoing war, Christian vs Muslim; instability; poverty esp. in Khartoum	++++(HOT)	*
Suriname	divided between coastal resorts and rebel activity in the jungle	++(HOT)	–
South Africa	violent crime (very dangerous for a non-war zone)	++(HOT)	*
Tanzania	armed robbery; carjacking; drugging tourists; unsafe travel after dark	++(HOT)	*
Turkey (1)	east and south-east—PKK	++++(HOT)	*
Turkey (2)	west coast—mostly terrorism free	++(TEPID)	*
Uganda	past civil unrest now overshadowed by its neighbours, which might flow over	+++(WARM)	*
United States	violent crime possible in cities; petty crime common, many gun owners	+HOT	–
Republic of Congo	described as 'dangerous and confused' (McManus 1999), esp. Brazzaville	+++(HOT)	*
Yemen	abduction of tourists at gunpoint; landmines (tourists killed December 1998)	++++(HOT)	*
Terrorism havens	Iran, Iraq, Sudan, Pakistan, Syria, Algeria, Afghanistan, Cuba (reports of ETA in Havana), Paris, Brussels (thought to have Algerian terrorist cells)		

Note: This table is obviously subject to significant change (even on a daily basis); however it serves a purpose in giving an indication of the sorts of problems faced by tourism principals in the face of terrorism and political unrest.

Legend:

+++++ extremely dangerous and unpredictable—not suitable for regular tourism or guidebook travellers

++++ highly dangerous, some access by experienced travellers; minimal regular tourism

+++ very dangerous and unsettling for experienced travellers; some regular tourism

++ dangerous possibilities persist; adventure travellers; confined regular tourism

+ somewhat dangerous due to specific elements; tourism functions

† mildly dangerous to regular tourism; considered exciting by experienced travellers

* destinations considered particularly dangerous for Australians according to *Herald Sun* (Melbourne) 3 January 1999 and Australian Dept Foreign Affairs

APHC All-Party Hurriyat Conference; CNDD Council for the Defence of Democracy; CNPZ

Nestor Paz Zamora Commission; DCM Dignity for Colombia Movement; DFC Dignity for Cuba; ELN Ejercito de Liberacion Nacional (or National Liberation Army); EPL/D Popular Liberation Army; ETA Euskal ta Askatasuna (Basque Homeland & Liberty); FARC Fuerzas Armadas Revolucionarias de Colombia; FIS Islamic Salvation Front; FRUD = Front pour la Restoration de l'Unité et de la Democratie; IRA Irish Republican Army; JKLF Jammu & Kashmir Liberation Front; MPLA Popular Movement for the Liberation of Angola; NADK National Army of Democratic Kampuchea; PKK = Kurdistan Workers Party; PLO Palestine Liberation Organisation; RPF Rwandan Patriotic Front (Paul Kagame); RUF Revolutionary United Front; ULFA United Liberation Front of Assam; UN United Nations; UNITA National Union for the Total Independence of Angola

Source: Author's presentation using information from Pelton, Aral & Dulles 1997, and updates from the (Melbourne) *Herald Sun*

Tourism Under Stress—the Israeli Example

With the exception of 1981–82, worldwide tourist arrivals have followed an upward trend for almost fifty years, but the growth registered by individual countries can be affected by a range of domestic and international factors. Table 7.6 (page 170) presents a detailed analysis of media events impacting upon arrivals by air in Israel. Israel is an interesting case to examine in detail as it is a relatively 'new' country and the evolution of tourism has been less influenced by what might be called 'traditional' or 'heritage' tourism trends, and more affected by 'micro-climatic' tourism conditions.

From the table, it is evident that, of the twenty-five years analysed, nine show a net decrease from year to year. Bar-On's (1996) research also states that:

> The effects of a major act (or a series of related acts) are different if it occurs: early in the year, off-season (Gulf War, for example), before the main tourist season (e.g. Six-Day War, June 1967) or during the high season, when it may be difficult for tourists to change their plans, reserve at another destination or postpone their trips (Gulf Crisis, from August 2nd, 1990). The loss of visitors may be spread over many months. The recovery may be rapid or slow and uneven . . .
>
> Bar-On 1996

This adds an interesting challenge for tourism professionals—to understand the actual impact of a specific event in terms of relative current demand (tourist arrivals) and the possible lag effect of previous events. Bar-On concludes that:

Terrorism and other violent events or series of crimes against tourists are notable in many tourist destinations, highlighted by instant news worldwide. They affect tourism in many ways: tourists may cancel or postpone trips to such destinations, often switching to alternative destinations. Their effects and the recovery from them and of promotion campaigns following them can best be studied by seasonal adjustments of monthly data and monitoring the smoothed short-term trends, by market segments and by tourist cities or regions (where possible).

Bar-On 1996

It is of interest (Table 7.6, page 170) that the two biggest positive changes on the previous year's visitor arrivals are:

- 1970–71 (+49%), which corresponds with a worldwide expansion of tourist traffic generated by the introduction of Boeing's 747 Jumbo in 1969–70 (international tourist arrivals increased by 15.5% compared with 1969–70, and again by 7.9% between 1970 and 1971); Israel's tourist arrival growth was positive growth as it does not appear to be recovery-based in nature (the previous year being a net growth year also); and

- 1991–92 (+61%), which is partially positive growth (theoretically about 8.4% worth, or the equivalent to the worldwide international arrivals growth from 1991–92), but in view of the two consecutive years of negative growth in Israel (–6% between 1989 and 1990 and –17% between 1990 and 1991) leading up to 1992, this might also account for some of this exceptional growth; it is, therefore, possibly a case of positive and lag-growth working together.

Table 7.6 Effects on Israeli visitor arrivals of major media events

Year	Visitor Arrivals ('000)	Change on previous	Tourists by air ('000)	Principal media events
1970	441	+8	382	Swissair plane to Israel blown up; 6 aircraft hijacked in Middle East; terror in Israel and Munich airport; War of Attrition (Suez Canal Nov. '69–Nov. '70)
1971	657	+49	566	Sabena hijack; El Al operates first jumbo (June)
1972	728	+11	627	terror at Tel Aviv airport (May, Aug.); attack on Israelis at Munich Olympics (Sept.)
1973	662	–9	562	Yom Kippur War (Oct. 6–24); World Oil Crisis; Lufthansa hijack; terror at Rome airport
1974	625	–6	526	terror attacks in Israel and at Rome airport
1975	620	–1	508	terror in Israel, Tel Aviv (Mar.)and Orly airports (Jan.); charters start to Eilat
1976	797	+29	672	Entebbe hijack (Jun.) and rescue; terror in Israel and Istanbul airport (Aug.); charters to Tel Aviv (Oct.)
1977	987	+24	820	Mogadishu hijack (Oct.) and rescue; terror in Israel, president Sadat visits Israel
1978	1071	+9	871	Iran revolution stopped tourism to Israel; attacks in Israel and at Orly airport (May), London (Aug.); Litani campaign in Lebanon (May)
1979	1139	+6	925	accord with Egypt (Washington, Mar.); terror in Israel
1980	1176	+3	956	economic crisis, USA and Europe; anti-Jewish terror, Paris (Oct.); flights Tel Aviv to Egypt direct (Feb.)
1981	1137	–3	922	Israel bombs Iraqi atomic pile (Jun.); rockets on Galilee
1982	998	–12	788	return Sinai to Egypt (Apr.); Israel ambassador London attacked (Jun.); Lebanon War (Jun. 1982–Jun. 1985); Sabra and Shatila massacres (Lebanon)
1983	1167	+17	852	France restricts travel allowance; US embassy in Beirut blown up (Apr.)
1984	1259	+8	936	attacks on Israeli embassies, Cairo, Nicosia (Jun., Oct.)
1985	1436	+14	1079	international terror, especially on airlines, US tourists (Jun. 1985–Sep. 1986) and Israelis; Eilat Free Trade Area
1986	1196	–17	930	international terror (Feb.–Sep.); USA bomb terrorist headquarters at Tripoli (Apr.)
1987	1518	+27	1151	stock exchange crisis, USA (Oct.); Intifada (Palestinian uprising, Dec. onward)

1988	1299	−14	979	terror in Nicosia (May), and on bus to Dimona (Mar.); PanAm bombed over Lockerbie (Dec.)
1989	1425	+10	1033	eastern Europe liberation, tourism to Israel; return of Taba to Egypt (Mar.)
1990	1342	−6	933	Iraq threats to Israel; invasion of Kuwait; Gulf Crisis (Aug.); terror in Israel; Muslims killed (Oct.)
1991	1118	−17	806	Gulf War, Iraq missiles on Israel (Jan.–Feb.)
1992	1805	+61	1257	attacks on Israeli embassies, Argentina, Ankara (Mar.); start of Arab–Israel peace process (Madrid Oct.); expulsion of Hamas activists to Lebanon (Dec.)
1993	1945	+8	1378	terror in New York (Feb.) & Egypt; US attacks on Iraq (Jan.); PLO agreement (Sept.); peace negotiations
1994	2170	+12	1503	transfer of Gaza & Jericho to Palestinian authority; peace with Jordan (Oct.); massacre of Arabs, Hebron (Feb.); bus bombed in Tel Aviv (Oct.)

Source: slightly altered from Bar-On, cited in Pizam & Mansfeld 1996

Figure 7.3   Evolutionary chart of visitor arrivals in divided Ireland

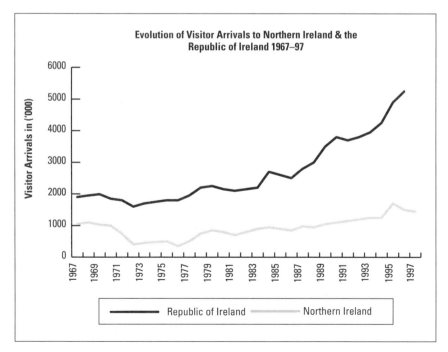

Source: Author's own chart; data in Wall 1996, and Northern Ireland Tourist Board 1998

The Terrorism Divide (North and South of Ireland)—a Tourism Barometer

Wall (1996), contributor to Pizam & Mansfeld (1996), believes that there is a clear connection between Northern Ireland's decreasing tourist arrivals and the political tensions afflicting the region from the 1960s until the 1970s.

Between 1967 and 1970, tourism to Northern Ireland was roughly on a par with the Republic of Ireland. For the next ten years or so, political instability and terrorism slowed tourism to the two Irelands with Northern Ireland reaching a record low of 423 000 arrivals. Whereas tourism began to recover slowly in the Republic from 1986 onward, the North stagnated well into the 1990s. By 1997, tourist arrivals in the Republic had almost quadrupled its northern neighbour.

The Republic has been aggressively promoting itself as a destination since 1992–93—which contributes significantly to the fast growth in arrivals between 1992 and 1997.

However, the apparent tourism stagnation (and even decline) in the North is the more interesting aspect of Figure 7.3. The Northern Ireland Tourist Board (NITB) has had a much smaller promotion budget at its disposal than Bord Fáilte (Republic of Ireland Tourism). Bord Fáilte spent US$28 million on promotion in 1992 (the 12th-biggest tourism promoter in the world) and, as part of its five-year program, increased this spending to US$41.8 million (9th in the world) in 1994. By 1995, the budget had been reduced by 11 per cent to US$37.8 million, but the benefits of this heavy promotion investment had already begun to show in the arrivals figures. The NITB has been promised approximately £14 million (BBC 1998a) as part of a broader economic development plan in Northern Ireland. This figure is roughly equivalent to the US$28 million available to Bord Fáilte in 1992—which puts the NITB approximately six years behind the Republic in the tourism catch-up race—but it is a firm starting block from which to begin the building process.

The Media Bring Bad Tidings

Comparison of tourism to Northern Ireland and the Republic of Ireland is interesting because the two regions are geographically close, are similar in climate, topography, scenery, and tourist attractions, and shared a common history and heritage before the split in the 1920s. Because of these similarities, Wall (1996) believes that, by comparing the Northern and Southern Ireland tourism industries, it provides decisive evidence of the effect of terrorism and political instability on tourism:

Regardless of whether visitor numbers are influenced predominantly by actual terrorist events or inaccurate perceptions of terrorist activities, it is clear that terrorism has affected tourism in Northern Ireland. Some believe that an inaccurate perception of violent events does more harm to the tourist industry than the events themselves.

Wall 1996

Lewis (1986) places the responsibility of tourism losses squarely in the hands of the media:

News coverage of terrorism and other dire events over the past eighteen months left the holiday industry wondering whether it didn't have more to fear from media hyperbole than from the crises themselves. Yet the experience, however bitter, taught the industry that the media in today's global village may come to play an even greater part in leading people to decide where they would—or rather wouldn't—spend their holidays.

Lewis 1986

The media appear to bear the brunt of the responsibility for Northern Ireland's flagging tourism in the past twenty-five years—allowing for the different promotional budgets noted above. Of course, the media focus on the region because of the political instability—political instability that has led to terrorism, deaths and, eventually, arrested economic and tourism development. The media might present the events in a sensational fashion—which damages tourism potential—but the energy and funds directed away from tourism promotion, and the failing will to progress during political strife, are as much to blame for the lack of development in the region.

Better Understanding of Terrorism and Tourism

The impact of terrorism tourism is better understood by tourism professionals and academics because of this interesting period in tourism's history—the 1980s through to the mid 1990s (that is, the 'terrorist years' in the Middle East and Europe) The power of image, marketing, and public relations in the destination 'healing process' (the ability of a destination to 'bounce back' after adversity) has been confirmed through experience. The challenge faced by tourism planners during the 1980s in overcoming a wave of terrorist activities that threatened tourism around the world was a learning experience on how best to tackle forces that have a direct and strong impact on tourism fundamentals (arrivals, revenues, transport communication, and so on). See Tables 1.1 (page 18) and 7.6 (page 170).

It could be argued that Turkey and Egypt's ability to bounce back consistently after terrorism acts is an example of quick-response or 'stop-the-bleeding' tourist industry healing. The Egyptian authorities defence against the spate of terrorism in 1992–94 was a combination of:

- communication strategies—aimed both internationally and at home (informing the Egyptian people of the damage that terrorism does to their country's image); and
- anti-terrorist police enforcement crackdowns and protection of tourists entering the country.

Wahab 1996

Tourism in Egypt was harmed for approximately two years following the terrorism period of the early 1990s, but a return to violence in 1996 saw a rapid response by the experienced Egyptian authorities—and the tourism turnaround was relatively fast.

A wide variety of methods [is] used by terrorists. However, hijacking and skyjacking of cruise ships and planes have been popular methods of terrorism, as well the destruction of such transportation systems by bombs or missiles. The link with tourism is obvious.

Wall 1996

The media have a tendency to cover such terrorist events with graphic visual detail—which builds a potentially distorted picture of the events and the apparent risks of travelling to countries that have come under the negative media gaze. Table 7.7 (page 178) shows an obvious relationship between the negative events and Northern Ireland's ailing tourism. Meanwhile, the Republic of Ireland steadily expanded its tourism in line with world growth trends. The chart in Figure 7.4 (page 175) shows this in linear form.

Marketing of destinations, and image implications, following negative media events are discussed in more detail in Chapter 9.

Signs of Change in Northern Ireland—Importance of Self-Image

Following the ground-breaking peace agreement in 1998, Northern Ireland's tourism industry received a great potential boost. Figure 7.4 (page 175) shows a small improvement in tourist arrivals to Northern Ireland—even in the lead-up to a possibly sustainable peace in the region. The Northern Ireland Tourist Board (NITB) reported that, despite a drop of one per cent in overall arrivals in 1996–97 (due to a fall in visitors from Great Britain, down three per cent, and the Republic of Ireland, down seven per cent), overseas markets picked up (continental Europe increased by eight per cent, and USA by nine per cent). The increased arrivals from the USA is a very good sign of the perceived general safety improvement in Northern Ireland—because the US market is extremely sensitive to terrorist threat.

Figure 7.4 Evolution of tourism's key indicators in Northern Ireland

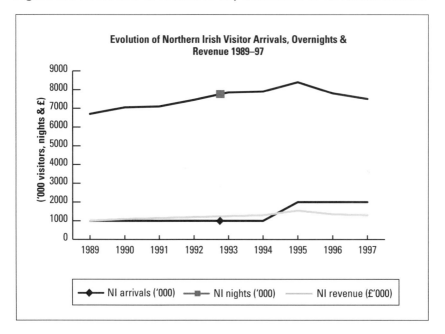

Source: Author's presentation (data from Northern Ireland Tourist Board 1998)

Before the softening of tensions in the early-to-mid 1990s, if one were to look at the chronology of terror striking Northern Ireland in the past thirty years (see Table 7.7, page 170), the prospects of a solution could never have been foreseen. Nor would it be possible to believe that tourism in Northern Ireland could be restored to normative levels or, at least, back on par with the Republic of Ireland. Yet it has . . .

> When the IRA [Irish Republican Army] hung up its holsters in 1994, the number of visitors shot up by 65%. Demand for accommodation soared and the tourist board had to set up an emergency 'welcome centre' to cope with requests for information . . . Whatever their reasons for visiting, the arrival of this new breed of tourist has created a 'boomlet' for those only too happy to cater for their curiosity
>
> Kelly 1997

It appeared that the more intrepid travellers were very quick to satisfy their curiosity about this small region that had received so much media attention over the previous twenty-five years. This is a type of tourism similar to 'war tourism'—but after the fact. In the Dutch language there is a compound word used to describe the phenomenon of people wanting to look at accidents on the road, and it can also be used to explain this tourist motivation. The word is *kijkfile*, which literally means 'look file'—or a traffic jam that occurs in the opposite lane of a freeway following an accident in the other direction. This version of 'rubber-necking' (as it is more commonly known in English) is also a tourist phenomenon—one that the Northern Irish tourism principals have been quick to capitalise upon.

The peace progress in 1998, culminating in the new Northern Ireland Assembly in May–June, led to renewed optimism in the tourist industry. A report on the BBC's news website elaborated on this:

> The recent progress in the peace process in Northern Ireland could create 8000 jobs in an expanding tourism industry, a minister said. Northern Ireland minister Paul Murphy hailed the potential for economic and industrial development following the creation of the new assembly.
>
> He was outlining £7000 million budget plans for the province to the Northern Ireland Grand Committee. From February, responsibility for the budget will pass to the new assembly's ministers.
>
> 'It seems to me with the advent of peace and political stability as a consequence of the assembly, that the money allocated to the department of economic development, particularly £160 million for the industrial development board, that the opportunities before us for economic and industrial development inevitably will be enhanced by what we've seen in the last few months,' he said. He believed the assembly will be able to expand on the 'good work that has been done' on inward investment. Some £14 million had been put aside for the Northern Ireland Tourist Board, which he said was significant because as peace became evident, people would want to see the provinces 'great treasures'.
>
> 'I believe the sort of tourist industry we have seen in the south could be extended to Northern Ireland as well,' he told the committee. 'There is the potential to create, if we had in Northern Ireland the same opportunities as in the south, 8000 extra jobs,' he said.
>
> BBC 1998a

One week later, the tone and optimism had changed rather dramatically. The headlines read 'Violence turns Belfast into a "ghost-town"' (BBC 1998b). Petrol bombings, hijackings, and shootings leading up to the stand-off at Drumcree over the Orange Order's contentious marching routes caused the atmosphere in Northern Ireland to sour during the course of a week. Informal estimates by inn keepers put the losses to their takings at 75% due to the return to violence in Belfast. The chairman of the Northern Ireland Tourist Board, Roy Bailie, estimated that peak season losses in potential revenues due to the renewed fighting could be up to £40 million. This perhaps adds weight to Bar-On's (1996) assertions that the impact of terrorism on tourism is higher in peak season.

The assistant editor of the Belfast politics and arts magazine *Fortnight* said that, 'fear is the factor keeping people away from normally busy areas' (BBC 1998b). He was speaking about areas such as South Belfast, Sandy Row, and the university area. He added, 'No tourists are going to come here with these kinds of pictures being beamed around the world' (BBC 1998b).

Roy Bailie, on the other hand, was not as pessimistic. He believed more strongly in the will of the Northern Irish people to continue the good progress being made:

> Should stability return to our streets, I have no doubt that everyone involved in tourism across Northern Ireland will do their utmost to turn this situation around.
>
> BBC 1998b

This suggests that the will of the people in Northern Ireland, and perhaps that of the people of other regions afflicted with terrorism violence, is very important in changing the tourism environment because an improved self-image in a tourism-challenged place ultimately reflects the outward image. It appears that the Northern Irish have a good-humoured, stoical disposition, which lends well to this change in tourism mentality—as illustrated in the following comment:

> This waggish tendency may also explain why this otherwise unprepossessing industrial city, riven by sectarian conflict and battered by economic misfortune, has continued to attract thousands of sightseers.
>
> Kelly 1997

Table 7.7   Principal media events and visitor arrivals in Northern
Ireland before 1990s peace process

Year	Nth Ire. Visitor Arrivals ('000)	Rep. Ire. Visitor Arrivals ('000)	Principal media events
Terror Years			
1972	435	1458	'Bloody Sunday', British army kill 13 Catholics in Londonderry (30 Jan.); IRA bomb kills 7 in Aldershot Eng. (Feb. 22); 'Bloody Friday', PIRA bombs Belfast killing 9, injuring 130 (21 July)
1973	487	1614	bombs in Belfast, Londonderry and London (8 March)
1974	486	1628	car bombs kill 22 in Dublin and 5 in Monaghan (17 May); 'Birmingham pubs bombing', 19 killed, 182 injured (21 Nov.)
1975	530	1688	no major incidents
1976	423	1720	5 Catholics killed (4 Jan.); 10 Protestants killed (5 Jan.)
1977	503	1953	no major incidents
1978	628	2299	PIRA fire bomb kills 12, injures 23 in County Down (17 Feb.); Oct.–Nov. rioting
1979	728	2360	PIRA kills Lord Mountbatten and 18 soldiers in Eire (27 Aug.)
1980	710	2258	no major incidents
1981	588	2188	riots in Belfast, Londonderry & Dublin when Bobby Sands (PIRA) dies of hunger strike (5 May)
1982	712	2250	PIRA bombs explode in Armagh, Ballmena, Belfast, Bessbrook, Londonderry, Magherafelt and Strabane (20 Apr.)
1983	865	2257	PIRA kill Catholic judge (16 Jan.) and land mine kills 4 UDR in County Tyrone (13 July); PIRA bomb kills 3 policemen, injures 33 at Ulster Polytechnic (4 Nov.); 3 killed in machine-gun attack on Pentocostal church in Armagh (17 Dec.)
1984	908	2579	PIRA assassinate assistant governor of Maze prison (6 Mar.) and kill 2 British soldiers in Fermanagh (18 May); PIRA bomb kills 5 in Brighton during Conservative Party conference (12 Oct.)
1985	863	2536	PIRA mortar attack kills 9 RUC officers in Newry (28 Feb.) and assassinate Catholic businessman (20 Aug.)
1986	824	2467	PIRA bomb kills 2 RUC officers in Armagh (1 Jan.)
1987	943	2664	Lord Gibson & wife killed by PIRA bomb (25 Apr.); RUC kill 8 IRA (8 May); PIRA bomb kills 11, injures 63 (8 Nov.)

1988	930	3007	3 PIRA shot in Gibraltar (6 Mar.); 3 killed at PIRA funeral (16 Mar.); 2 killed at IRA funeral (19 Mar.); PIRA kill 2 British airmen (1 in Germany, 1 in Netherlands) (1 May); UVF kill 3 Catholics in Belfast (15 May); PIRA kill 6 soldiers in Lisbon (6 June); PIRA blast kills 1 wounds 9 in London (1 Aug.); 8 soldiers killed, 28 injured by PIRA (20 Aug.); 3 PIRA killed by British army (30 Aug.)
1989	1091	3484	4 PIRA bombs hit British army barracks in Shrewsbury, 1 injured (20 Feb.); PIRA bomb Royal Marine School of Music, 9 killed, 22 injured (22 Sept.); soldier & daughter killed by PIRA in Germany (25 Oct.)
1990	1152	3666	PIRA bomb wounds 7 (14 May), kills 1 (16 May) in London; 3 shot and 1 dead in Lichfield and Germany (1 Jun.); PIRA bomb injures 8 in London (25 June), bomb kills member of parliament near London (30 July)

Peace Train

1991	1186	3535	PIRA fires mortars at Downing St. (Prime Minister's residence) injuring 3 (7 Feb.); bomb kills 1, injures 41 at railway station (18 Feb.); PIRA firebomb 5 London stores (1 Dec.); bombs in Armagh injuring 70 (12 Dec.); 25 PIRA bombs cause US$70 million in lost business (1–16 Dec.); Peter Brooke (Nth Ire. Sec.) says peace talks are 'a possibility, not a probability' (31 Jan.); IRA launches 3 mortars at 10 Downing St. (7 Feb.); talks between four parties renewed (25 Mar.), UVF and UFF announce joint ceasefire (22 Apr.), UFF breaches ceasefire killing Sinn Féin councillor Eddie Fullerton (25 May); 3 UDR soldiers killed in IRA lorry bomb (30 May); Sir Ninian Stephen announced as independent chairman for North–South talks (14 June); Stormont talks begin and end (3 July); Loyalist command ends ceasefire (5 July); Brooke attempts to broker talks again, but fails (16 Sep.)
1992	1254	3666	IRA bomb kills 8 Protestant workers (17 Jan.); 3 shot at Sinn Féin office on Falls Road by off-duty RUC officer (4 Feb.); Loyalists shoot 5 Catholics in Belfast (5 Feb.); delegates from North's 4 main parties meet at Stormont for 1st plenary session in new talks (9 Mar.); deadlock in talks (12 June), Ulster Defence Association banned from talks (10 Aug.); Strand 2 of talks resume after summer, Ian Paisley and Peter Robinson walk out, but return a week later (2 Sep.); talks flagging and 2000-lb bomb destroys forensic science labs in Belfast (23 Sep), Unionists walk from talks (10 Nov.)
1993	1262	3888	Warrington bomb kills 2 children, prompting peace initiative (20 Mar.); Hume and Adams meet and assert a right to 'national self-determination' of the Irish people (10 Apr.); document drafted by Hume presenting the broad principles of agreement (7 Oct.); 10 people killed after IRA bomb in Belfast (23 Oct.); 7 killed in UFF gun attack in Derry (30 Oct.); a channel of communication has existed between IRA and British for years—revealed by Observer (28 Nov.); Downing St. declares Nth Ire. will decide its future and IRA permanently renounces violence (15 Dec.)

Terror Tourism

1994	1294	4309	Irish government removes Section 31 broadcasting ban (19 Jan.); 6 Catholic men shot by loyalists in Loughinisland pub (18 June); IRA announces complete cessation of violence (6 Sep.); combined loyalist ceasefire called (13 Oct.); first official meeting between government officials and Sinn Féin—decommissioning of weapons a stumbling block (9 Dec.)
1995	1557	4821	British army ends daytime Belfast patrols (12 Jan.); Sinn Féin pulls out of talks, but 4 weeks later Adams states, 'IRA has not gone away' (17 June); Pres. Clinton shakes Gerry Adams hand in Falls Rd cafe (30 Nov.), George Mitchell (head of decommissioning body) calls for submissions from all parties (5 Dec.)
1996	1436	5282	Mitchell report published, laying down 6 principles of non-violence as a precursor for all-party talks (26 Jan.); 16 months of IRA ceasefires end with 1-tonne bomb detonated in London's Canary Wharf (9 Feb.); Sinn Féin polls very well in Nth Ire. Forum elections (30 May); significant loyalist figure shot IRA-style in a post office raid in Adare (7 Jun.); Sinn Féin barred from the opening inter-party talks (10 Jun.); 1.5-tonne bombs explodes in Manchester city centre (15 Jun.); Catholic taxi-driver shot by UVF (7 Jul.); 1.2-tonne bomb explodes in Killyhevlin Hotel, injuring 40 (following Orange March rioting in Portadown)—INLA blamed for explosion (13 July); IRA bombs go off at British army barracks in Nth Ire.—1 soldier killed (7 Oct.)

Tourism Derailed

1997	1415	n/a	Blitz of IRA bomb threats (5 Apr.); Labour Party wins in British general election opens the door to 10 Downing St. for Gerry Adams (1 May); PM Blair visits Nth Ire. and pushes contacts between govt officials (16 May); Blair bans any further talks with IRA following shooting of 2 RUC men (16 Jun.); Orange March leads to Portadown riots (6 July); Adams seeks a renewed ceasefire from IRA (20 Jul.); no progress in decommissioning (26 Aug.); IRA ceasefire validated by Mo Mowlam (Nth Ire. Sec.), IRA return to talks (29 Aug.); Sinn Féin signs up to Mitchell Principles (9 Sep.); Ulster Unionists join talks (17 Sep.); Adams and McGuinness meet Blair for the first time at Stormont Castle (13 Oct.), Gerry Devlin murdered by loyalists (5 Dec.); Adams and McGuinness meet at 10 Downing St. (9 Dec.); LVF leader shot in Maze prison by INLA (Republican splinter group)—killings on both sides in 4 weeks that follow (27 Dec.)

Countdown to Peace Tourism

1998	n/a	n/a	Sinn Féin rejects British and Irish governments' new settlement (17 Jan.); urgent meeting between Adams, McGuinness and Blair at 10 Downing St. (19 Jan.), IRA rejects Anglo–Irish paper, claiming it to be too Unionist (21 Jan.); Ulster Freedom Fighters accused of spate of killings and later admit it (22/23 Jan.); Catholic taxi-driver killed, bomb planted in Belfast club (24 Jan.); peace talks move to London, UDP leave (26 Jan.); Blair announces new inquiry into Bloody Sunday (29 Jan.); drug

dealer shot by Direct Action Against Drugs (alias IRA) (9 Feb.); 2 UDA men shot (10 Feb.); IRA suspects charged with 10 Feb. murders (14 Feb.); peace talks in Dublin (16 Feb.); Catholic executed IRA-style (18 Feb.), leading to Sinn Féin suspension from talks (20 Feb.); 2 bombs explode—blamed on Continuity IRA (23 Feb.); Catholic and Protestant friends shot by LVF (3 Mar.); mortar attack on police station—dissident Republicans blamed (10 Mar.); suspected RUC informant shot in Maze prison (15 Mar.); 1-tonne bomb discovered (22 Mar.); peace talks resume at Stormont with Sinn Féin back (23 Mar.); Republican dissident mortar attack on Forkhill RUC (24 Mar.); deadline for resolution set by Mitchell—Apr. 9 (26 Mar.); INLA shoot former RUC reservist (27 Mar.); enormous bomb intercepted at port bound for England (2 Apr.); Ulster Unionists threat to block final resolution 72 hours before deadline—Blair flies to Dublin to rescue peace deal (7 Apr.); Irish premier Ahern meets parties at Stormont, last-minute frantic negotiations, final deal on verge when Gerry Adams claims it to be impossible without a change in the position of the Ulster Unionists (8 Apr.); after sleepless night all parties broker a future for Nth Ire. amidst much jubilation and hope (9 Apr.)

Legend: IRA (Irish Republican Army); PIRA (Provisional Irish Republican Army); UDR (Ulster Defence Regiment); UVF (Ulster Volunteer Force), n/a (not available)

Source: author's table; data 1972–91 from Wall 1996; data 1991–98 from *Irish Times* 1998

A Chronology of Peace Tourism

Amid the chronology of fighting and terrorism, reciprocal murders, and executions in Northern Ireland (as shown in Table 7.7, page 178), it is not surprising to note the parallel failure of tourism. It is also not surprising to see tourism begin to flourish as peace beckoned—as shown by the improved international arrivals in 1988, but showing more marked improvement from 1991. The growth trend dipped a little in 1997, but a glance at the opposing forces of terror and mayhem might shed some light on why the 'peace train' did not generate a continuing upward improvement in tourism.

It will be interesting to see what happens to Northern Ireland tourism when the ugly face of terrorism serves only as a curio for *kijk* tourists ('look tourists'), and to see whether the NITB can use some of the millions of pounds on offer to develop and sustain tourism beyond the 'terrorism factor' into 'peace tourism'. We might see Northern Ireland rivalling the Republic of Ireland before too long.

Conclusion

Studies suggests a high sensitivity level to terrorism—perhaps irrationally high in the case of respondents from the USA, who are generally much more risk-averse in their tourism decision-making. This affects the tourism industry in more than merely financial terms. It damages the overall public image of the industry as being capable of resisting such outside forces and threats. It is also interesting to note the evidence that suggests that there is an irrational over-emphasis on the relative risk of terrorism to tourists—perhaps explained by media reports that concentrate on the horrors and the tactics, rather than the objective facts. Events in Northern Ireland compared with the Republic of Ireland, and terror and tourism in Israel, also throw interesting light on the relationship between terrorism and tourism.

There is a triangular relationship that ties the terrorist to the audience, and hence to tourism. Figure 7.5 shows this relationship in its simplest form—a connection that has grown stronger with the ever-expanding grip of the public media over world audiences. This is not to accuse the mass media of being a partner in terrorism, but it does suggest an important link between terrorist modes and objectives, and the potential publicity to be gained—such as the Tamil Tiger bombings in Colombo timed to achieve maximum world media coverage in the lead up to the cricket World Cup of March 1996. In this case, the short-term result was the cancellation of the Australian and West Indian cricket matches in Sri Lanka. The terrorist attack on Israeli Olympic athletes in the 1972 Munich Olympics is also a good example of terrorist opportunism—capitalising on impeccable timing, media exposure, and the impact on sports tourism.

Figure 7.5   The triangular relationship:
tourism–the media–terrorism

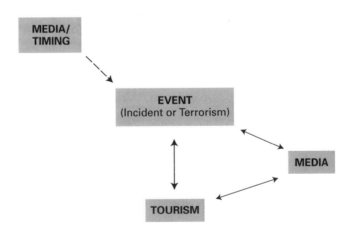

Source: original presentation

In the case of the Tamil Tiger bombings in Colombo, of the countries scheduled to play in the competition, two decided to boycott Sri Lanka. Why not the others? And why just Sri Lanka—in view of Pakistan's having also experienced bombings and threats for many years?

These are difficult questions to answer. It might reflect the conservative nature of the individual players, or their country of origin, or perhaps the image of the country even before the terrorist events took place. In the end the tourism industry has little say in the way the event is portrayed by the mass media. This process is summarised within the triangular relationship: Tourism–The Media–Event (see Figure 7.5).

Sri Lankan tourist authorities and government bodies, having a vested interest in creating the image of Sri Lanka as a safe place to visit, attempted to lobby the boycotting nations into changing their decision—in the knowledge that the publicity from such decisions would adversely affect their country in time to come.

The mass media clearly have a role to play as a critical source of information to potential tourists and to providers of tourist information. The degree of direct impact that this information has upon tourists, juxtaposed with the information being recycled and relayed indirectly through tourism professionals, is undefined. More specific research on tourism and the media is required to define the exact relationship. Enough is known currently to suggest that tourism managers should take more care to present safety elements with their product—as thoroughly and honestly as resources and information constrictions allow.

Discussion Time

- The full group is subdivided into smaller groups. Each group (of 3–5 members) chooses a different country from the table in *Fast Facts: The World's Most Dangerous Places*. Choose a country that interests the group, is well known for tourism of some kind, and has received some form of media attention in recent weeks or months. The group is to draw up an anti-terrorism strategy for the tourism industry in the country. The information in Chapter 7 should act as a guide to the areas of interest in this exercise—for example, air-travel strategy, airport security, promotional issues, and perceptions of terrorism.
- The anti-terrorism tourism strategies can be presented as case studies to the full group, or submitted to the group facilitator in report format.

8

Case Study II
Mega-events as a Tourism/Media Merry-Go-Round—The Olympics Example

SYNOPSIS OF CHAPTER

- What a mega-event is and how it relates to tourism

- The intrinsic importance to tourism and the media of the Olympics

- The links among sports, tourism, and communication

- *Fast Facts:* TV sports rights in Europe

A mega-event is a critical example of tourism that, without the influence of the media, would not exist in the form that we presently understand it.

What is a Mega-Event?

A mega-event has been (perhaps too narrowly) defined in the following terms:

> We shall define a mega-event as an event with (a) large numbers of participants or visitors and (b) worldwide publicity. We shall exclude, however, those events which have a special local touch like festivals in Bayreuth or Salzburg and events which take place in existing large congress halls because in both cases the facilities exist already. Our main concern are those mega-events which could take place almost anywhere in the world, like olympic games, world cups, etc.
>
> Socher & Tschurtschenthaler 1987

Perhaps to properly understand the term 'mega-event', we need to break the term into two parts—taking the second part first.

An Event

Socher and Tschurtschenthaler's definition (quoted above) excludes purely local events and those that occur in pre-existing congress halls—which means, implicitly, that an event must be temporary in nature and only in a temporary structure to be truly called an event. The most important element, to be genuinely able to call an event a 'mega' event, is that it receive worldwide publicity. Why this should preclude events that happen to be conducted in or on pre-existing structures is beyond reason.

A tourist event is any short-term happening that, by express purpose or coincidence, attracts a significant number of local, national, or international visitors. It might be once-off, annual, biannual, triannual, and so on. In the cases where the event is manufactured (a world-renowned music festival such as Woodstock, USA, or the little-known Antique Fair in Kyneton, Australia), there is a clear intention to amuse, entertain, or simply attract attention to itself for whatever purpose—whether it be profit, political motivation, gifts, rewards, and so on. A 'coincidental event' might be a natural phenomenon that occurs on a regular basis (regular enough for visitors to plan to witness it)—such as a solar eclipse. Others might be the crazy antics of a small group of devotees performing dangerous or amusing acts that draw visitors. These might begin to attract attention through word-of-mouth and eventually become a regular tourist event (for example, the cliff divers in Acapulco). Other examples of 'events' include swimming with the dolphins at Monkey Mia in Western Australia, or the return of the penguins at Phillip Island in Victoria.

In tourism circles, both business and academic, the expression 'an event' has, in more recent years, been associated with the grouping of like-motivated tourism exercises, under the anagram 'MICE':

Meetings;
Incentives;
Conference/Convention/Congress;
Exhibition/Exposition.

What is Mega?

A word of ancient times, but popular in modern usage, 'mega' means something that is exceptionally large—whether that be in physical terms or in terms of prestige. The modern colloquial usage fits in with the original Greek term—which really means 'great', but is often taken to mean 'multiplied by a million' (as in 'megahertz' or 'megabyte').

A Mega-Event

Combining the two terms, a 'mega-event' is a happening or unique event (an exhibition, fair, sports event, concert, and so on) that is limited in duration and, through mass attention, is magnified in physical or fiscal size. Attention might be drawn to the event through paid advertising, or be gained through free publicity and snowballing media attention.

Ritchie (1984) also calls mega-events 'hallmark events' and goes on to give seven classifications and some (rather Canadian-oriented) examples under each (see Table 8.1, page 187). Some additional, more recent examples have been added to this table.

Ritchie & Yangzhou (1987) also define mega-events in more technical terms as being:

> ... major one-time or recurring events of limited duration, which serve to enhance the awareness, appeal and profitability of a tourism destination in the short- and/or long-term. Such events rely for their success on uniqueness, status, or timely significance to create interest and attract attention.
>
> Ritchie & Yangzhou 1987

This definition speaks of the importance of attracting attention to the event, but does not elaborate on how this should be done. More explicit reference to the role of the media is needed to capture the nature of a mega-event.

Following the first academic conference dedicated to the study of mega-event tourism, conducted in the Mid-Sweden University in 1997, the 'Ostersund Declaration of Mega Event Tourism' was created. It examined:

- the effects of mega-events in image creation for countries, regions, and local tourism;
- the short- and long-term effects of mega-events relating to the attraction of visitors, and the social and economic consequences derived from them;
- the importance of mega-events for the achievement of key economic and social goals;
- developing strategies for hallmark events to be conducted within the general framework of local, regional, and national tourism policy planning; and
- the approaches to optimise the tourism impacts of mega-events.

The following recommendations were made:

- that research should be directed towards better understanding of the above relationships;
- that mega-events be analysed in terms of the social, economic, environmental, cultural, and physical effects;

- that there be an improvement in global coordination of mega-event handling and research;
- that there be an improvement in the standards and methodology of research to enable consistent global comparisons between events;
- that there be greater cooperation between governments, universities, and professional sectors to aid social and economic development stemming from mega-events.

Fayos-Sola 1997

Table 8.1 Hallmark/mega-events by classification

Classification	Examples
World fairs or expositions	Expo 1967 Montreal; Expo 1986 Vancouver; Expo 1988 Brisbane; Expo 1992 Seville; Expo 1998 Lisbon; Expo 2000 Hannover
Unique carnivals and festivals	Mardi Gras Rio De Janeiro, New Orleans, Sydney; Nottingham Festival; Melbourne Big Day Out; Oktoberfest Munich; Calgary Stampede; Running of the Bulls, Pamplona
Major sports events	Summer Olympics; Winter Olympics; World Cup Soccer; AFL Grand Final; State of Origin Rugby League
Significant cultural and religious events	Oberammergau Germany; Papal Coronation Rome; Royal Wedding London; Death of Diana, Princess of Wales; Pilgrimage to Mecca; Mexico's Day of the Dead
Historical milestones	Los Angeles Bicentennial; ANZAC Day marches; Australia's Bicentennial; Mexico's Day of Independence
Commercial & agricultural events	Wine Purchasing in France; Royal Winter Fair, Toronto; Melbourne Show; Floriade 1982 Amsterdam
Major political events	Presidential inaugurations; papal/royal visits; funerals; political handovers

Source: based on Ritchie 1984, and Ritchie & Yangzhou 1987

Tourism, Mega-Events, and the Media

Figure 8.1 (page 188) represents tourism and the media, treated as a linked entity, working together to generate a mega-event. Tourism can influence a mega-event (when the event draws on a known tourist destination or attraction for its audience or publicity) and, in turn, a mega-event can influence tourism (because people will travel to experience an important event). However, the media's influence is critical, taking a simple event and transforming it into a mega-event through mass audience potential and, according to Roche:

Publicity effects, together with scale of media and sponsorship income, need to be built into our definition of what counts as a mega-event.

Roche 1992

Thus the suggestion is that, without the media, a mega-event is basically a simple event.

In the other direction, a mega-event also has some influence or 'bargaining power' over the media. For example, the Olympic Games wield substantial power over television channels bidding for the right to televise the event worldwide. This bidding process, in itself, possibly has valuable publicity effects for both the bidding city and the event.

. . . advertising time on world media, equivalent to £25 million sterling, was gained by the £5 million bid. Cynics are suggesting that mega-events bids, without the event, give a greater weight of net benefits!

Travis & Croize, cited by Roche 1992

Following the 1999 corruption scandal surrounding the Salt Lake City Winter Olympics bid, and questions being asked about earlier bids by unsuccessful bidding cities (for example, Beijing, China), even more media attention is cast on this fiercely competitive bidding process.

Figure 8.1 The mega-event molecule

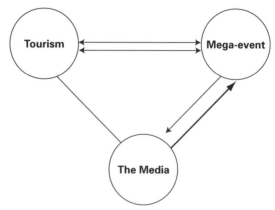

Source: Author's presentation

The Olympic Games

The IOC [International Olympic Committee] is known for putting on the biggest show on earth . . . the most participants in history . . . spectators on site and the greatest television audience ever.

Rozin 1996

The modern Olympic Games are a mega-event in every facet. As Roche observes:

> ... media presentation of the event also inevitably provides a certain amount of free and generally positive publicity for the host city.
>
> Roche 1992

Although this publicity is difficult to quantify, there is fervent competition to host the Games. During the 17-day event every four years, virtually the whole world pays attention to the Games through television, radio, and print. Summer and winter Olympic events are now staggered, alternating every two years, so the spotlight returns to the Olympic flag, rings, and motto (*Citius, Altius, Fortius*—'faster, higher, stronger') twice as often.

History of the Olympic Games

The rise of the Olympic Games to mega-event status has not been as smooth a ride as a contemporary observer might believe. From the beginning of the modern Games in 1896, the founder of the new Olympic movement, Baron Pierre de Coubertin, faced financial concerns in the lead-up to the event. He was eventually bankrolled by two eminent Greek industrialists. The Games fought its way to the top over the following hundred years (see Table 8.2).

Table 8.2 Olympic Games comparisons (1896–1996)

Description	Athens	Atlanta
Days	5	17
Sports	9	26
Events	32	271
Countries	13	200
Athletes	311	10 000+
Tickets available	60 000 (est.)	11.2 million
Funding	Donations 67%; Stamps 22%; Tickets/coins/medals 11%	Television 34%; Sponsors 32%; Tickets/retail/other 8%

Source: Based on tables from IOC 1996a

The Games' calling is to promote higher achievement in sport and peace in the tradition of the ancient games in Greece. Ironically, the modern Games have suffered from war and political considerations. World Wars I and II affected the successful running of the Games (see Table 8.9, page 204). Rioting in Mexico City (1968) was intended to raise awareness of the urban poverty in this city, and the hypocrisy of conducting what was felt to be a glamour event at the heavy expense of the local people.

In 1972, the Games reached their lowest point after terrorism found its way into the heart of the Olympic movement. Using the Munich Games as a backdrop, Islamic fundamentalists kidnapped and murdered Israeli Olympians to direct attention to their cause. The Games slid a little further in Moscow in 1980, again under the watchful eyes of millions of viewers, when the US government officially boycotted the Games.

Negative media attention and skyrocketing costs almost crushed the modern Games completely. However, the Los Angeles Games in 1984:

> ... proved that sophisticated marketing could transform an almost bankrupt Olympic Movement (Montreal is still paying for the 1976 Games) into the greatest sports marketing event of the twentieth century. For companies who can link their names and products to the Olympics, the Games are a commercial goldmine.
>
> Stephens 1996

Despite this, at the 1988 Calgary Winter Olympics, early experimenting with the economics of television rights failed to pay dividends for the American Broadcasting Company (ABC) in the USA. ABC paid US$309 million for the rights, but underestimated advertising demand—resulting in a net loss of approximately US$100 million (Roche 1992). Nevertheless, the television networks soon regrouped with the value of hindsight and, at present:

> The role of media and sponsorship is most clear in the case of premier mega-events like the Summer and Winter Olympic Games. The sale of television rights has, for many years, contributed a major and (unusually) continually inflating proportion of the *gross income* earned by Olympic event organizers, for instance.
>
> Roche 1992

For example, in the centennial Games (1996), television represented 34 per cent of Games funding (IOC 1996a).

The broadcasting history of the Games has, on the whole, been an example of success—through continuous growth in the number of countries where broadcasts are available. Organisers of the Games tend to pride themselves on being able to deliver their message of hope, peace, and goodwill to every corner of the globe. As Richard Pound (IOC) put it:

You turn on the [television] set and see athletes of the world . . . trying as hard as they can to win and yet remaining friendly. It says something to the rest of the world about what is really possible.

Rozin 1996

The first experiments with television coverage of the Olympics occurred with the Berlin Games in 1936. Television became a genuine force in the Games in 1960, when the first European-wide live broadcast by the European Broadcasting Group (EBU) was negotiated. Incidentally, the EBU still has the right to transmit the Games, having been given the continuing rights despite a much higher bid (US$2 billion) by the rather more commercially oriented News Corporation—headed by Rupert Murdoch. Murdoch has had, and continues to have, great success in televising sports via pay-per-view television in Europe and the USA. He has also attempted to branch out into sports-team ownership with his bid to purchase the Manchester United soccer team (September 1998).

The IOC's decision to take the lower (EBU) bid reflects its desire to remain available to as wide an audience as possible, and to stay with a proven entity (EBU) with more than 25 years' experience (Rozin 1996). The IOC's goal is to be watched by the entire world, and this appears increasingly more feasible—with every Games being made available to more and more countries, as shown in Table 8.3 (page 192). (The exception was Melbourne, where distance and technology limited exposure.)

Much of this continuing improvement can be attributed to improvements in technology, but a great deal must also be put down to the globalisation and recognition of the Olympics name and what it symbolises (see Figure 8.2, page 194). The build-up of expectation over four years is also a factor in this.

It is interesting to compare the average television audiences and the number of countries televising the Olympics compared with other significant sporting mega-events of our times (Tables 8.4a, 8.4b).

Table 8.3   Number of countries broadcasting the Olympic Games

Year	Host City	Number of Countries
1936	Berlin	1
WWII	WWII	WWII
1948	London	1
1952	Helsinki	2
1956	Melbourne	1
1960	Rome	21
1964	Tokyo	40
1968	Mexico City	n/a
1972	Munich	98
1980	Moscow	111
1984	Los Angeles	156
1988	Seoul	160
1992	Barcelona	193
1996	Atlanta	220

Source: IOC 1996/97, Zenith Media 1996/97

Table 8.4a   Rankings of worldwide sport programs (audience)

Ranking	Year	Event	Daily Av. Cumulative Audience ('000)
1	1996	Olympic Games	1208
2	1994	Olympic Winter Games	669
3	1994	World Cup (soccer)	618
4	1996	Euro '96 (soccer)	445
5	1995	World Athletics Championships	412
6	1995	Formula 1 (racing cars)	366
7	1996	US Superbowl (gridiron)	134
8	1995	Wimbledon (tennis)	106
9	not provided	World Cup (rugby)	84
10	not provided	World Series (US baseball)	5

Source: IOC 1996/97

Table 8.4b   Rankings of worldwide sport programs (number countries televising)

Ranking	Year	Sports Event	Number of countries televising
1	1996	Olympic Games	214
2	1995	World Athletics Championships	207
3	1996	Europe '96 (Finals) (soccer)	192
4	1994	World Cup (soccer)	188
5	1996	US Superbowl (gridiron)	187
6	1996	Wimbledon (tennis)	167
7	1996	NBA Finals (US basketball)	151
8	1995	Formula 1 (racing cars; av. race)	127
9	1994	Olympic Winter Games	120
10	not provided	World Cup Rugby	100

Source: IOC 1996/97

The recognition of certain entities around the world has become possible with the globalisation of names, people, companies, and so on through the media. The world's response to the death of Diana, Princess of Wales in 1997 is a sign of the times—the power of the media to elicit emotional responses in their audiences. In the wake of her tragic accident, people wept, sent flowers, and donated copious amounts of money to a fund that had not yet been set up to manage the money. One person was even quoted as saying that the experience was as if a member of the immediate family had been lost. It would be interesting to know how the real members of this person's family would respond to the comparison between them and (essentially) a fictitious character in their 'real' lives.

Individuals recognise and often recall symbols or images with uncanny accuracy. The Olympic Games has benefited from this unusual phenomenon. This is exemplified in the results of a survey conducted to examine company logo recognition (Figure 8.2, page 194).

The Games as a Media Merry-Go-Round

Although the spirit of the Olympic Games remains a showcasing of the 'best of the best' in certain sports, there is a very prominent battle for supremacy being fought by the 'best of the best' in media and sponsor boardrooms around the world. The Games 'got smart'. According to Richard Pound (IOC member and chairman of the Atlanta Coordination Commission):

Figure 8.2 Company logo recognition

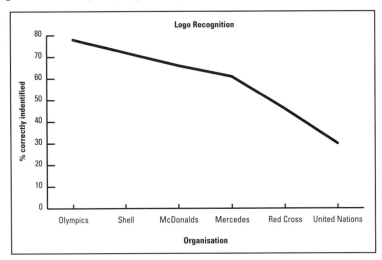

Source: Rozin 1996

The progress of sport as an international phenomenon over the last 100 years could not have been possible without the support of sponsors and the business community.

IOC 1996a

Television and the media have certainly intensified the commercial appeal of the Games (and Olympic logo) in the past two decades, shown in the comparison between the 1992 and 1996 Games' media facts and figures in Table 8.5.

Table 8.5 Media Olympic broadcasters 1992, 1996

Description	Barcelona 1992	Atlanta 1996
No. countries	193	220
Host coverage	2700 hours	3000 hours
Cumulative global audience	16.6 billion	20 billion
Unduplicated audience	4 billion	3.5 billion
No. hours	161	171
No. advertisers	130	59
Peak audience rating (USA)	22.2	27.2
Television rights (per quadrennium)	US$0.8 billion	US$1.7 billion

Source: IOC 1996a

It is interesting to note that the 1996 Games showed increases in all categories, from number of broadcasters to the highest-rating programme (number of people tuning in to watch television at the same given time), but that the number of advertisers was smaller. This was part of a new approach to marketing the Olympics and sport in general.

The new approach involved having fewer sponsors/advertisers who were locked-in to the Games at much higher premiums to advertise, and who were required to make 'up-front' payments to associate themselves with the Games as 'official sponsors'. Different classes of official sponsors were defined, with different rights to use the Olympic name and symbols under different guidelines. For example, in 1996, TOP III ('The Olympic Partners, phase III') worldwide sponsors paid the most, and had the greatest liberty to use Olympic references. These companies included: Coca-Cola, Kodak, Visa, Bausch & Lomb, *Sports Illustrated*, Xerox, Matsushita/Panasonic, IBM, UPS, and John Hancock. There were also local host Games sponsors, who paid less and had less Olympic Games entitlements. In 1996, ACOG (Atlantic Committee for the Olympic Games) sponsors included: Sensormatic, York, Randstad, Bellsouth, Georgia Power, Blue Cross, Scientific-Atlanta, Borg-Warner Security, Wheel of Fortune, General Motors, BMW, Holiday Inn, Nissan, Avon, Worldtravel Partners, Texaco, American Gas Association, International Paper, Textron, General Mills, Brunswick Corporation, Dial, and Merill Lynch). There were also advertisers and partners on a country-by-country basis (through Olympic broadcasters in each country).

The Centennial Games (1996)

The centennial Olympic Games presented the world with many memorable firsts on the playing fields of the elite, but the Games also represented a giant step forward in the relationship between the media and the Games. The president of the International Olympic Committee, Juan Antonio Samaranch, usually proudly proclaims at the closing of each Games that they were 'the best Games ever'. Improvement and progress are highly valued principles in the Olympic Movement, and the role that the media play in this continuing ascendancy is very important. However, reports throughout the centennial Games highlighted the difficulties experienced by organisers in coordinating the activities of almost 11 000 athletes, 17 000 media representatives, and more than 2 million spectators spread around the various venues in Atlanta, USA. Some crucial communication problems between the organisers and the media caused severe public-relations tensions in the early part of the Games. Sports results were not being transmitted in a timely fashion to the media centre, leaving journalists little alternative—in lieu of sports stories—but to report on the poor organisation of the Games. Hence, the story behind the story is that the Games must continue to grow in terms of media hype and television coverage to justify being called 'the best Games ever', but the physical event itself perhaps needs to be scaled down to a more manageable size in future

Mega-Results from the Centennial Games

The centennial Games were available to an estimated 226 countries worldwide—33 more than in Barcelona in 1992. It was estimated that 142 countries showed the Games on national channels, 89 with additional foreign channel access, and that 66 countries received satellite coverage. The IOC estimated that, in its major television markets, multiple broadcasters averaged approximately 23 hours a day over the 17-day event. From this almost 24-hour coverage, they calculated their cumulative gross audience to be 19.7 billion viewers, an increase of 2.9 billion over Barcelona's—with the largest improvements being experienced in Asia and America. Western Europe showed more coverage than any other region (24 per cent of the total 1996 Games coverage), followed by Africa (14 per cent), eastern Europe (12 per cent) and east Asia (10 per cent). Broadcasters worldwide paid more for the rights to show the centennial Games than any previous Games—the magnitude of which is shown in Table 8.6 (page 197).

As for the kind of attention that the Olympics is capable of attracting on a country-by-country basis, the consumption-per-inhabitant figures in Table 8.7 (page 198) show some astounding results. Such calculations give broadcasters and the IOC an indication of the penetration they have into the average household. For example, the average weighted audience per minute of Olympic coverage is estimated and extrapolated to arrive at a consumption per individual—based on national populations and program ratings. It is of interest that the Australian consumption of the Atlanta Games exceeded that of all other countries. Sporting interest in Australia is known to very high—with active participation and spectatorship well above average. Viewership and spectatorship of Australian Football League (AFL) matches reflects this. The AFL Grand Final in September each year consistently scores extremely high sports ratings in southern & western Australia, followed closely by State of Origin Rugby League matches in New South Wales and Queensland. The opening ceremony of the 1996 Olympic Games received a very good rating for a sporting program in Australia (40.0)—see Table 8.8 (page 199) for the top five rated Olympic events in 1996 in Australia.

Table 8.6   Worldwide 1996 Olympic Games broadcasters and rights fees

Countries	Broadcasters	Rights Fees 1992 (US$)	Rights Fees 1996 (US$)
Europe	EBU	94.5 mill	250 mill
Canada	CBC	16.5 mill	20.7 mill
USA	NBC	401 mill	456 mill (+30 mill revenue share)
Central/Sth America	OTI	3.55 mill	5.45 mill
Australia	Channel 7	33.87 mill	30 mill
New Zealand	TVNZ	5.9 mill	5.0 mill
Japan	Japan pool	62.5 mill	99.5 mill
Korea	Korea pool	7.5 mill	9.75 mill
Philippines		0.3 mill	1.0 mill
Chinese Taipei		1.1 mill	1.9 mill
Africa	URTNA	0.1 mill	IOC paid
South Africa	SABC	6.0 mill	6.7 mill
Caribbean	CBU	0.14 mill	0.19 mill
Asia	ABU/ASC	2.2 mill	8.0 mill
Arab States	ASBU	0.5 mill	3.4 mill
Puerto Rico		0.3 mill	0.75 mill

Legend: ASBU Arab States Broadcasting Union; CBC Canadian Broadcasting Corporation; CBU Caribbean Broadcasting Union; EBU European Broadcasting Union; NBC National Broadcasting Corporation; OTI Organisation of Television in Iberoamerica; SABC South Africa Broadcasting Corporation; TVNZ Television New Zealand; URTNA Union of National Radio and Television Organisations of Africa

Source: IOC 1996a; Sydney Olympics 2000

Table 8.7 Olympic Games television consumption per inhabitant per selected countries in 1996

Key Countries	Total Hours Watched 1996	Total Hours Watched 1992
Australia	66:27	21:30
Brazil	42:28	18:42
Great Britain	12:05	17:33
Japan	31:42	22:58
South Africa	11:18	06:05
USA	25:03	18:32

Source: derived from figures of IOC 1996/97, Zenith Media 1996/97

Figure 8.3 Television rights fees—total per quadrennial (in US$ millions)

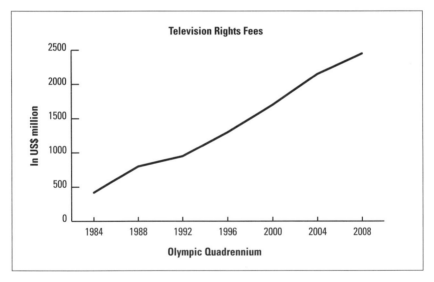

Source: Rozin 1996

Table 8.8 Top-rated sports programs on Channel 7, Australia, in the 1996 Games

Ranking	Olympic Program	Live/Highlights	Rating Achieved*
1	Opening Ceremony	Live	40.0
2	Swimming—Kieren Perkins 1500 m	Live	36.6
3	Women's basketball—Aust. vs USA	Live	35.9
4	Basketball & softball coverage	Highlights	32.8
5	Opening Ceremony	Highlights	29.5

Note: * see *Focus* on Nielsen ratings [page 33]

Source: Channel 7 Australia 1996

The results in Table 8.8 indicate that the Olympic Games have a powerful influence on sports-viewing patterns. Although not indicated here, they also compare very well to high rating non-sporting programs. The timing of the event is important. Its mega-status is orientated around the quadrennial nature of the event, the hype and buildup in all forms of media related to the hosting of the Games, the bidding wars, and the venue building (political and financial capital invested in running it successfully).

The IOC's Investment in the Media-Effects Argument

Chapter 5 of this book examined the media-effects argument and came to the conclusion that 'there is no direct relationship between *exposure* to information and *learning* of information' (Carter 1971). However Piel (1979), in his study examining the impact of free time and the mass media in Belgium, claims that 'no general criteria can be set to measure the impact of the mass media on leisure activities'. Despite this, as has been shown in this case study, the IOC places much value on the media, particularly television and sponsorship rights, as a source of income and, indeed, as a source of rejuvenation for the Olympic Movement. With so much at stake in these exclusive rights deals, what does the IOC do to protect its interests?

The IOC invests millions of dollars to protect the international television and sponsorship rights through monitoring schemes employed in important television and sports markets—such as western Europe, USA, Australia, China, and Russia. Professionals scan the various media during the Olympics looking for infringements of the Olympic television and sponsorships contracts.

Fast Facts: TV Sports Rights in Europe

Event	Period	Bought by	Price	Transmission
Olympics	2000–08	EBU	US$1.44 bn	Free to air
World Cup (soccer)	1998	EBU	US$1.35 mill	Free to air
World Cup (soccer)	2002–06	Kirch Group	US$2.27 bn	Pay TV
English Premiership (soccer)	1997–2001	BSkyB	US$1 bn	Pay TV
Dutch First Division (soccer)	1996–2004	Sport 7	US$7 mill (est.)	Free to air
Italian Premier (soccer)	1996–98	Telepiu	unknown	Pay TV
Formula 1 (Digital)	1996	BSkyB/Kirch	unknown	Pay TV
Formula 1 (UK)	1997–2001	ITV	US$100 mill	Free to air
Formula 1 (Italy)	1997–2001	RAI	US$100 mill	Free to air

Legend: EBU European Broadcasting Union; ITV Independent Television (UK); RAI Radio Televisione Italiana

Source: Short 1996

The monitoring of 'good sponsorship practice' is a fundamental in the continuing success of these television and sponsorship deals.

According to John Krimsky, the secretary-general of the United States Olympic Committee (USOC):

> Parasite marketing [or ambush marketing] jeopardises the ability to stage the Games . . . taking food out of the mouths of young athletes.
>
> Quoted by Rozin 1996

Stephens (1996) supports this view, and also quotes marketing director of the IOC, Michael Payne as saying that ambush marketing:

> . . . is extremely serious for us as it has the potential to destroy the value of paid-for sponsorship.
>
> Quoted by Stephens 1996

Ambush marketing is the misappropriation of Olympic copyrights (rings, flag, name) without the paid-up, official right to do so. The objective of the IOC is to protect the official sponsors who have paid millions of dollars for commercial exposure from others attempting to get such exposure for free. Hence the IOC protects its partners with vigilant television monitoring around the world—particularly in and around the Olympic sites. The IOC is concerned enough about this issue to invest significant sums of money to police their territory.

Relationship Between the Games and Tourism

To this point, we have looked at the Olympic Games as an example of a mega sporting and media event, but we have not examined the tourism implications directly.

Standeven and De Knop make this very important connection between sport and tourism:

> Sport during holidays is becoming popular. The main sports are walking, hiking and swimming, but also new sports like sailing and tennis.
>
> Standeven & De Knop 1999

This began with 'Club' formula holidays, which were popular in the 1970s and 1980s, and evolved into 'sport tourism'—which first came to the attention of tourism observers in the 1990s.

Definition of 'Sport Tourism'

> All forms of active and passive involvement in sporting activity, participated in casually or in an organised way for non-commercial or business/commercial reasons, that necessitate travel away from home and work locality.
>
> Standeven & De Knop 1999

More and more people are interested in activity vacations. From this has arisen a very lucrative niche market for tourism providers. Examples include horse-riding, rafting, hang-gliding, paraflying, parachuting, and so on. The trips are arranged with the exclusive intention of practising a sport with which the tourist is familiar, or trying something new.

Some sport-specific tourism is directed at the spectator rather than at the participant. For example, agents and operators made a very healthy profit arranging tickets and trips to cater for the 'connoisseur observers' in France for the 1998 (soccer) World Cup. The interrelationship between sport and tourism is shown in Figure 8.4 (page 202).

Tourism and Sport: a Two-Way Relationship

Standeven and De Knop (1999) also posit that sport might as easily flow from tourism experiences as it does in the reverse. They offer the example of ski vacationers, whose interest in the sport, despite having no local (natural) facilities, leads to the development of the ski industry elsewhere to cater for the incoming enthusiasts. Another example is a resort holiday that exposes tourists to a sport—such as diving—and ignites interest in the sport at home. When the sport is pursued locally it eventually leads to a

Figure 8.4   Tourism as it flows through sport

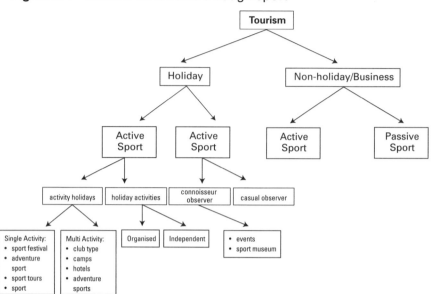

Source: Standeven & De Knop 1999

sub-industry of dive centres and schools in source destinations. The Olympics, if viewed from the tourism side of the relationship, contributes to this.

> Examples of tourism bringing permanent value to sport in the local community may be found in facilities constructed with a tourist objective but which have spin-offs beyond their initial function such as those for the Los Angeles or Barcelona Games or the World Student Games in Sheffield. However, it is important to remember that facilities constructed to international standards are generally over-sophisticated for community use.
>
> Standeven and De Knop 1999

The two-way relationship discussed here is shown in Figure 8.5 (page 203).

The Role of Tourism in Sporting Mega-Events

> The Olympics are not just a global quadrennial sports event, but, summer or winter alike, a major tourist attraction.
>
> Ahn et al. 1987, cited in Standeven & De Knop 1999

Figure 8.5 The interrelationship between sport and tourism

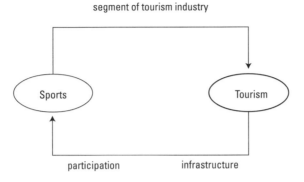

Source: Standeven & De Knop 1999

The weight of evidence suggests that localised participative or spectator sports contribute to tourism (for example, local teams travelling to play away from home), and that tourism leads to local sports development (infrastructure and participation; Figure 8.5). When the sport is a mega-event, there is an added ingredient to the equation—the media which provide a communication between the sporting event and a much wider audience. Hence, the relationship between tourism and sports mega-events is slightly different from that between tourism and sport in general. See Figure 8.6.

Figure 8.6 The interrelationship between sports mega-events and tourism

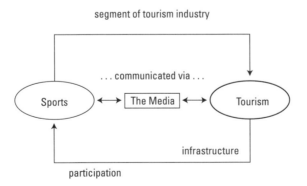

Source: based on Standeven & De Knop 1999

Table 8.9 Chronology of the Olympics

Year	Dates	City	Nations	Events	Competitors
1896	6 Apr.–15 Apr.	Athens	14	43	245
1900	14 May–28 Oct.	Paris	19	86	1 078
1904	1 Jul.–23 Nov.	St Louis	13	89	689
1908	27 Apr.–31 Oct.	London	22	107	2 035
1912	5 May–27 Jul.	Stockholm	28	102	2 437
1916	First World War				
1920	20 Apr.–12 Sep.	Antwerp	29	152	2 607
1924	4 May–27 Jul.	Paris	44	126	2 972
1928	17 May–12 Aug.	Amsterdam	46	109	2 884
1932	30 Jul.–14 Aug.	Los Angeles	37	117	1 333
1936	1–16 Aug.	Berlin	49	129	3 936
1940	Second World War				
1944	Second World War				
1948	29 Jul.–14 Aug.	London	59	136	4 092
1952	19 Jul.–3 Aug.	Helsinki	69	149	5 429
1956	22 Nov.–8 Dec.	Melbourne	67	145	3 178
1960	25 Aug.–11 Sep.	Rome	83	150	5 313
1964	10 Oct.–24 Oct.	Tokyo	93	163	5 133
1968	12–27 Oct.	Mexico	112	172	5 498
1972	26 Aug.–11 Sep.	Munich	121	195	7 121
1976	17 Jul.–1 Aug.	Montreal	92	198	6 043
1980	19 Jul.–3 Aug.	Moscow	80	203	5 283
1984	28 Jul.–12 Aug.	Los Angeles	140	221	6 802
1988	17 Sep.–2 Oct.	Seoul	159	237	8 473
1992	25 Jul.–9 Aug.	Barcelona	169	257	9 368
1996	19 Jul.–4 Aug.	Atlanta	197	271	10 000

Source: IOC 1996b

Conclusion

Mega-events, the media and tourism are inextricably linked. The Olympic Games is the biggest mega-event in the world, and marketing tactics harnessing the media and television rights have played an important part in this development. The marketing of sponsorship involving Olympic logos and other Olympic copyright materials has also been important.

Discussion Time

- There has been a lot of attention in the media about the over-commercialisation of mega-events—especially the Olympic Games. In small groups, discuss the importance of having sponsorship and commercialism in mega-events. In a simple figure or diagram of the group's own making, try to find the best place to insert or link commercialism and sponsorship to the other chief components in the tourism, media, and mega-events relationship. What are the implications of removing one of the components on the remaining ones?
- The group should be divided into smaller, working groups of 3–5. Each group should compose a list of the mega-events of which they are aware, and discuss what makes it a mega-event. In a table format, the group is then asked to write down all that they know about each mega-event in the first column (dates, features, attractions, audience, and so on) and, in the next column, write the source of this information. Was it television, newspapers, word-of-mouth . . . etc.? Once completed, the groups can reform into the larger group and, one by one, compare their lists with those of the other groups. Note the differences in facts and details among groups describing the same events. Also note the predominant information sources about mega-events—with the final objective being to establish a theory on which medium dominates mega-events.

9

Case Study III
Tourist Destination Marketing Following Negative Media Events

SYNOPSIS OF CHAPTER

- Destination marketing and the impact of negative media events

- Different forces affecting destination image and marketing—government travel warnings; Internet travel marketing; information as a self-fulfilling prophecy

- Travel promotion and public-relations strategies after media disasters vs promotion under normal conditions

- *Focus* on US State Department Travel Warnings and Classifications

- Tourism crisis management

Hurricane Mitch, which struck towards the end of [1998], has helped to blast Central America back into the headlines. The resulting crisis has been met with the usual muted response from the international community, and the press has embraced another horror story from the region with gusto. It's a tragedy made all the greater by the fact that Central America seemed on the point of emerging from its years of political upheaval—the signing of the Guatemalan peace accords at the end of 1996 marked the end of the region's final conflict—and asserting itself as a major travel destination. Having seen the pictures in the newspapers and on TV, you may be tempted to stay away. But it's worth remembering that contact can only help, rather than hinder, Central America, as it tries to recover from this latest natural disaster.

Lilley 1999

Introduction

Destination marketing can be used in three situations:

- to attract new visitors to an obscure destination;
- to encourage visitors to a destination with established, but flagging, tourism credentials;
- to re-market a destination that is, as a result of a disaster, experiencing a severe decline in tourism.

In the second scenario, the decline is usually over a relatively prolonged period. For example, Spain's Costa Del Sol experienced a growth in tourism from 1960 (0.4 million UK visitors) until 1988 (7.5 million UK visitors), but then suffered a gradual but worrying fall (to 7.0 million UK visitors in 1990). Tourism policy, after a valuable lesson, was changed (Waugh 1995)—with an improvement in the trend.

The third scenario can occur relatively quickly from a specific incident. For example, over a period of twelve months in 1993, Egypt lost an estimated US$1 billion in lost tourism following the publicity given to the murder of three tourists and the wounding of another dozen by Muslim extremists (Pizam & Mansfeld 1996).

This Case Study is concerned with this third scenario—the sudden loss (or potential loss) of tourism following 'bad press'. Even an event that has not been substantiated can still lead to a tourism 'disaster' if the media coverage is adverse.

What is Destination Marketing?

> Place promotion is defined as the conscious use of publicity and marketing to communicate selective images of specific geographical localities or areas to a target audience.
>
> Ward & Gold 1994

According to Kotler, Haider and Rein:

> . . . places increasingly compete with other places to attract their share of tourists, businesses, and investment. The marketing of places has become a leading economic activity and, in some cases, the dominant generator of local wealth.
>
> Kotler, Haider & Rein 1993

Promoting a destination in normal circumstances is a difficult task, but promoting a destination that faces tourism challenges—whether from negative press, or from infrastructural damage caused by natural or man-made disaster—is an altogether more arduous task. The first concern is to survive, followed by rebuilding the destination and its image while waiting for circumstances to change (recognising that this could take months or even years).

This Case Study will develop the theme of media effects from the demand side of destination marketing, but one must never ignore the supply side (the product). The old adage 'take care of the pennies and the pounds take care of themselves' might be reworded in this situation to 'take care of the supply and the demand takes care of itself'. However, this ignores a basic marketing ethos—that without demand there is no product (a destination to bother caring for) (De Groote & Nielsen 1998b). Taken a little further, given that a destination, by definition (Keller 1998), is a 'travel objective . . . tourists will visit because of the attractions they find there', it should be no surprise to find tourists reluctant to visit a place devastated by floods, famine, or internal turmoil. This Case Study aims to examine the relationship between demand-side marketing and tourism-challenged or obscured destinations.

What is a Negative Media Event?

A negative media event is the communication by the media of bad news, danger, annoyances, or other matters that would be considered unfavourably by the majority.

It should be noted that the event being communicated might or might not be factual. The net result is more or less the same whether or not the event actually occurred. People feel reviled, shocked, or afraid, and their degree of concern is reflected in their decision to 'decide', 'defer' or 'decline'—according to the '3Ds' model of travel decision-making (see Figure 6.1, page 127).

This phenomenon refers back to the concept of the 'abstract truth' (Lombardi 1990) attached to a media event in the face of little or no contradictory first-hand or eye-witness evidence. Essentially, this means people believe what they see, hear, and read in the media, viewing the media as the legitimate authority where no higher order authority (government warnings, airlines, first-hand accounts) makes assertions to the contrary.

An example of this occurred in the southern Mexican state of Chiapas, which hit the world headlines on 1 January 1994, following the uprising of a small band calling itself the *Ejercito Zapatista de Liberacion Nacional* (Zapatista National Liberation Army, or 'Zapatistas'), in San Cristóbal de las Casas and neighbouring towns. The primary intention of their uprising was to attract world media attention to the plight of the peasants of Chiapas—a mostly Indian underclass who suffered from a poor standard of health care, education, and civil rights. Some argued that this was a successful action in that it led to social reform (previously evicted peasants took over hundreds of farms in the region), and that its effects might even have been great enough to have contributed to the crash of the Mexican peso in 1995.

The Zapatistas' leader, Rafael Guillen, a former university lecturer from Tampico, fled deep into the jungle once the Mexican army targeted him for arrest. Chiapas received minor concessions—such as limited autonomy to Indians, redrawn voting boundaries, and acknowledgment of native languages and education. However these were never enacted into law. Over the years, the group received a sympathetic ear from Mexicans and foreigners alike, and high-profile visits from Oliver Stone to the Zapatista hideout added to their celebrity status. However, despite the good intentions of drawing media attention to the plight of the underprivileged, the fact remains that the action of the rebels has severely arrested tourism development in the region—despite the localisation of violence and the fact that tourists were never directly threatened.

By the beginning of 1997, the area had cooled off to the point where the more intrepid travellers or 'war tourists' returned. A magazine article (cited in Pizam & Mansfeld 1996), published around the time that the Zapatistas first hit the headlines, reported a Canadian tourist as saying that she wanted to visit Chiapas for three reasons: 'journalism, a tan and a revolution' Before the regional conflict, ethnic tourism predominated in Chiapas, but these would-be tourists were deterred by the danger and were replaced by tourists visiting explicitly because of the danger.

Then reports of a bus massacre in Chiapas reached the headlines, fanning the flames anew.

Discussions in Mexico regarding Chiapas have reached an impasse. Some in the country say it is better if tourism does not develop—because it would conceal the difficulties still faced by the peasant population under a veneer of tourist-inflated wealth that, without the full implementation of the Zapatistas' proposed reforms, would inevitably end up in the hands of a wealthy elite. Others, particularly those involved in tourism, say it is a great shame that tourists do not go to the state so they can see how beautiful it is, and see that it is *not* unsafe. After a discussion in August 1998 with a well-meaning Mexican restaurateur in a village on the Pacific coast, the present author was vehemently reassured that the area was perfectly safe, and that the media in Europe was ill-informed.

Effects of Travel Advice on Destination Marketing

In Chapter 4 of this book, the issue of public safety and government travel warnings was discussed. The issuing of public warnings is generally made via a nation's own diplomatic missions. Government travel warnings (see Figure 9.1, page 211) are not always published outright in the traditional mass media because this can cause political tension between the source and destination countries.

Sometimes, however, the production of diplomatic tension is the political intention of the source country—in order to take a moral or economic stand. For example, the violation of human rights in Mynamar (Burma) and Turkey has produced such reactions. This has been referred to previously as 'guilt-edged' tourism (see page 109). In these circumstances, the threat to tourists *per se* is not of principal importance, but the act of travelling to such countries apparently condones the regimes that perpetrate violations of human rights.

The consequences of these political manoeuvres are wide-ranging, affecting tourism principals in both the source and destination countries.

Impact of Travel Warnings on Destination Countries

From the point of view of the tourist destinations, it is vitally important that they actively conduct a full tourist security assessment—particularly related to their chief source markets—and that they engage in honest dialogue with national tourist offices (NTOs) and consular travel/ information services on safety issues. The aim is to rebuild confidence in the destination as fast as possible. Many foreign missions have much of this information online—such as the US State Department's *Travel Warnings & Consular Information Sheets*, or the Australian Department of Foreign Affairs & Trade's *Consular Information*.

In some cases, a source government with underlying political agenda actively courts the media to publicise their views on travel to a certain destination while ostensibly protecting the safety of tourists. This makes the tourism-resuscitation process after major negative media events all the more difficult. For example, the Reagan administration published warnings against flying to Athens airport in 1986—thereby nearly strangling tourism to Greece, and affecting tourism on a pan-European scale. In this situation, the fastest way to rebuild the tourism economy is to comply with the requests of source tourist governments. Tourism is a resilient force and, given the right encouragement and the outward signs of improvement to the problem in question, it can return to pre-disaster levels.

According to Geoffrey Lipmann, president of the World Travel & Tourism Council (WTTC), leisure tourism:

. . . is susceptible to external shocks. And it doesn't recover as quickly as business travel. The one certainty is tourism bounces back. Over the last 50 years the industry has grown faster than global gross domestic product.

Knight 1998

An example of this was the state of tourism in Indonesia in 1998. *Time* magazine reported (21 September 1998) that tourists entering through Ngura Rai airport decreased by 30 per cent in May 1998 compared with the same period in 1997. Hotel occupancy rates reached as low as 20 per cent in June/July 1998. However, within only five months of the highly publicised unrest in Indonesia, hotel rooms' occupancy had rallied back to 40 per cent in the Grand Hyatt Nusa Dua.

Figure 9.1   US State Department Travel Announcement Warning—Iraq

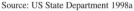

Source: US State Department 1998a

Impact of Travel Warnings on Source Countries

At home, good tourism providers, as principal information providers for tourists, should be up to date on travel conditions in destinations.

This was not the case in the present author's experience, however, when plans to go to Indonesia were put under a cloud by the student riots of May/June 1998. With flights reserved but not paid for (through a travel agency specialising in travel to South-East Asia), the author's expectation was that some sort of travel update would be issued by the provider to ask their clients if they still wished to travel—seeing that a potential coup d'état was under way in Indonesia. Weeks passed and it became clear that the client would have to contact the agent—rather than the reverse. Friends of the author in Indonesia advised, in early June, that they expected political unrest caused by growing economic hardship to spread slowly throughout the country.

Contact was made with the Belgian and Australian embassies. Both recommended a deferral—pending future events. The Belgian government actively issued warnings against travel to Indonesia—using state radio (Studio Brussels) and newspapers (in both French and Dutch). The Belgian government then took the unusual step of forcing tour operators to cancel their forthcoming trips to Java and the rest of Indonesia (even to Bali, which had attracted only a low-level warning at this time). In the USA warnings were issued that were 'picked up' by the media (*International Herald Tribune* 1998).

In the meantime, the author received no contact from the travel agent. Eventually, the author contacted the agent to advise that the flight option to Indonesia would not be taken up—with an explanation of the reasons for this decision. The attendant had apparently heard nothing of the difficulties in Indonesia. It is apparent that some travel agencies do not seek the most up-to-date travel-status information—either actively (by contacting consulates), or passively (by simply watching the daily news or reading newspapers).

A knowledge of whom to contact is obviously important in this situation, and more effort should be put into promoting the existence of the various associations, companies and institutions available to help travellers.

From the perspective of the tourism destination, a high priority should be their keeping the market well informed of the rebuilding process (after war, for example) or of safety improvements (after published criticism of safety issues).

Focus on US Travel Warnings

What are Travel Warnings, Consular Information Sheets & Public Announcements?

The US State Department has an orderly and practical method of distinguishing levels of travel safety. This is based on a basket of up-to-date political, health, economic, and social factors.

The State Department uses three classifications of notification. In decreasing order of importance, these are:

*   Travel Warnings;
*   Public Announcements; and
*   Consular Information Sheets

See Table 9.1 (page 215) for examples of countries in different classifications in 1998.

Travel Warnings

These are issued when the State Department decides to recommend that Americans should definitely avoid travel to a certain country.

Public Announcements

These are a means to disseminate information about terrorist threats and other relatively short-term situations posing significant risk to American travellers. In the past, Public Announcements have been issued to deal with short-term coups, bomb threats to airlines, violence by terrorists, and anniversary dates of specific terrorist events.

An example is Figure 9.2 which illustrates the US response to Indonesian student riots in June–July 1998.

Figure 9.2 US public announcement for Indonesia

PUBLIC ANNOUNCEMENT

U.S. DEPARTMENT OF STATE
Office of the Spokesman

INDONESIA

July 13, 1998

Sporadic small-scale demonstrations and disturbances continue to occur in various parts of Indonesia. Tourist areas in Bali have not been affected.

The political and economic situation remains unsettled.

Americans in all parts of Indonesia should avoid crowds and disturbances, and exercise prudence and caution.

Because of the possibility of robbery and two confirmed instances of expatriates being killed after entering taxis, Americans in Jakarta who require taxis are advised to engage a taxi from a major hotel queue or by calling a taxi company, rather than hailing one on the street.

All Americans in Indonesia should register with the U.S. Embassy in Jakarta (tel: 62 021 344-2211), the U.S. Consulate General in Surabaya (tel: 62 031 568-2287), or the U.S. Consular Agency in Bali (tel: 62 0361 233-605). Updated information is available from the U.S. Embassy in Jakarta or through the Embassy's home page at http://www.embassyjakarta.org.

This Public Announcement supercedes the Public Announcement for Indonesia issued June 11, 1998 and expires September 15, 1998.

Source: US State Department 1998a

Consular Information Sheets

This information is available for virtually every country in the world. Information Sheets include such information as location of the US embassy or consulate in the country, unusual immigration practices, health conditions, minor political disturbances, unusual currency and entry regulations, crime and security information, and drug penalties.

If an unstable condition exists in a country that is not severe enough to warrant a Travel Warning, a description of the condition(s) might be included under an optional section entitled 'Areas of Instability'.

Consular Information Sheets generally do not include advice, but present the information in a factual manner so travellers can make their own decisions concerning travel to a particular country.

Simple Precautions Before Risky Travel

- show an intelligent interest in the media news about the intended destination;
- analyse and balance the media representation of events;
- conduct Internet research; reports, maps, commentaries, consular websites, etc.;
- elicit the 'official attitude' on the destination from relevant embassies and authorities;
- weigh official policy against reported activities;
- assess recent terrorist activity (reported by the RAND corporation)—when, where, how, by whom?;
- check to see if planned flight path is potentially dangerous (for example, over Afghanistan in 1998).

Simple Caution During Risky Travel

- wide-bodied aircraft are less favoured as terrorist targets because it is harder to control passengers in these aircraft;
- the safest seats are said to be window seats or non-prominent seats, preferably close to exits;
- reputable airlines and hotels are the safest option when travelling;
- when at a destination, keep a low profile;
- avoid routine behaviour (to deter kidnapping or becoming a predictable target);
- keep friends and family informed of whereabouts;
- do not use public transport—contact reputable or hotel-recommended taxis;
- avoid public crowds or demonstrations;
- do not book hotels in the company name, dress down, and do not carry expensive accessories;
- avoid hotels with no apparent safety installations; check lock efficacy, 24-hour reception, safe deposits (or a safe in the room).

Table 9.1 US State Department's different travel safety
classifications

Travel Warnings	Public Announcements	Consular Information Sheets
Afghanistan	Azerbaijan	All Countries (plus special briefs)
Albania	Bolivia	
Algeria	Burma (Myanmar)	
Angola	Croatia	
Bosnia-Hertzegovina	China	
Burundi	Ecuador (Galapagos Is.)	
Cambodia	Egypt	
Central African Republic	Ethiopia	
Colombia	France	
Congo (Brazzaville)	Georgia	
Dem. Republic of Congo	Ghana	
Eritrea	Indonesia	
Guinea-Bissau	Honduras	
Iran	Kenya	
Iraq	Lesotho	
Israel & Occupied Territory	Madagascar	
Kuwait	Malaysia	
Lebanon	Mexico	
Liberia	Nicaragua	
Libya	Mongolia	
Monserrat	Saudi Arabia	
Nigeria	South Africa	
Pakistan	Taiwan	
Rwanda	Tanzania (Zanzibar)	
Serbia & Montenegro	Togo	
Sierra Leone	Uganda	
Somalia	Yemen	
Sudan		
Tajikistan		

Note: Travel status can change quickly; this table is presented as an example only (as at 17 November 1998).

Source: Author's presentation based on information from US State Department 1998a

Travel Information as a Self-Fulfilling Prophecy

Some travel information might not be factual in any objective sense, but might become a self-fulfilling prophecy if enough people believe it. The recommendation of particular hotels, beaches, restaurants, and so on can be of this nature. For example, if a travel guidebook recommends a city as being 'a centre for backpackers', and if the guidebook also recommends a particular budget-priced hotel in that city as being 'very popular with foreign travellers', the end result is that the hotel is likely to become popular with foreign backpackers—regardless of whether it really was so before the guidebook promoted the idea.

This sort of promotion is successful with certain travellers who plan independently but enjoy having like-minded people around at certain points in their travel—described by Plog (1990) as allocentric tendencies.

The order in which items appear in guidebooks is influential. Hotels and restaurants are often divided into budget, middle and top-end price categories—and then ranked from cheapest to most expensive within each of these categories. The ordering here is logical and practical and, even if the publisher does not intend to indicate a preference of one over another, readers tend to remember the first and last items in a list. This is significant in the context of all published information—whether it be in a book, brochure, map, or website homepage.

Travel/Destination Promotion After a Media Disaster

The media's presentation of an event determines the response of tourism providers and national tourism organisations (NTOs) in attempting to control and rectify the damage.

Destination Promotion Under Normal Conditions

In an average, uneventful year NTOs spend a significant amount of their annual budgets on promoting their country's tourism resources. The top spenders on national tourism promotion for 1992–95 are shown in Table 9.2 (page 217).

Sometimes investing substantial money on tourism promotion does not reap the rewards expected. One might assume that the greater the amount spent, the greater will be the net benefits in terms of tourist arrivals and revenue. In Australia's case this does not appear to be so—as Table 9.3 (page 217) indicates.

Table 9.2 Top tourism promotion budgets 1992–95 (in million US$)

Rank	Country	1992	1993	1994	1995	% change (1994–95)
1	Australia	51.1	64.3	75.8	87.9	16.0
2	UK	60.2	na	77.9	78.7	1.0
3	Spain	85.1	77.7	77.5	78.6	1.4
4	France	72.0	69.2	62.7	72.9	16.3
5	Singapore	na	na	49.7	53.6	7.8
6	Thailand	na	na	42.9	51.2	19.3
7	Netherlands	30.9	30.0	43.9	49.7	13.2
8	Austria	na	na	45.7	47.3	3.5
9	Ireland	28.0	25.0	41.8	37.8	−9.6
10	Portugal	30.5	36.2	34.9	37.3	6.9

na = not available

Source: De Groote & Nielsen 1999 and World Tourism Organization Yearbook, Budgets of National Tourism Administrations 1995/96.

Table 9.3 Top promotional performance for 1992 vs 1995

Rank	Country	Promotional spending per tourist arrival 1992	Promotional spending per tourist arrival 1995	Revenues per US$1 spent on promotion 1992	Revenues per US$1 spent on promotion 1995
1	France	1.21	1.20	347.00	375.00
2	Spain	2.15	1.74	261.00	319.00
3	UK	3.25	3.47	227.00	222.00
4	Thailand	na	7.42	na	148.00
5	Singapore	na	8.35	na	141.00
6	Netherlands	5.12	7.88	162.00	122.00
7	Portugal	na	3.92	na	121.00
8	Australia	21.29	23.76	78.00	78.00
9	Israel	na	15.97	na	77.00
10	Ireland	na	8.60	na	48.00

na= not available

Source: De Groote & Nielsen 1999, and World Tourism Organization Yearbook, Budgets of National Tourism Administrations 1995/96.

Australia is an interesting case to examine. After a heavy campaign aimed at putting 'brand Australia' on the tourist map, the 'Passport to Growth' strategy (Commonwealth Department of Tourism 1992) set out to build Australia's tourism product in line with marketing promises being made via international advertising. The plan was relatively successful with overseas arrivals increasing from 2.4 million in 1991 to 3.7 million in 1995. However, when compared with the return on investment gained by France, Spain, and the UK—as measured in promotional spending per tourist arrival and revenues per US$ spent on tourism promotion—Australia still lags behind some European and Asian destinations.

Perhaps the conclusion that can be drawn from Tables 9.2 and 9.3 is that some destinations are better able to draw tourists with minimal effort, thus entitling them to be called 'flagship destinations' (Keller 1998) or 'traditional products in developed tourism destinations' (De Groote & Nielsen 1998b). Other countries such as Australia have had to establish themselves or affirm their tourism credentials through intensive marketing.

But it is important for national tourism organisations to be conscious of the law of diminishing returns where the extra promotional spending does not lead to extra tourist arrivals. Despite Australia's increased tourism spending from US$51.1 million in 1992 to US$87.9 million in 1995 (the world's biggest spender in that year), the returns of US$78 per US$1 invested did not improve.

Destination Promotion Under Duress

Applying Image and Promotion to a Media Disaster Theory

There have been many attempts to describe or define 'image'. Baloglu and Brinberg say:

> Image differentiates tourist destinations from each other and is an integral and influential part of a traveler's decision process. Several definitions of image suggest that it has both cognitive and affective components.
>
> Baloglu & Brinberg 1997

According to Kotler, Haider and Rein (1993) image is the sum of beliefs, ideas, and impressions that people have of a place or destinations, whereas Dichter (1985) talks about image as being an overall impression of a destination with some emotional content.

It is clear that 'image' means different things to different people. Therefore it stands to reason that influencing or changing the prevailing image of a destination is a difficult task. Lilley (1999) says that it is not made any easier when:

The only stories that get substantially reported by the Western media are natural disasters and the sporadic and sometimes violent attacks on visitors, with immediate consequences for tourism-dependent local economies.

Lilley 1999

This raises the question of whether academic research can provide a theoretical recipe to handle such an unpredictable and complex concept as destination image. The following paragraphs will attempt to answer this question.

Promoting Tourism Winners

Table 9.3 (page 217) shows a cross-section of the winning tourism destinations—those countries that yielded the best results from a given promotional input. They are popular destinations with generally positive affective images. However, even the winners cannot afford to rest on their laurels with regard to tourism image because disaster, bad press, and negative events can strike anywhere.

France experienced a near tourism disaster following Algerian terrorist bomb attacks in the Paris Metro. Domestic and international tourism activity was hindered between June and December 1995. The branch manager for Royal Tours (Interviews 1995) in Belgium said that Belgians were afraid to go to France, and that the travel agents 'hadn't sold Paris since June [1995]'. The public service strike in the same year almost crippled the Paris tourism industry. Yet, within months (perhaps six months after the bombs) business was back to usual. A strike usually will affect a place only while it is occurring—unless strikes become endemic and, thus, permanently associated with the place. A 'flagship destination'—because of its inherent popularity—recovers quickly from adverse publicity.

The United Kingdom (especially London and Manchester) has also experienced sporadic terrorist threats that affected its long-haul tourist arrivals. It is of interest, however, that its short-haul (intra-European) market was not as severely affected. Travellers from the USA were deterred more than others but, as previously noted (see Chapter 7), Americans tend to be more sensitive to terrorism due to their increased likelihood of being targets. As with the experience of Paris, UK-bound tourism returned to normal very quickly after the memory of these events had subsided.

Spain has had some problems managing the media's portrayal of the ETA (Basque separatists) actions in the north of the country, but it has rarely posed a problem to Spanish tourism—because the bulk of arrivals in Spain are located in the south and along the coast (Costa del Sol, Costa Brava).

Israel (see Table 9.3) poses a somewhat different problem. The negative media portrayals of Israel are a combination of sporadic disaster and 'business as usual' (living with the hidden tensions between Palestinians and Israelis over land rights, and border disputes between Israel and its neighbours). Israel's situation is a difficult one to examine—because it is a protracted problem that is repeatedly in and out of the media's attention.

Hall and O'Sullivan observe that:

> Three elements are identified as leading to the creation of destination images: returning tourists through word-of-mouth reporting of their experiences, the media, and the government of the tourist-generating region. Governments, through their foreign policy settings can have a dramatic impact on perceptions of potential destinations.
>
> Hall & O'Sullivan 1996

Hall and O'Sullivan offer a useful figure to illustrate this communication flow (Figure 9.3).

Figure 9.3   Political instability, violence, and the image-making process

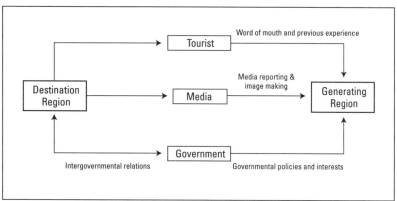

Source: Hall & O'Sullivan 1996

For a more detailed examination of the events that have shaped the image of Israel in the minds of potential visitors, see pages 168–71.

The other countries in Tables 9.2 and 9.3 (page 217) have not had grave disasters that affected tourism. The crash of the Thai currency (the bhat) probably improved tourism arrivals on the whole—despite being a disaster from an investor's perspective.

The Connection Between Expectation and Outcome

Tourists who anticipate danger, frustration, poor facilities, or generally tough travelling conditions, do not have high expectations, and it can be to the advantage of the tourist destination to promote this image. The vitality of the tourist industry in Vietnam and Laos, for example, following two decades of misery for those countries, is that they represent a 'playground' for the intrepid traveller—and a 'gold mine' for tour operators who have started up group tours in those countries.

However, establishing such an image can be complicated. Should the host country promote itself in terms of the exotic nature of the place, the unpredictabil~~ity~~ and perhaps even the dangers? Or should they emphasise the co~~mfort away~~ from home in the untamed lands once forgotten? An ~~intricate p~~sychological relationship between expectation and ~~reality faces~~ tourism principals faced with the dilemma of ~~marketing~~ their destination.

~~The four p~~ossible outcomes of joining these two ~~dimensi~~ons of travel

	satisfied tourists / first-time tourists / repeat tourists / reputation builds	satisfied tourists / low first-time tourists / high repeat tourists / eventually reputation builds
Outcome	dissatisfied tourists / first-time tourists / no repeat tourists / reputation fails	dissatisfied tourists / low first-time tourists / low repeat tourists / poor overall reputation

High — Low

Source: Author's presentation

Public Relations and Managing Tourism Crises

What is the role of public relations in tourist decision-making and destination image formation? We first need to look at some definitions of public relations.

Lubbe observes:

> When viewing destination image as a relationship which is established and maintained between a tourist destination and potential tourists and other groups in a tourist generating country, promoting the attributes of the destination is not sufficient. A tourist destination cannot only promote an image which will influence potential tourists to visit that destination but also ensure that the image has the capacity to meet the needs and expectations of potential tourists.
>
> Lubbe 1997

Lubbe then explains the importance of public relations as:

> ... essentially a function concerned with image, public opinion and the establishment and maintenance of positive relationship[s] between individuals, institutions, social groupings, organisations and even governments. The theoretical principles and concepts on which public relations is built makes it the most appropriate process for developing the image of a destination.
>
> Lubbe 1997

In this context, public relations is a very important function in the crises management or (media) damage control process.

Public Relations—Definition and Application

Hilton International's definition of public relations is:

> The process by which we create a positive image and customer preference through third-party endorsement.
>
> Kotler, Bowen & Makens 1999

Moore and Kalupa (1985, cited in Lubbe 1997) define public relations as something that 'measures, analyses and influences public opinion' which stems from a public that share similar interests and common opinions. Kelman (1965, cited in Lubbe 1997) says that research should focus not only on the description of an object, but also on the conception of an object in terms of how the individual behaves towards it.

The goal of public relations as it pertains to normative destination image should be to foster and communicate a positive image. This is achieved in two primary steps:

- develop a positive destination image; and
- target the appropriate market.

In the case of a damaged image—resulting from a negative media event relayed to the world via the mass media—an extra step needs to be inserted. To construct an effective public-relations and marketing program, it is important to begin with a clean, stable foundation. In the first instance, the negative image must be extinguished. See Figure 9.5.

Figure 9.5 Fostering a positive public-relations image

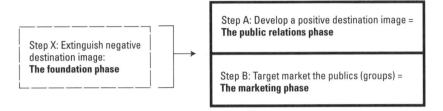

Source: Author's presentation

In general, there are two approaches to extinguishing this initial negative image.

1. Crisis Management

The destination should exercise damage control at the time of the negative event. This includes such activities as:

- monitoring and managing media coverage—ensuring that all reports present a balanced and accurate picture;
- conducting background briefings for journalists, key tourism players (especially in the source countries from which tourists come), tour operators, and travel agents;
- limiting harm to tourists already on location;
- restricting damage to tourism infrastructure and showing tourism services operating normally;
- seeking assurances from source governments that they will support a destination's attempts to control the problems and the image damage resulting.

In this context, Kotler, Bowen & Makens (1999) recommend four critical elements in crisis management for individual companies—but these elements can apply to a destination just as well:

- the destination should appoint a spokesperson to handle the media;
- the spokesperson should gather the facts and stick to them in reporting; (the authors also recommend that the spokesperson should say: 'I don't know at this time'—rather than 'no comment');
- if the destination uses a particular PR agency, contact them immediately; and

- notify the press and keep them informed—they will find out anyway!

For more information on 'do' and 'don't' in destination crisis-handling, refer to Table 9.4.

2. Post-crisis Management

In cases where immediate crisis management is not possible or not performed adequately, time will be needed for the event to fade in the public mind—unless another event reverses the original event, thus improving the damaged image faster (for example, South Africa's image was improved almost overnight when Nelson Mandela was released from prison). But recovery is generally a longer process—particularly in the context of protracted political or economic crises. In these circumstances, the destination might be forced to reinvent itself before tourists will again accept it as a possible travel alternative. According to Durocher (1994), the speed of recovery depends on:

- the extent of damage caused by the disaster;
- the efficiency with which tourism partners bring facilities back on line; and
- an effective marketing message that clearly states that the destination is once again open and ready for business.

Of course, prevention is always the best cure. Although it might help to monitor the negative media attention generated by a tourism disaster, it is preferable that the destination uses public relations as an open communications process, purposefully scanning or 'gatekeeping' their sphere of interest in order to take any corrective action that might be necessary to maintain the positive relationship it has formed with key source countries. Lubbe (1997) suggests that corrective action can be taken *internally* (within the destination) '. . . to ensure that the desired image reflects the reality of what is offered', or can be taken *externally* by using inducements to '. . . affect the knowledge, predispositions and behaviours of the publics'. A two-way communication process is preferable—as advocated in Chapter 2 of the present book.

Table 9.4 Crisis communication 'Do' and 'Don't'

DO	DON'T
Do have a crisis plan that includes natural disasters, security breaches, safety issues, strikes, and so on	Don't wait for a crisis to design a plan
Do update the plan often	Don't assume that the plan will cater for changing circumstances
Do train tourism participants to handle crisis and do attend to the injured immediately	Don't wait for a crisis to train tourism staff; don't treat the injured as liabilities

Do be aware of legal issues; do document training of staff and the updated crisis plan	Don't admit fault until an investigation and don't offer to pay injured parties' medical costs or compensation until all the facts are in
Do cooperate fully with all government entities	Don't appear difficult or defensive
Do have one spokesperson (and only one) available at all times to discuss the crisis	Don't let anyone but the spokesperson answer questions; don't speak off the record to anyone
Do speak truthfully, authoritatively, and factually	Don't speak in tourism or industry jargon; don't provide lurid descriptions
Do provide facts to the media and respect their deadlines and job functions; do say 'I don't have that information yet'	Don't frustrate media by lack of cooperation; don't answer reporters with 'no comment'
Do deal equally with all media	Don't favour one reporter over another
Do keep tourists informed	Don't put up a defensive wall of silence
Do show concern for tourism workers also affected by the crisis	Don't appear indifferent to wider economic consequences on others
Do be prepared for possible questions; tackle negative issues	Don't freeze when interviewed on television; don't become defensive when asked questions; don't fail to respond to all questions; don't leave a negative impression without making a response
Do verify all callers asking for statements	Don't respond to anonymous enquiries
Do increase security if necessary, making it highly visible at tourist sites if advisable	Don't appear inactive or incompetent
Do respect privacy	Don't release names of any victims
Do keep detailed notes of disclosed information	Don't inadvertently contradict what has previously been said
Do initiate information/press update sessions	Don't be cast in the defensive role of being pursued—initiate contact with media
Do thank a reporter if information has been reported accurately	Don't assume that accurate reporting will happen automatically
Do show concern for tourists, stressing past safety records and actions	Don't assume that others know what has been done in the past
Do forgive after a labour strike	Don't maintain grievances and disputes
Do create a positive follow-up campaign	Don't allow matters to take their own course
Do review crisis policy after an event	Don't assume that everything worked well

Source: Author's presentation (adapted from Miller 1997)

Opinion Shapers and the Tourist Determination Process

Destination marketers, through their public-relations systems, seek to understand the way in which information is spread throughout society, and how this information influences the adoption of new ideas. Kotler (1991) says that new ideas are adopted in society through a process called 'diffusion' (from its source to users of the information), and that information is dispersed through critical channels that influence whether or not an idea (for example, whether a destination is desirable or dangerous) will be adopted or rejected by the target audience (for example, tourism source countries).

Baskin and Aranoff (1998) describe this adoption of information as taking place through five stages, and say that there are five fundamental channels of influence. The interaction between the adoption of information and the channels of influence is shown in Figure 9.6.

Figure 9.6 The critical paths of influence in the adoption and changing of tourism ideas

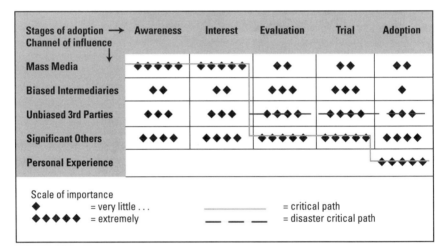

Source: adapted from Baskin & Aranoff 1988

Figure 9.6 illustrates that, in the early stages of awareness of a new destination, the mass media (television, radio, newspapers, magazines, and Internet) are most effective in disseminating information to an often distant target audience. In the middle stages of the acquisition of information, it appears that 'significant others'—such as friends, neighbours, respected people—play a decisive role. Finally, 'personal experience' confirms that the information was sound, and reaffirms the decision to adopt or reject.

To complete the Figure, 'biased intermediaries' are those who stand to benefit from another's adoption of the information (for example, a salesperson), and 'unbiased third parties' are those who have a credible input without a stake in the adopter's choices (for example, consulates, consumer groups).

From the perspective of a destination that is known but suffers from a fractured image (due to a disaster of some kind), the critical path might differ somewhat. If risk is perceived and substantiated (at least as an abstract truth), it is suggested that the critical path would follow the same path as a normative diffusion process, but would diverge at the point of evaluation by the unbiased third party—until it is adopted or not.

Image Reversal Promotional Campaigns

According to Lilley, talking about the Central American region:

> . . . there's a long way to go—and a lot of PR to be done—before the region's reputation recovers from a decade of apocalyptic images of civil war, human rights violations and . . . Hurricane Mitch.
>
> Lilley 1999

Different representations or ideas about a place are formed through various channels of influence at different stages of the image-adoption process. This can, in turn, be affected by cultural or preconceptual bases in different countries—such as traditions, values, customs, biases, preferences, and communication networks (Lubbe 1997).

A promotional campaign specifically intended to reverse a destination's sour image will probably be aimed at a target audience of the most important tourism source countries. Therefore, from the destination's perspective, an understanding of the value systems of each of their key source markets should greatly enhance the fine tuning of a successful image-reversal campaign. A destination would be advised at this stage to do some research to answer some basic questions.

Preparation for an Image-Reversal Campaign

There is a number of important questions to ask before undertaking a destination image-reversal campaign:

- What image does the destination presently have in key markets (source countries)?
- What are the present cultural and social values of importance in these markets (religion, social customs, prejudice, preferences, taboos)?
- How is information diffused in these markets (formal/informal channels, mass media, grapevine, open/closed networks)?
- What image would the tourist destination like these markets to have of it (fun, challenging, lazy, relaxing, safe, boring)?
- How can the destination influence these markets (by waiting, advertising, educating)?

- Who should be targeted within these markets (mass media, biased interested parties, unbiased parties, significant others, decision leaders)?
- When should the destination begin to reverse the image (during or after adverse event, after the height of media interest has passed, before it becomes too great a problem)?
- How much should be invested in the image reversal (financial investment, psychological commitment)?
- Should the campaign be focused internally as well as externally (educating/re-educating host people)?
- Should the campaign be conducted in-house, or should it use external marketing strategists (try to conduct promotional campaign internally or hire consultants)?
- Once the campaign is under way, how is it to be monitored (assessment of whether desired image is being created)?

According to Kotler, Bowen and Makens (1999), the power of mass advertising is weakening. This is due to increased advertising costs and clutter, rising costs of sales-promotion and personal selling and, in the present author's opinion, more sophisticated consumers with higher expectations. In a survey of 286 US marketing managers, 75 per cent declared that they used PR marketing—which indicates that the current alternative to mass advertising and promotion is PR.

Following careful research of the target public, and how best to reach these audiences, a destination must then examine which of the most important marketing PR tools would suit its needs. These include:

- publications—annual reports, brochures, cards, articles, newsletters, magazines, and audiovisual material;
- events—anniversary celebrations, art exhibitions, auctions, benefit evenings, bingo, book sales, cake sales, contests, dances, dinners, fairs, fashion shows, parties, parties in unusual places, 'phonathons', rummage sales, tours, and walkathons;
- news—develop story line, research it, write press releases;
- speeches—quality preparation, charismatic delivery, and thorough distribution of copies of the speech to staff, press, and stakeholders in the tourist destination;
- public service activities—boost goodwill, showing destination's philanthropy, and so on;
- logo—and application of logo to signs, brochures, stationery, documents, cards, buildings, and uniforms;

- focused PR—build PR around an owner of the property, a national icon or leader, the distinctive location; a distinctive product or service

Based on Kotler, Bowen & Makens 1999

It should also be borne in mind that such preparations can be made *before* a crisis has occurred. Destination image-shaping can be undertaken for preventive purposes—in cases where it is predicted that the image, although currently healthy, can become harmful to the destination in the longer term. For example, certain Greek and Spanish islands have lucrative tourist industries focused on particular markets—Lesbos for lesbian tourism, Myckynos for gay tourism, and Ibiza for rave party tourists. These markets can be extremely fickle. A risk-aversion solution—to reshape or broaden the image before problems arise—can assist in avoiding difficulties if market preferences should change.

Process Approach to Destination Image-Reversal

When answers to the above questions have been established, a destination is in a better position to begin with the process of trying to repair its ailing image. The process begins with a clear understanding of the pre-existing image.

With this existing image in mind, the process of reshaping follows the critical path illustrated in Figure 9.7. This figure emphasises the ability of

Figure 9.7 Process approach to destination negative image reversal

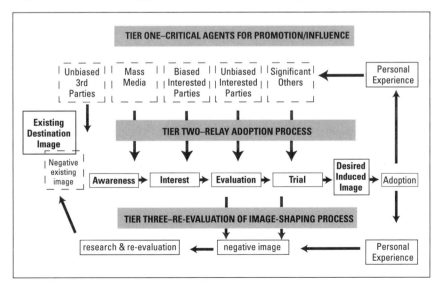

Source: Author's presentation adapted from Lubbe 1997

the mass media to coax the relevant tourist groups from 'awareness' through 'interest' to 'evaluation'. Thereafter 'significant others' nurture the potential tourist until 'trial' and eventual 'adoption' takes place (after positive 'personal experience').

At this point, if the experience is 'negative' (or if there has been a negative existing image from the outset), the process follows a 'disaster-critical' path. This path differs in that the initial medium of communication is not through the mass media directly. Rather, it is the unbiased third parties—in the form of government authorities (via source country's embassies). The embassies can then choose to relay the message via the mass media to potential tourists. Thus, the process is filtered through a legitimate authority line.

Promotional campaigns, therefore, will be communicated via the upper (influence) tier of Figure 9.7. The middle tier illustrates the adoption process through the pertinent influences. The lower tier indicates a need to re-evaluate the image-shaping process.

Putting the Theory into Practice

News and Information Releases

Tourism professionals need to work with the media—as the most important conduit for their products and services. Careful, selective planning needs to go into the preparation of subjects for a pending news release. Controlling the flow and content of information is important—given that a large proportion of tourism media coverage is allocated to disasters, failures, strikes, break-downs. A typical example is:

> Hurricane Mitch . . . has helped to blast Central America back into the headlines.
>
> Lilley 1999

A positive angle on a news story is one way of encouraging new tourists, or converting disenchanted old tourists. Effective communication in this regard is therefore extremely important.

Effective Tourism Communications/Writing

Some important characteristics of good tourism communications/writing include:
- developing a sense of newsworthiness (or employing someone who has this skill);
- maintaining professional relations between tourist entities and the media; being aware that relationships with the media require

adherence to accepted norms and standards;

- assessing the probable impact of statements or words on different audiences;
- being aware that tourism has inherent newsworthiness—that it interests and excites people;
- being aware that dramatic stories sell themselves (crime, disaster, romance, humour), but that they have different impacts on the destinations about which they speak;
- recognising the newsworthiness of the release of scientific research results, or statistics from authorities such as the World Tourism Organization (WTO) or World Travel Tourism Council (WTTC);
- being aware that timing is very important;
- carefully checking and editing of text before release;
- ensuring that all facts and figures are correct (reputations depend upon them);
- being mindful of deadlines when delivering text or copy to printers, publishers, or the media;
- indicating sources of all facts;
- giving release instructions for a news release (such as 'for immediate release' or 'hold for a later date', and so on);
- writing simply and objectively, usually in third person (but often in first and second person for advertising writing);
- applying what is called the 'Hey-You-See-So' approval system to writing a press release—'Hey' (gain attention), 'You' (identify audience), 'See' (subject), 'So' (plan of action or next move);
- recognising that editors might remove some material for space reasons, and therefore presenting the bulk of the important information in the first paragraph (that is, think of press copy as a pyramid upside-down with the heavier material being presented at the top).

Influenced by Reilly 1990, and by Kotler, Bowen & Makens 1999

Conclusions

In the Introduction, reference was made to Dubrovnik and the disastrous impact of a bitter civil war on tourism in that town. Years later, it might be difficult to see that a war ever took place—except for the continuing lack of tourists, as illustrated in the following:

On the hill just to the south of Dubrovnik, the Serbian-Montenegrin artillery set up its batteries and, in the winter of 1991/92, rained thousands of shells down on to the old town. Miraculously, Dubrovnik held out; even more amazingly, it has quickly recovered. Any visitor to the city who was unaware of its recent history would have no inkling of the experience. Dubrovnik today is one of the most attractive, cohesive, intriguing cities in Europe. The only sign of change is that its heart—the square between the Sponza Palace and the Church of St Blaise—is not crammed with tourists as it was in the past.

Thorncroft 1998

Dubrovnik has not fully overcome its damaged image of the early 1990s. The war in the neighbouring Kosovo region has done little to help the tourism-rebuilding process. Nevertheless, more could have been done to restore the image of Dubrovnik through public relations—with better image-reversal promotion campaigns, the application of primary research on the town's potential new target markets, and focusing on the opinion shapers within these audiences. More attention could have been given at the height of the war in Dubrovnik to crisis-management techniques. When more information had been collected on the extent of the damage to the tourist industry (research on number of arrivals and altered image), a re-positioning program could have been implemented. This would have involved extinguishing the present negative image, creating a new market position, carrying out public relations, and undertaking active marketing towards revitalising the ravished tourism economy.

Discussion Time

- Both Israel and Northern Ireland face the challenge of marketing their destination for tourism while the wheels of peace turn slowly. After splitting a larger group into two working groups, each group chooses one of the above countries as their home destination. Formulate a comprehensive communication strategy given the special circumstances of the country. This will involve an assessment of:
  - its chief assumed markets;
  - any recent media coverage (negative or positive) of the conflicts affecting the country;
  - expected outcomes of marketing and PR efforts;
  - possible budget constraints;
  - strengths, weaknesses, opportunities and threats (SWOT).
- Having completed the above analysis, an evaluation chart should be prepared as a useful tool to set down the goals of the communication program (see sample chart).

- While peace talks are in progress, news of a car bomb explosion reaches the government. The groups have to write a press release for the chosen destination. This press release should be designed to allay the doubts of tourists and tourism principals concerning possible dangers. Present the press release to the rest of the group. Discuss whether the press release would serve its purpose, and what rewording would improve it.

Figure 9.8 Sample evaluation chart

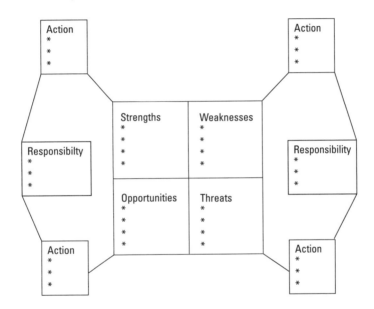

Source: Author's presentation

Bibliography
and References

Africa Economic Digest 1989, UK, July 1989.

Age 1998, 'Traveller's Check; Travel Bestsellers', *Age, Saturday Extra*, 19 December 1998.

Art of European and World Travel Backpacking 1998, <www.artoftravel.com>.

Ashworth, G. & Goodall, B. 1990, *Marketing Tourism Places*, Routledge, New York.

Ashworth, G. & Voogd, H. 1990, *Selling the City*, Belhaven Press, London.

Australian Broadcasting Corporation 1998, <www.abc.net.au>, 1998.

Australian Embassy/Consulate Brussels (Public Affairs) 1995.

Australian Tourism Commission (ATC) 1998, *Tourism Speech Notes*, ATC Corporate Affairs, Sydney, <www.atc.net.au>.

Baloglu, S. & Brinberg, D. 1997, 'Affective Images of Tourism Destinations', *Journal of Travel Research*, Vol. 35(4), 1997.

Bar-On, R. 1996, 'Measuring the effects on tourism of violence and of promotion following violent acts', in *Tourism, Crime and International Security Issues*, Pizam, A. & Mansfeld, Y. (eds), John Wiley & Sons, Chichester.

Barraclough, C. 1996, 'Born-Again Beirut', *Age*, Melbourne, 6 January 1996.

Baskin, O. & Aranoff, C. 1988, *Public Relations: The Professional and the Practice*, 3rd edn, Brown, Dupuque.

Bell, E. 1996, 'Information Media-circulation', *Observer*, London, 21 January 1996.

Benelux Travel Express 1998, 'Le Grandes Famille dans L' Aviation Internationale', *Benelux Travel Express*, Belgium, 16 October 1998.

Beni, M. 1996, 'Travel Trade and Globalization: Communication and Competition on the International Market', *AIEST Congress Report 46, New Zealand*, Vol. 38, St Gall, 1996, pp. 115–25.

Bennett, M. & Radburn, M. 1991, 'Information Technology in Tourism: The Impact on the Industry and Supply of Holidays', in *The Tourism Industry: An International Analysis*, Sinclair, T. & Stabler, M. (eds), CAB International, Wallingford.

Berthon, P., Pitt, L. & Watson, R. 1996, 'Marketing Communication & the World Wide Web', *Business Horizons*, September–October 1996, pp. 24–32.

Beyer, L. 1996, 'Peres Terrible Choices', *Time* magazine, New York, 18 March 1996.

Bigness, J. 1996, 'Travelers Abandon Hospitality for Ease of Computer Service', *Wall Street Journal*, Brussels, 12 July 1996.

Bodlender, S. 1990, 'Managing the Future', in *Horwarth Book of Tourism*, Quest, M. (ed.), Horwarth & Horwarth, Macmillan Press, London.

Boeing 1998, <www.boeing.com>.

Bord Fáilte (Irish Tourist Board), Public Relations, Dublin.

Bordas, E. 1990, 'Marketing Research—Marketing Strategy: Design of a Communication Strategy for a Tourist Destination', *AIEST Congress Report 32 (Tourist Research as a Commitment)*, 1990, St Gall.

Boyd, A. 1994, *Broadcast Journalism; Techniques of Radio and TV News*, Focal Press (Butterworth-Heinemann), Oxford.

Brady, J. & Widdows, R. 1988, 'The impact of world events on travel to Europe during the summer of 1986', *Journal of Travel Research*, 26(3), 1988, pp. 8–10.

Brenchley, F. 1986, 'Living with Terrorism: The Problem of Air Piracy', Institute for the Study of Conflict & Terrorism (RISCT), London.

Briggs, S. 1997, *Successful Tourism Marketing: A Practical Handbook*, Kogan Page, London.

British Broadcasting Corporation (BBC) 1998a (2 July), 'Hopes for Northern Ireland Tourism Boost', <www.news.bbc.co.uk>, 2 July 1998.

British Broadcasting Corporation (BBC) 1998b (10 July), 'Violence Turns Belfast into Ghost Town', <www.news.bbc.co.uk>, 10 July 1998.

British Embassy Brussels (Press and Public Affairs) 1998, 'Foreign and Commonwealth Office Travel Advice—Indonesia', Brussels, 20 May 1998–11 June 1998.

British Tourist Authority 1990, 'Factors affecting the slow of international tourism', *Tourism Intelligence Quarterly* 12(2), 1990, p. 14.

Brotherton, B. & Himmetoglu, B. 1997, 'Beyond Destinations—Special Interest Tourism', *Anatolia (Journal of Tourism and Hospitality Research)*, Vol. 8(3), 1997, pp. 11–30.

Buckley, P. & Klemm, M. 1993, 'The decline of tourism in Northern Ireland', *Tourism Management* 14(2), pp. 184–94.

Buhalis, D. 1996, 'Information Technology as a Strategic Tool for Tourism', *The Tourist Review*, Vol. 2., 1996, pp. 34–6.

Burns, P. & Holden, A. 1995, *Tourism: A New Perspective*, Prentice-Hall, Hemel Hempstead.

Cairns Port Authority (CPA) 1992, Cairns.

Cano, V. & Prentice, R. 1998, 'Opportunities for Endearment to Place Through Electronic Visiting: WWW Homepage and the Tourism Promotion of Scotland', *Tourism Management*, Vol. 19 (1), Pergamon Press, UK, 1998, pp. 67–73.

Carter, A. 1971, *Mass Media*, Macmillan, London.

Castles, I. 1996, *Yearbook Australia 1995*, Australian Bureau of Statistics, No. 77, 1996, Canberra.

Casty, A. 1973, *Mass Media and Mass Man*, Holt-Reinhart, Winston.

Chaliand, G. 1987, *Terrorism from Popular Struggle to Media Spectacle*, Sagis Books, London.

Channel 7 Australia 1996, 'Olympic Broadcasting Programme Ratings', Melbourne, 1996.

Cialdini, R 1988, *Influence; Science & Practice*, Harper Collins, UK.

Cohen, E. 1974, 'Who is a Tourist? A Conceptual Clarification', *Sociological Review*, No. 22(4), 1974, pp. 164–82.

Cohen, R. 1993, 'Ad Gains Could Exceed 6% This Year', *Advertising Age* (Melbourne), 3 May 1993.

Commonwealth Department of Tourism 1992 (now Department of Industry, Science & Tourism), 'Tourism: Australia's Passport to Growth—A National Tourism Strategy', Canberra, June 1992.

Cooper, C. & Wanhill, S. 1998, *Tourism Development: Environment & Community Issues*, John Wiley & Sons, Chichester.

Crompton, J. 1979, 'Motivations for Pleasure Vacation', *Annals of Tourism Research*, Vol. 6(4), Pergamon Press, UK, 1979, pp. 408–24.

Crompton, J. 1992, 'Structure of Vacation Destination Choice Sets', *Annals of Tourism Research*, Pergamon Press, UK.

Crompton, J. & Ankomah, P. 1993, 'Choice Set Propositions in Destination Decisions', *Annals of Tourism Research*, Vol. 20, Pergamon Press, UK, pp. 461–76.

Curren, J. & Gurevitch, M. 1984, *Mass Media and Society*, Edward Arnold, Kent.

Curtis, L. 1984, *Ireland: The Propaganda War*, Pluto, London.

Cutlip, S., Center, A. & Broom, G. 1985, *Effective Public Relations*, 6th edn, Prentice-Hall, New Jersey.

Davidoff, P. & Davidoff, M. 1983, *Sales and Marketing for Travel and Tourism*, Prentice-Hall, New Jersey.

Davison, W., Boylan, J. & Yu, F. 1976, *Mass Media Systems and Effects*, Praeger Publishers, New York.

Davo (Royal Tours), Travel Agency, Louvain.

De Groote, P. 1997, 'A Multidisciplinary Analysis of World Fairs and Their Effects', *Toeractua* 1997(1), Limburg University Centre publication, Diepenbeek.

De Groote, P. & Nielsen, C. 1998a, 'Hasselt's Green Boulevard Project: A New Challenge for Urban Living, Mobility and Tourism', *Toeractua* 1998(3), Limburg University Centre publication, Diepenbeek.

De Groote, P. & Nielsen, C. 1998b, 'Regional Tourist City Destination Marketing Case Study: Hasselt's Visitors (Marketing Considerations)', *AIEST Congress Report 48*, Morocco (Destination Marketing—Scope and Limitations), St Gall, 1998.

De Groote, P. & Nielsen, C. 1998c, 'The Evolution of Tourist Information Centres; From Humble Booth to Hopeful Tourist Office to Holistic Visitor (Information) Centre', *Toeractua* 1998(2), Limburg University Centre publication, Diepenbeek.

De Groote, P. & Nielsen, C. 1999, 'Strategy-Based Tourism Policy as a factor for Australia's Tourism Development and Success', *AIEST Congress Report 41 (Future-Oriented Tourism Policy: a contribution to the strategic development of places)*, St Gall, 1999.

De Groote, P. & Ooms, C. 1998, *Stilte . . . in Vergadering: De Congres—en Meetingbranche in Belgie en Nederland*, Garant, Leuven-Apeldoorn.

De Knop, P. 1998, 'Oorsprong en Evolutie van het Sportief Toerisme', *Recreatie en Toerisme*, August 1998, Netherlands.

De Lisser, E. 1996, 'A Summer of Tragedies Scares Travelling Children', *Wall Street Journal*, Brussels, 30 August 1996.

Department of Foreign Affairs and Trade (Australia) 1998, 'Foreign Affairs and Trade Australia—Travel Advice', 1998, <www.dfat.gov.au>.

Department of Foreign Affairs and Trade (Australia) nd, 'Public Relations and Travel Advice', Melbourne.

Department of Industry, Science and Tourism 1997 (Australia), *Industry Science Tourism Annual Report 1996/97*, Canberra.

Department of Industry, Science and Tourism 1998a (Australia), *Impact Monthly Fact Sheets*, April–November 1998, Canberra.

Department of Industry, Science and Tourism 1998b (Australia), *Talking Tourism*, No. 13, Office of National Tourism, Canberra, March 1998.

Department of Industry, Science and Tourism 1998c (Australia), *Tourism Industry Trends*, Office of National Tourism, Canberra, 1998.

Department of Industry, Science and Tourism 1998/99 (Australia), *Impact: Monthly facts sheet on the economic impact of tourism & the latest visitor arrival trends*, June 1998–July 1999, Office of National Tourism, Canberra, 1998/99.

Department of Industry, Science and Tourism 1999 (Australia), *Talking Tourism*, No. 14,

Office of National Tourism, Canberra, March 1999.

Dichter, E. 1985, 'What is image?', *Journal of Consumer Research*, No. 13, 1985, pp. 455–72.

Dolnicar, S. & Mazanec, J. 1998, 'Destination Marketing: Reinventing the Wheel or Conceptual Progress?', *AIEST Congress Report 48*, Morocco (Destination Marketing—Scope and Limitations), St Gall.

Dorman, C. 1997, 'HK Tourism Looks Down the Barrel', *Age*, Melbourne, 1997.

Dorsey, J. 1996, 'Turkey Aims to Ignite Explosive Tourism Potential', *Wall Street Journal*, Brussels, 1996.

Durocher, J. 1994, 'Recovery Marketing: What to do after a natural disaster', *Cornell Hotel and Restaurant Administration Quarterly 35*, No. 2, 1994, p. 66.

Eisenberg, D. 1998, 'Acting Up in the Air', *Time* magazine, New York, 21 December 1998.

Elias-Varotsis, S. nd, 'Le Tourisme Evenementiel en Australie: enjeux et perspectives', unpublished paper, Université Paris XII, 199X.

European Commission 1998, *European Tourism Partnerships for Jobs (Conclusions and Recommendations of the High Level Group on Tourism Employment)*, European Commission, DG XXIII, Brussels, 1998.

Evans, M. 1998, 'Broadcasters to make sure they get their money's worth', *Sydney Morning Herald*, 25 September 1998.

Explora 1998, 'Le Tourisme en Croatie . . . enfin!', *Explora* No. 1, May 1998.

Eysenck, M. 1994, *Handbook of Cognitive Psychology*, Laurence Erlbaum, New Jersey.

Fayos-Sola, E. 1997, 'Conference Report: The Impact of Mega Events', *Journal of Travel Research*, Vol. X, September 1997.

Federal Airports Corporation (FAC) 1992, Australia.

Federal Aviation Administration (FAA) 1998, 'Facts and Figures', <www.faa.gov>.

Fodness, D. & Murray, B. 1997, 'Tourist Information Search', *Annals of Tourism Research*, Vol. 24(3), Pergamon Press, UK, 1997, pp. 503–25.

Foreign and Commonwealth Office (UK) 1998, 'Travel Advice' (various).

Fortune 1996, 'The Brand's the Thing—Research on Media Dynamics', *Fortune* magazine, 4 March 1996.

Freesun News 1998, 'United Airlines: A Rising Star (Alliance)', *Freesun News*, November 1998.

Gartner, W. & Shen, J. 1992, 'The Impact of Tiananmen Square on China's Tourism Image', *Journal of Travel Research*, Vol. 30 (4), 1992, pp. 47–52.

Goddard, J. 1981, 'Leisure, Recreation and Tourism', *Regional Studies*, 15 (5), 1981, pp. 311–411.

Goddard, J. 1995, 'Away for the Day: Gone to the Exhibition', *Family Tree Magazine*, No. 8, 1995.

Goeldner, C. 1995, 'Tourist Information Systems', in *Tourism Marketing and Management Handbook—Student Edition*, Prentice-Hall, Hempel Hempstead.

Goeldner, C. 1997, 'Conference Report . . . Travel and Tourism Industry and Academic Institutions in a True Alliance', *Journal of Travel Research*, Vol. 36(2), 1997.

Gold, J. & Ward, S. 1994, *Place Promotion; the Use of Publicity and Marketing to Sell Towns and Regions*, John Wiley & Sons, Chichester, 1994.

Goodall, B. 1991, 'Understanding Holiday Choice', *Progress in Tourism, Recreation & Hospitality Management* (Cooper, C., ed.), Vol. 3, Belhaven Press, London.

Goodall, B. & Ashworth, G. 1988, 'How Tourists Choose Their Holidays; An Analytical Framework', in *Marketing in the Tourism Industry—The Promotion of Destination Regions*, Croom Helm, New York.

Gow, H. & Otway, H. (eds) 1990, 'Communicating with the Public About Major Accident Hazards', Report: Commission of the E.C., Elsevier, London.

Grabler, K., Maier, G., Mazanec, J. & Wober, K. 1997, *International City Tourism—Analysis and Strategy*, Pinter, London.

Greenslade, R. 1998, 'All change on the tabloid carousel', national newspaper circulation, ABC, in *Guardian*, London, 14 December 1998.

Gunn, C. 1972, *Vacationscape: Designing Tourist Regions*, University of Texas, Austin.

Haines, M. (ed.) 1994, *The Travellers Handbook*, WEXAS International, London.

Hall, C. 1992, *Hallmark Tourist Events: Impacts, Management and Planning*, Belhaven Press, London.

Hall, C. & O'Sullivan, V. 1996, 'Tourism, political stability and violence', in Pizam & Mansfeld 1996 (op. cit.).

Hawkins, D. 1989, *Tourism in Contemporary Society: An Introductory Text*, Prentice-Hall, New Jersey.

Hawkins, D., Leventhal, M., & Olden, W. 1998, 'The Virtual Environment: Utilisation of Information Technology to Enhance Strategic Travel Marketing, in *Tourism Development: Environment & Community Issues*, Cooper, C. & Wanhill, S. (eds), John Wiley & Sons, Chichester.

Health Publications Unit (UK) 1992, *Health Advice for Travellers Handbook*, UK.

Healy, M. 1998, 'Targets Shared Insidious Links, US Intelligence Officials Say', *Los Angeles Times*, Los Angeles, USA.

Hewitt, C. 1992, cited in Paletz, D. & Schmid, A. 1992, *Terrorism and The Media*, Sage, California.

Hill, D. 1998, 'Stop Card Thieves Taking Off', *Sunday Times (Money)*, 19 July 1998.

Hiroi, O., Mikami, S. & Miyata, K. 1995, *A Study of Mass Media Reporting in Emergencies*, DRC, Delaware.

Hoffman, B. 1998, 'Curbing Terrorism' (book review), *Economist*, UK, 1998.

Hoffman, B. & Gardela, K. 1986, *RAND Chronology of International Terrorism*, Rand, USA.

Holloway, C. 1991, *The Business of Tourism*, Pitman, London.

Holloway, C. 1994, *The Business of Tourism*, 4th edn, Pitman, London.

Holloway, J. & Plant, R. 1998, *Marketing for Tourism*, Pitman, London.

Horner, S. & Swarbrooke, J. 1996, *Marketing Tourism, Hospitality and Leisure in Europe*, International Thomson Business Press, London.

Hotel Rankings 1997, *Hotels*, July 1997.

Hutchison, J. 1997, *Tourism: Getting it Right for the Millennium*, Department of Industry, Science and Tourism, Canberra.

Index of International Opinion 1994, London.

Infotravel 1998a (October), 'Assurances et Sports d'Hiver, Le Travail sur Mesure s'Impose: Une Variete de Primes et de Garanties', *Infotravel* No. 9, October 1998.

Infotravel 1998b (November), 'ACE: The Front-, Mid- & Back- Office Solution for the Future!', *Infotravel* No. 10, November 1998.

'Inside Track' 1996, as quoted in *Independent*, London, 9 March 1996.

Interavia Business & Technology 1989, Aerospace Media, <http://aerospacemedia.mdeo.com/interavia.htm>.

International Herald Tribune 1998, 'US Warns on Travel to Indonesia', *International Herald Tribune*, 5 June 1998.

International Olympic Committee (IOC) 1996a, 'Marketing Matters' (The Olympic Marketing Newsletter), IOC Marketing Department, No. 9, Summer, Lausanne, 1996, pp. 1–16.

International Olympic Committee (IOC) 1996b, *Olympic Movement Directory*, Lausanne.

International Olympic Committee (IOC) 1996/97, 'Marketing Matters' (The Olympic Marketing Newsletter), IOC Marketing Department, No. 10, Winter, Lausanne, 1996/97, pp. 1–16.

Internet Advertising Bureau (IAB) 1998a, 'Airline Reservation Systems Face Internet Threat', <www.hospitalitynet.nl>.

Internet Advertising Bureau (IAB) 1998b, 'Internet Direct Marketing Bureau Slams Spamming, Endorses Opt-in Email and calls on all Marketeers to Support', <www.hospitalitynet.nl>.

Internet Advertising Bureau (IAB) 1998c, 'Destination Management Systems—A Tool for Growth', <www.hospitalitynet.nl>.

Internet Advertising Bureau (IAB) 1998d, 'Internet Direct Marketing Bureau Slams Spamming, Endorses Opt-in Email and calls on all Marketeers to Support', <www.hospitalitynet.nl>.

Internet Advertising Bureau (IAB) 1998e, 'The Impact of Information Technology on Travel and Transportation', <www.hospitalitynet.nl>.

Internet Link 1997, 'A Beginners Guide to the Internet', No. 1, March 1997.

Irish Times 1998, 'The Path to Peace—The Troubles', <www.irish-times.com>.

Jansen-Verbeke, M. 1994, *Tourism: Quo Vadis? From Business as Usual to Crisis Management*, Centre for Tourism Management, Erasmus University, Rotterdam.

Jenkins, B. 1988, 'Future Trends in International Terrorism', in *Current Perspectives on International Terrorism*, Slater, R. & Stohl, M. (eds), Macmillan Press, London, pp. 246–66.

Jenkins, C. 1990, 'Tourism: Is Future Demand Changing?, in *Horwarth Book of Tourism*, Quest, M. (ed.), Horwarth & Horwarth, Macmillan Press, London.

Jenkins, R. 1978, 'Vacation Decision Making', *Journal of Travel Research*, Vol. 16, 1978.

Johnson, J., Snepenger, D. & Akis, S. 1994, 'Resident's Perceptions of Tourism Development', *Journal of Travel Research*, Vol. X(X), 1994.

Keller, P. 1998, 'Invitation to AIEST Annual Congress No. 48', *Destination Marketing—Scope and Limitations*, St Gall, 1998.

Kelly, P. 1997, 'Belfast: The Crack is Good and the Streets Are Safe', *Independent on Sunday—Travel*, London, 21 September 1997.

King, E. 1995, 'Year To Go', *Age*, Melbourne, 30 December 1995.

Knight, R. 1997, 'The Global Voyage—Special Report', *Time* magazine, New York, 16 June 1997.

Knight, R. 1998, 'Back on Track—Travel', *Time* magazine, New York, 21 September 1998.

Knowles, M. 1990, 'Packaging the Tourism Product', in *Horwarth Book of Tourism*, Quest, M. (ed.), Horwarth & Horwarth, Macmillan Press, London.

Kotler, P. 1991, 'Marketing Management: Analysis, Planning and Control', 7th edn, Prentice-Hall, New Jersey.

Kotler, P., Bowen, J. & Makens, J. 1999, *Marketing for Hospitality and Tourism*, 2nd edn, Prentice-Hall, New Jersey.

Kotler, P., Haider, D. & Rein, I. 1993, *Marketing Places*, The Free Press (Macmillan Press), New York.

Landmark Travel Channel 1998, 'Travel TV Logo (TV That Takes You There)', literature and program, London.

Lanquar, R. & Hollier, R. 1986, *Le Marketing Touristique*, Presses Universitaires de France, Paris.

Laws, E. 1991, *Tourism Marketing: Service & Quality Management Perspective*, Stanley Thomas Publishers, Cheltenham.

Lenthall, K. 1994, 'The Public at Risk', *Age*, Melbourne, 20 October 1994.

Lewis, P. 1986, 'Tourism and Terrorism', *Report on Business* magazine, Vol. 3 (5), 1986, pp. 102–8.

Lickorish, L., Jefferson, A., Bodlender, J. & Jenkins, C. 1991, *Developing Tourism Destinations*, Longman, Harlow.

Lieberman, D. 1996, 'Sports Illustrated Plots Course for Growth', *USA Today* (International Edition), 20 August 1996.

Lilley, P. 1999, 'Visiting Central America in the Aftermath of Hurricane Mitch', *Rough News*, Issue No. 7, 1999.

Lombardi, R. 1990, cited in Gow, H. & Otway, H. (eds) 1990, 'Communicating with the Public About Major Accident Hazards', Report: Commission of the E.C., Elsevier, London.

Lonely Planet 1998, 'Lonely Planet Online', *Lonely Planet Catalogue*, March–August 1998.

Lubbe, B. 1997, 'Applying an Open Systems Public Relations Model to Destination Image Development', *TTRA European Chapter Conference Report 1*, Lillehammer, Norway, 17–20 August 1997.

MacLean, S. 1994, 'Ansett Jumbo Safety Probe', *Age*, Melbourne, 20 October 1994.

MacLeod, S. 1996, 'Targeting the Tourist', *Time* magazine, New York, 29 April 1996.

Manfredo, S. 1989, 'An Investigation of the Basis of External Information Search in Recreation and Tourism', *Leisure Studies Series*, 1989.

Mansfeld, Y. 1992, 'From Motivation to Actual Travel', *Annals of Travel Research*, Vol. 19, Pergamon Press, UK.

Mansfeld, Y. 1996, 'Wars, tourism and the "Middle East" factor', in *Tourism, Crime and International Security Issues*, Pizam, A. & Mansfeld, Y. (eds), John Wiley & Sons, Chichester.

Marling, K. 1994, *As Seen on TV: The Visual Culture of Everyday Life in the 1950s*, Harvard University Press, Cambridge, Mass., USA.

Maslow, A. 1970, *Motivation & Personality*, 2nd edn, Harper & Row, New York.

Mathieson, A. & Wall 1982, G., *Tourism: economic, physical & social impacts*, Longman, London/New York.

Maxa, R. 1999, 'Are the skies safer since 1978?', <www.msnbc.com>, 31 March 1999.

McGuinness, S. 1994, 'Ansett Jumbo Safety Probe, *Age*, Melbourne, 20 October 1994.

McIntosh, R. & Goeldner, C. 1986, *Tourism Principles, Practices & Philosophy*, John Wiley & Sons, New Jersey.

McLeod, J., Kosicki, G. & Zhangdang, P. 1991, 'On Understanding and Misunderstanding Media Effects', in *Mass Media and Society*, Curren, J. & Gurevitch, M. (eds), Hodder & Staughton, Kent.

McManus, G. 1999, 'No-Go Zones', *Herald Sun*, Melbourne, 3 January 1999.

McWhinney, E. 1987, *Aerial Piracy and International Terrorism: The Illegal Diversion of Aircraft & International Law*, Martinus Nijhoff Publishers, Dortrecht.

Medlik, S. 1991, *Managing Tourism*, Butterworth-Heinemann, Oxford.

Medlik, S. 1996, *Dictionary of travel, tourism and hospitality*, Butterworth-Heinemann, Oxford.

Merrill, J., Lee, J. & Fiendlander, E. 1990, *Modern Mass Media*, Harper & Row, USA.

Middleton, V. 1988, *Marketing in Travel and Tourism*, Heinemann, Oxford.

Middleton, V. 1994, 'The Marketing and Management of Tourism Destinations—Research Directions for the Next Decade', *AIEST Congress Report 44*, St Gall.

Mill, R. & Morrison, A. 1985, *The Tourism System; an introductory text*, Prentice-Hall, New Jersey.

Miller, J. 1997, 'Crisis to Calm, It's the Crisis Communication Do's and Don'ts', *Hotel and Motel Management*, Vol. 211 (16), 1997, p. 18.

Mitchell, A. 1996, 'Coke is First Off the Blocks in the Big Race', *Marketing Week*, 2 August 1996.

Mitchell, B. 1994, 'CAA Safety Approach Will Lead to More Crashes', *Sunday Age*, Melbourne, 9 October 1994.

Morison, A. 1995, 'After the War', *Age*, Melbourne, 9 December 1995.

Moutinho, L. 1987, 'Consumer Behaviour in Tourism', *European Journal of Marketing*, 21(10), 1987, pp. 1–44.

MSNBC (News) 1998a, ' Are the skies safer since 1978?', <www.msnbc.com>, 1998.

MSNBC (News) 1998b, 'Flying the crowded skies', <www.msnbc.com>, 1998.

MSNBS (News) 1998c, ' Tourists flee Club Med holiday hell', <www.msnbc.com>, 1998.

Neckermans, Tour Operator, Louvain.

Needham 1996, P., 'Can You Trust Your Travel Agent?', *Age Travel* (Melbourne), 3 February 1996.

Netherlands Board of Tourism (NBT) 1989, *Tourism, 10 Years Ahead* (literature and research), Amsterdam, March 1989.

Netherlands Board of Tourism (NBT) nd, Public Relations & Advertising, Amsterdam.

Nielsen, C. nd, 'Consumer Behaviour: The Role of Stable, Secure and Safe Tourism in Travel Decision Making', Free University Brussels report, Brussels.

Nielsen Media 1998, 'What TV Ratings Really Mean and Other Frequently Asked Questions', <www.nielsenmedia.com>, 1998.

Noble, J., Bernhardson, W., Brosnahan, T., Doggett, S., Forsyth, S., Honan, N. & Lyon, J. 1998, *Lonely Planet Mexico*, Lonely Planet, Hawthorn.

Northern Ireland Tourist Board (NITB) 1998, 'Tourism Facts 1997', NITB Press Office, Belfast.

Odasuo, Kenoye 1991, *Methods of Diffusion*, Sage, London.

Official Publication of the European Community 1992, *Tourism in Europe*, Luxembourg.

Official Publication of the European Community 1997, *Europe from A to Z*, Luxembourg.

Olympic Notebook 1997, 'February in Nagano', *Time* magazine, New York, 15 December 1997.

Office de Promotion du Tourisme (OPT) nd, Press Department, Brussels.

Outside 1998, 'Outside Grote Reisgidsen-Test', *Outside* No. 2., Brussels, 1998.

Page, S. 1994, *Urban Tourism*, Routledge, London.

Paletz, D. & Schmid, A. 1992, *Terrorism and the Media*, Sage, California.

Pearce, D. 1982, *The Social Psychology of Tourism Behaviour*, Pergamon Press, UK.

Pearce, D. 1991, 'Challenge and Change in East European Tourism: A Yugoslav Example, in *The Tourism Industry: An International Analysis*, Sinclair, T. & Stabler, M. (eds), CAB International, Wallingford.

Pearce, D. & Stringer, P. 1990, 'Psychology and Tourism', *Annals of Tourism Research*, Vol. XX, Pergamon Press, UK.

Pelton, R., Aral, C. & Dulles, W. 1997, *The World's Most Dangerous Places*, Fieldings Worldwide, Redondo Beach, California.

Pethiyagoda, L. 1996, 'The Effects of Political and Security Concerns on Tourism', Victorian University of Technology newsletter *Backchatts*, Melbourne.

Piel, J. 1979, Report: 'Relations Entre le Temps Libre, les Mass Media at l'Evolution des Principaux Indicateurs Economiques et Sociaux de la Belgique', 3rd World Congress,

The Contemporary Societies Towards Free Time, Brussels, 1979.

Pilandonn, P. nd, 'Les Relations Economique Exteriere de Mayotte', *Annuare des Pays de L'Ocean*, 19XX.

Pizam, A. 1982, 'Tourism and Crime: is there a relationship?', *Journal of Travel Research* 20(3), 1982, pp. 8–20.

Pizam. A. 1996, 'Does tourism promote peace and understanding between unfriendly nations?', in *Tourism, Crime and International Security Issues*, Pizam, A. & Mansfeld, Y. (eds), John Wiley & Sons, Chichester.

Pizam, A. & Mansfeld, Y. (eds) 1996, *Tourism, Crime and International Security Issues*, John Wiley & Sons, Chichester.

Plog, S. 1974, 'Why destination areas rise and fall in popularity', *Cornell Hotel and Restaurant Administration Quarterly*, Vol. 14(4), 1974, pp. 55–8.

Plog, S. 1990, 'A Carpenter's Tool: An Answer to Stephen L. J. Smith's Review of Psychocentrism/Allocentrism', *Journal of Travel Research*, Vol. 28(4), 1990, pp. 43–5.

Pottorf, S. & Neal, D. 1994, 'Marketing Implications for Post-Disaster Tourism Destinations', *Journal of Travel & Tourism Marketing*, 3(1), 1994, pp. 115–22.

Prentice, R., Witt, S. & Wydenbach, E. 1994, 'The Endearment Behaviour of Tourists Through Their Interaction with the Host Community', *Tourism Management*, No. 15, 1994, pp. 117–25.

Rajecki, D. 1982, *Attitudes: Themes and Advances*, Sinaver Associates Publishers, Sunderland.

Quest, M. (ed.) 1990, *Horwarth Book of Tourism*, Horwarth & Horwarth, Macmillan Press, London.

Rand Organisation 1999, <www.rand.org>, 1999.

Reed, R. 1996, 'Sole Power Rules', *Herald Sun*, Melbourne, 20 July 1996.

Reilly, R. 1990, *Effective Communication in the Travel Industry*, Delmar Publishers (Merton House Travel & Tourism Publishers), USA.

Richardson, J. 1995, *Travel and Tourism in Australia: The Economic Perspective*, Hospitality Press, Melbourne.

Rimmington, M. & Kozak, M. 1997, 'Developments in Information Technology: Implications for the Tourism Industry and Tourism Marketing', *Anatolia (International Journal of Tourism and Research)*, Vol. 8(3), 1997, pp. 59–80.

Ritchie, B. 1984, 'Assessing the Impact of Hallmark Events: Conceptual and Research Issues', *Journal of Travel Research*, Vol. 23(1), 1984, pp. 2–11.

Ritchie, J. 1990, 'New Realities, New Horizons: Leisure, Tourism and Society in the Third Millennium', *Summary of Talks at the First International Tourism Policy Forum*, Washington 1990.

Ritchie, B. & Yangzhou, Y. 1987, 'The Role and Impact of Mega-Events and Attractions on National and Regional Tourism—a conceptual and methodological overview', *AIEST Conference Report 37*, Vol. 28, St Gall, 1987, pp. 17–58.

Roche, M. 1992, 'Mega-Events and Micro-Modernization; On the Sociology of the New Urban Tourism', *British Journal of Sociology*, Vol. 43, 1992, pp. 563–600.

Royal Automobile Club Victoria (RACV) nd, Insurance Division, Melbourne.

Rozin, S. 1996, 'Empowering the Olympic Movement—A Look at the Business Dynamics Behind the Olympics', *Fortune* magazine, Special Report, May 1996.

Ryan, C. 1991a, *Recreational Tourism, A Social Science Perspective*, Routledge, London.

Ryan, C. 1991b., 'Tourism, Terrorism and Violence, The Risk of Wider World Travel', *Conflict Studies 244*, Research Institute for the Study of Conflict & Terrorism (RISCT), London.

Ryan, C. 1993, 'Crime, violence, terrorism and tourism: an accidental or intrinsic relationship?', *Tourism Management*, 14(3), 1993, pp. 173–83.

Ryan, C. & Kinder, R. 1996, 'The deviant tourist and the crimogenic place—the case of the tourist and the New Zealand prostitute', in *Tourism, Crime and International Security Issues*, Pizam, A. & Mansfeld, Y. (eds), John Wiley & Sons, Chichester.

Schramm, W. 1960, *Mass Communication*, University of Illinois Press, USA.

Schulian, J. 1996, 'Protecting the Investment—NBC's Opening Night Coverage Was as Commercial as the Games Themselves', *Sports Illustrated*, 29 July 1996.

Schwer, K. & Daneshvary, R. 1997, 'The Effect of Information on Attitudes Regarding Tour Fees: The Case of Hoover Dam Power Plant Tour', *Journal of Travel Research*, Vol. 36(2), 1997.

Seaton, A. & Bennett, M. 1996, *The Marketing of Tourism Products—Concepts, Issues and Cases*, International Thomson Business Press, London.

Serfaty, S. 1990, *Media and Foreign Policy*, Macmillan Press, London.

Sheraton Hotels 1990, *Sheraton Hotels Employee Handbook*, ITT Sheraton Hotels, Port Douglas, 1990.

Short, D. 1996, 'TV Sports Contenders Get a New Referee', *European*, Brussels, 1996.

Sinclair, T. & Stabler, M. (eds) 1991, *The Tourism Industry: An International Analysis*, CAB International, Wallingford.

Sirakaya, E. & McLellan, R. 1997, 'Factors Affecting Vacation Destination Choices of College Students', *Anatolia*, Vol. 8(3) (*International Journal of Tourism & Hospitality Research*), 1997, pp. 31–44.

Snepenger, D., Collins, W. & Snepenger, M. 1992, 'Media Viewing Behaviour—Research Notes', *Annals of Tourism Research*, Vol. 19(3), 1992, pp. 562–4, Pergamon Press, UK.

Snepenger, D. & Karahan, S. 1991, '1991 Visitation to Yellowstone National Park after the Fires of 1988', *Annals of Tourism Research*, Vol. 18, 1991, pp. 319–20, Pergamon Press, UK.

Socher, K. & Tschurtschenthaler, P. 1987, 'The Role and Impact of Mega-Events: Economic Perspectives—The Case of the Winter Olympic Games 1964 and 1976 in Innsbruck', *AIEST Conference Report 37*, Vol. 28, St Gall, 1987.

Sonmez, S. & Burnett, G. 1997, 'Make No Enemies: The Tourist Contending with the Terrorist', *Anatolia* (*International Journal of Tourism and Hospitality Research*), Vol. 8(3), 1997, pp. 45–58.

Sonmez, S. & Graefe, A. 1998, 'Influence of Terrorism Risk on Foreign Tourism Decisions', *Annals of Tourism Research*, Vol. 25(1), Pergamon Press, UK, 1998, pp. 112–44.

Southwest Airlines nd, Marketing and Public Relations, Dallas.

Sports Marketing Surveys 1996, *1996 Centennial Olympic Games Television Coverage Around the World*, Brussels.

Standeven, J. & De Knop, P. 1999, 'Sport Tourism', in *Human Kinetics*, Champaign (Ill.).

Stephens, A. 1996, 'Game for Business—Interview with the IOC's Michael Payne', *Business Life*, February 1996.

Sters, R. 1991, *Introduction to Organisational Behaviour*, 4th edn, Harper Collins, New York.

Sunday Times 1990, 'The David Creasy Case', *Sunday Times*, London, 27 May 1990.

Sunday Times 1995, 'Schadenfreude', *Sunday Times*, London, 22 May 1995.

Sunday Times 1997a (7 September), 'Kashmiri Hopes', *Sunday Times Travel*, 7 September 1997.

Sunday Times 1997b (14 September), 'Cuban Tourism Bomber Arrested', *Sunday Times Travel*, London, 14 September 1997.

Sunday Times 1997c (October), 'Directions: Thomson Buys Austravel', *Sunday Times*, London, 19 October 1997.

Suzy Waffles nd, Marketing Department, Brussels.

Swedish Consulate 1996, Country Fact Sheet, Brussels.

Swinglehurst, E. 1996, *Global Tourism—The Next Decade: Face-To-Face the Sociocultural Impacts of Tourism*, Butterworth-Heinemann, Oxford.

Swissair 1998, <www.swissair.com>.

Sydney Morning Herald 1998, 'Broadcasters to Make Sure They Get Their Money's Worth', <www.smh.com.au>,1998.

Sydney Olympics nd, 'Technical Information', Sydney Olympics 2000 Bid Ltd., 19XX.

Sydney Olympics 2000, <www.sydney.olympic.org>.

Theuns, H. 1992, 'Rejoinders and Commentary—Media Use in Third Word Tourism Research', *Annals of Tourism*, Vol. 19, Pergamon Press, UK.

Thorncroft 1998, 'Dubrovnik', *Weekend Financial Times*, London, 4–5 December 1998.

Tourism Forecasting Council 1998 (Australia), *Forecast: Seventh Report on the Tourism Forecasting Council*, Vol. 4(1) March 1998, Canberra.

Tourism Victoria nd, Public Relations and Advertising, Melbourne.

Travel 1998, 'Internet, Wat, Waarom en Wanner?', *Travel* magazine No. 98, Netherlands, 1998.

Travis, A. 1982, 'Physical Impacts: Trends Affecting Tourism—Managing the Cultural Environmental Impacts', *Journal of Tourism Management*, 3(4), pp. 256–62.

Travlang (Foreign Languages for Travelers) nd, <www.travlang.com>.

Trenholm, S. 1986, *Human Communication Theory*, Prentice-Hall, New Jersey.

Tribe, J. 1995, *The Economics of Leisure and Tourism Environments, Markets and Impacts*, Butterworth-Heinemann, Oxford.

Ungoed-Thomas, J. 1998, 'What to Pack for Holidays: A Lawyer', *Sunday Times*, London, 19 July 1998.

US State Department 1997, 'Patterns of Global Terrorism: 1997—Europe and Eurasia Overview', <www.state.gov>, 1997.

US State Department 1998a, US State Department Services—Travel Warnings and Consular Information Sheets, <www.state.gov>, 1998.

US State Department 1998b, 'International Terrorist Incidents', <www.state.gov>, 1998.

US Travel Data Center, USA, 1995.

US Travel & Tourism Administration (USTTA), USA, various years statistics.

Usher, R. 1997, 'Flight or Fright?—Special Report', *Time* magazine, New York, 16 June 1997.

Van Dinh, T. 1987, *Communication and Diplomacy in a Changing World*, Ablex Publishing, New Jersey.

van Raaij, W. & Francken, D. 1984, 'Vacation, Activities and Satisfaction', *Annals of Tourism Research*, Vol. 11, Pergamon Press, UK.

Verblen, T. 1953, *The Theory of the Leisure Class*, 7th edn, New American Library, Macmillan Press, New York.

Verchere, I., 'Airlines Play Down Risks to Travellers', *European*, Brussels, 15 November 1995.

Voase, R. 1995, *Tourism: The Human Perspective*, Hodder & Staughton, London.

Wahab, S. 1996, 'Tourism and terrorism: synthesis of the problem with emphasis on Egypt', in *Tourism, Crime and International Security Issues*, Pizam, A. & Mansfeld, Y. (eds), John Wiley & Sons, Chichester.

Walker, J. 1999, *Introduction to Hospitality*, 2nd edn, Prentice-Hall, New Jersey.

Wall, G. 1996, 'Terrorism and tourism: an overview and an Irish example', in *Tourism, Crime and International Security Issues* (Pizam, A. & Mansfeld, Y. eds), John Wiley & Sons, Chichester.

Wall Street Journal 1998, 'Europe Travel Survey', Dow Jones & Company, New York.

Walsh, G. 1995, 'Great Escapes', *Age*, Melbourne, 4 February 1995.

Ward, S. & Gold, J. 1994, *Place Promotion; The Use of Publicity and Marketing to Sell Towns and Regions*, John Wiley & Sons, New York.

Waugh, D. 1995, *Geography: An Integrated Approach*, Nelson, UK.

Wells, M. 1996, 'Games Could Provide Biggest Ad Blitz Ever', *USA Today*, 15 July 1996.

Wilkinson, P.1989, *Lessons of Lockerbie*, Research Institute for the Study of Conflict & Terrorism (RISCT), London.

Wilkinson, P. 1990, 'Terrorists Targets and Tactics: New Risks to World Order', Research Institute for the Study of Conflict & Terrorism (RISCT), London.

Williams, P., Bascombe, P., Brenner, N. & Green, D. 1996, 'Using the Internet for Tourism Research: Information Highway or Dirt Road?', *Journal of Travel Research*, Spring 1996, pp. 63–70.

Witt, S. & Martin, C. 1987, 'Measuring the Impacts of Mega-Events on Tourist Flows', *AIEST Conference Report 37*, Vol. 28, 1987, pp. 213–21.

Witt, S. & Moutinho, L. 1995, *Tourism Marketing and Management Handbook*, Prentice-Hall, UK.

World Tourism Organization (WTO) 1994, 'The Future Ain't What It Used To Be', *WTO News*, No. 5, Madrid, 1994.

World Tourism Organization (WTO) 1994–98, *Yearbook of Tourism Statistics*, various edns 1994–98, Madrid.

World Tourism Organization (WTO) 1995/96, *World Tourism Organization Yearbook, Budgets of National Tourism Administrations*, 1995/96, Madrid.

World Tourism Organization (WTO), *WTO Tourism Compendium*, various edns, 1996–99, Madrid.

World Tourism Organization (WTO) 1997, *International Tourism; A Global Perspective*, 1997, Madrid.

World Travel and Tourism Council (WTTC) 1997, 'The European Union Travel and Tourism-Creating Jobs', *1996/97 WTTC Travel & Tourism Report*, London.

Yallop, D. 1995, 'The Maltese Falcon', *Australian Magazine*, Canberra, 6 May 1995.

Youell, R. 1995, *Leisure and Tourism (Advanced GNVQ)*, 2nd edn, Longman, Harlow.

Youell, R. 1996, *A–Z Leisure, Travel and Tourism Handbook*, Hodder & Staughton, London.

Zenith Media 1996/97, television and population information: 'Zenith on TV', 'UK Media Yearbooks', London, 1996/97.

Interviews

1995

Holt, D., former airport manager, Air New Zealand, Melbourne, Australia, 1995.

McAlister, P., Royal Automobile Club Victoria; Insurance Branch Consultant, Melbourne, Australia, 1995.

Royal Tours, Branch Manager, Royal Tours (Davo) Travel Agents and Tour Operator, Louvain Branch, Belgium, 1995.

1996

Boutris, A., Office de Promotion du Tourisme (OPT) (National Tourism Organisation); Press Department, Brussels, Belgium, 1996.

Fuller, P., Australian Embassy/Consulate; Counsellor Public Affairs, Brussels, Belgium, 1996.

Neckerman Tour Operator, Branch Manager, Louvain Branch, Belgium, 1996.

Suzy Waffles, Marketing Manager, Brussels, Belgium, 1996.

1998

British Embassy Brussels, Press Officer, Press and Public Affairs Section, Brussels, Belgium, 1998.

1999

Denis, M., Advertising Administration, Tourism Victoria, Melbourne, Australia, 1999.

Index